LAND VALUATION

ADJUSTMENT PROCEDURES AND ASSIGNMENTS

Readers of this text may be interested in the following books published by the Appraisal Institute:

- *The Appraisal of Real Estate*
- *The Appraisal of Rural Property*
- *Appraising Residential Properties*
- *The Dictionary of Real Estate Appraisal*

LAND VALUATION

ADJUSTMENT PROCEDURES AND ASSIGNMENTS

by James H. Boykin, PhD, MAI, SREA, CRE

APPRAISAL INSTITUTE®

875 North Michigan Avenue Chicago, IL 60611-1980

Reviewers: Don M. Emerson, MAI, SRA
Dianne G. Hays, MAI, SRA
Mark R. Linne, MAI
Michael S. MaRous, MAI, SRA

*Vice President, Educational
Programs and Publications:* Larisa Phillips
*Director, Content Development and
Quality Assurance:* Margo Wright
Manager, Book Development: Stephanie Shea-Joyce
Supervisor, Book Design/Production: Michael Landis

For Educational Purposes Only

The material presented in this text has been reviewed by members of the Appraisal Institute, but the opinions and procedures set forth by the author are not necessarily endorsed as the only methodology consistent with proper appraisal practice. While a great deal of care has been taken to provide accurate and current information, neither the Appraisal Institute nor its editors and staff assume responsibility for the accuracy of the data contained herein. Further, the general principles and conclusions presented in this text are subject to local, state, and federal laws and regulations, court cases, and any revisions of the same. This publication is sold for educational purposes with the understanding that the publisher is not engaged in rendering legal, accounting, or other professional service.

Nondiscrimination Policy

Library of Congress Cataloging-in-Publication Data

Boykin, James H., 1936–
    Land valuation : adjustment procedures and assignments / James H. Boykin.
        p. cm.
    ISBN 0-922154-64-3
        1. Real property—Valuation. I. Title
HD1387 .B693 2000
333.33'2—dc21

00-053118

Contents

List of Figures

List of Tables

About the Author

James H. Boykin is the Alfred L. Blake Professor of Real Estate in the School of Business at Virginia Commonwealth University. Before becoming an educator, Dr. Boykin served with the Federal Housing Administration in Detroit and Richmond, Virginia. Later he was with the Richmond-based firm of Rountrey and Associates, where he specialized in eminent domain valuation. He has also worked with the Urban Land Institute in Washington, D.C. and has had his own real estate appraising and consulting business. Boykin has qualified in 14 different courts of law and has lectured to Appraisal Institute and mortgage banking classes throughout the United States.

Dr. Boykin holds the MAI, SREA, and CRE professional designations of the Appraisal Institute and the Counselors of Real Estate. He has held various positions in these organizations, including serving as a member of the governing council and regional vice president of the Appraisal Institute. He has been chairman of the Real Estate Research Centers and Chair Holders Association and has served on the board of directors of the American Institute of Corporate Asset Management, the Virginia Real Estate Appraiser Board, the RF&P Corporation, and the real estate advisory committee of the Virginia Retirement System.

Dr. Boykin has been listed in numerous bibliographies, including *Outstanding Educators of America, Who's Who in Real Estate,* and *Who's Who in Finance and Industry.* He is a member of Lambda Alpha honorary land economics fraternity, a fellow of the Homer Hoyt Advanced Studies Institute, and a faculty fellow of the School of Mortgage Banking. In addition to numerous professional journal articles, research monographs, and reports, he has written the following books: *Mortgage Loan Underwriting* (Mortgage Bankers Association of America) and *Transfer Methods and Valuation Procedures for Conservation Easements* (International Right of Way Association). He is coauthor of *Basic Income Property Appraisal* (Addison-Wesley), *Financing Real Estate* (Prentice Hall), and *Valuation of Real Estate* (Prentice Hall); the editor-in-chief of *Real Estate*

Counseling (Counselors of Real Estate); consulting editor of *Industrial Real Estate* (Society of Industrial and Office Realtors) and *The Appraisal of Real Estate,* sixth edition (Appraisal Institute); and co-editor of *The Real Estate Handbook* (Dow Jones-Irwin) and *Real Estate Analysis* (Counselors of Real Estate).

Foreword

The Appraisal Institute is pleased to present *Land Valuation: Adjustment Procedures and Assignments* by James H. Boykin, PhD, MAI, SREA, CRE, a basic guidebook to help appraisers successfully complete new or difficult land valuation assignments. This practical, hands-on text provides benchmarks for property analysis and illustrates how various land valuation assignments can be performed, using both traditional techniques and appropriate alternative methods. In addition, it offers readers a wide array of valuation-related data sources, formats, procedures, and references to help them develop new insights and undertake further research into land valuation issues.

Land Valuation: Adjustment Procedures and Assignments addresses the appraisal of sites in mature neighborhoods and prospective subdivisions as well as residential waterfront property, industrial and commercial land, farmland and timberland, historic and scenic land, resort lots, wetlands, contaminated sites, and rights of way. It demonstrates how to locate properties in the field, conduct site analysis, and determine highest and best use. A variety of adjustment techniques are explained, including adjusting for size differences, changing market conditions, accessibility, public utilities, and location. Also covered are ways to use property listings, improved property sales, and paired sales analysis to estimate land value and the selection of appropriate units of comparison.

This text can be used as a desk reference by all appraisers involved in the valuation of land, regardless of their level of experience. Illustrations and computations reinforce the discussion of various valuation methods and assignments. Numerous graphics, photographs, and charts are incorporated into the book to facilitate the reader's understanding of the material presented.

Brian A. Glanville, MAI
2001 President
Appraisal Institute

Acknowledgments

The author acknowledges with deep appreciation the valuable suggestions offered by the following persons: Frank O. Brooks, Jr., ACF, King William, Virginia; David M. Keating, MAI, Jacksonville, Florida; Peter J. Patchin, MAI, Burnsville, Minnesota; Robert S. Sutte, MAI, Winter Park, Florida; Robert J. Callaway, MAI, West Palm Beach, Florida; A. Scruggs Love, Jr., MAI, Hondo, Texas; James L. Quinn, MAI, Greenwood, Mississippi; Charles M. Tarver, Atlanta, Georgia; J. Carl Schultz, MAI, Atlanta, Georgia; William L. Christensen, MAI, Salt Lake City, Utah; Blaine B. Chase, MAI, Denver, Colorado; Stuart A. Waymack, Richmond, Virginia; Don M. Emerson, MAI, Gainesville, Florida; and Kevin M. McMillion, my graduate research assistant.

PART

I

Introduction

CHAPTER

1

Overview of Land Valuation Assignments and Adjustment Procedures

This introductory chapter provides an overview of the purpose and organization of the text. It is followed by Chapter 2, "Economic Significance of Land," which traces the historical growth of the United States and its urbanization. Developed urban areas still represent a comparatively small share of the entire U.S. land mass. Land ownership trends involving private and federally owned land are discussed in Chapter 2.

Chapter 3, "Locating Properties in the Field," stresses the necessity for accurately locating a parcel in the field. Suggestions are offered for mastering this part of the appraisal process. Also discussed is the use of tools such as assessor's map section sheets, scaled distances in conjunction with vehicle odometer readings, computer-generated maps, and landmarks established via topographical maps. In some instances, utility pole markers can be referenced on highway construction plans. Aerial photographs are yet other means for locating property boundary lines, remote buildings, and prominent changes in ground cover. Deed books contain land plats, which are used to determine a parcel's size, shape, location, and boundary lines. Chapter 3 also provides instructions on how to use a compass in navigating from point to point, either in a car or at a property site.

"Site Analysis" is the subject of Chapter 4. A site analysis, in which the appraiser evaluates a site's usefulness and optimum use, includes an analysis of the site's ownership rights, mineral rights, riparian rights, zoning, private restrictions, boundary lines, easements, terrain, soil conditions, and flood hazards. An owner's legal rights to a property may include mineral and royalty interests. The fundamentals of zoning, the probability of rezoning, and related price adjustments are addressed. Private restrictions and their value implications are illustrated and discussed. Guidelines are offered for determining and measuring a parcel's boundary lines and slope.

Chapter 5, "Judging Highest and Best Use," explores each of the criteria used to determine the highest and best use of a parcel. Most probable use and probable present site value are also covered. The most probable use concept is preferred by some appraisers because it is rooted in the marketplace and reflects the actual behavioral patterns of active market participants. A comprehensive highest and best use analysis is performed to determine the optimal use for a site. An example is presented to explain this analytical concept and the issue of excess land is explored.

Part II of the text, "Adjustment Procedures," opens with Chapter 6, "Adjusting for Size Differences." The comparable sales and the appraised parcel should have the same highest and best use. That is, the sale sites should be possible substitutes for the appraised site. Whenever possible, appraisers should avoid using sales that differ substantially from the appraised parcel in terms of size. Several judicial rulings on the subject of land size adjustments are presented in the chapter. Generally, unit land prices decline exponentially as the parcel size increases. Land size adjustments may be based on a unit price rate of change and calculated by interpolation. It may be beneficial to use land sale listings and the value extraction method to appraise a parcel when sales data are scarce.

According to Chapter 7, "Adjusting for Changing Market Conditions," when adjusting the prices of comparable land sales, the appraiser should 1) adjust for changing market conditions before adjusting for physical, legal, or sale conditions; 2) improve the accuracy of time adjustments by using a series of periods rather than one long period; and 3) be familiar with the zoning, utilities, and physical state of each sale when it was transferred. Whenever possible, several sets of sales and resales of the same parcel should be analyzed. This technique is illustrated as is the analysis of similar land sales at different times. The importance of using sales in the same community and sales that are physically similar to the appraised parcel is stressed. The appraiser must recognize periods of both declining and increasing land prices and make the appropriate adjustments.

Chapter 8, "Using Property Listings," acknowledges that land listings are not consummated sales and should never be used as the sole indicator of value. Still, during periods of relatively inactive market sales, listings can provide an additional corroboration of value. Options to purchase land are another measure of a parcel's value. In addition to serving as an indicator of the value of an appraised parcel, listings can be used to set an upper limit of value and reveal how long listed parcels have been on the market. Moreover, they can be used to estimate the exposure time and reasonable marketing time for the appraised parcel. By studying a large number of listings and sales of a particular class of land, an analyst can determine the ratio of sale prices to listing prices.

In Chapter 9, "Handling Improved Property Sales," readers learn that improved property sales may provide an indication of an appraised parcel's value. The best results are achieved when the improvements have only nominal value—e.g., sales of land with dilapidated buildings or buildings that no longer serve a useful purpose. Two possibilities are presented when the underlying land value is extracted from marginally improved sale properties: 1) the improvements may add to the value of the parcel and, thus, their value must be deducted to reveal the price paid for the land, or 2) the improvements may have negative value and thus a positive adjustment needs to be made to reflect the full amount of the purchase price.

"Paired Sales Analysis" is the focus of Chapter 10. The steps involved in the paired land sales adjustment technique, also known as the *matched pair* method, are discussed and illustrated. Although the paired sales rarely provide clear-cut indications of the relative values of property attributes, this analytical method imposes order on the valuation of land. The steps used in this method are:

1. Identify similar features of the sales.

2. Isolate a value-influencing difference.

3. Adjust the price to reflect a single feature.

4. Apply the adjustment to reflect the subject's value.

In Chapter 11, "Sale Units of Comparison," the two basic units of comparison discussed are density units and physical units. Density units are specified by zoning ordinances and physical units relate to physical measurements, either linear or square units. When several units of comparison are applied to an appraised parcel, they may be expected to produce corroborating indications of value. Analysis of land sales based on the prospective number of productive units, such as hospital beds, is generally not satisfactory. An essential step in using the comparative-unit method is to ascertain the size of both the sale and appraised parcels accurately.

According to Chapter 12, "Accessibility Adjustments," a corner site generally is preferred and considered more valuable for traffic-dependent businesses like convenience stores, service stations, fast-food restaurants, and other retail establishments. Corner sites offer advantages such as better merchandise display, enhanced store visibility, and easier ingress and egress. Contrastingly, residential land uses and office buildings often do not benefit from the added traffic exposure produced by a location at an intersection. Each parcel must be appraised based on the peculiar value influences affecting land value in that particular location. At first glance, two physically similar parcels with the same zoning may appear to have similar values. Yet, different traffic volumes may cause one of the parcels to have a higher and better use than the other. Also discussed in Chapter 12 is the positive effect that close proximity to expressway interchanges has on the land values of industrial and distribution facilities and the opposite effect such proximity has on land values for residential properties.

"Adjusting for Public Utilities" is covered in Chapter 13. The ability to detect value patterns for parcels with and without public utilities is of tremendous importance to appraisers. The availability of public sewers is of greater concern than water service in making utility value adjustments because sewers are more expensive and have a greater effect on land values. Land uses such as apartments, which have high water consumption, require public water and sewer service. Therefore, sales of similar parcels lacking public water and sewer probably will not be comparable unless the distance to extend these lines to a sale parcel is fairly short. If a land sale is sufficiently similar to an appraised parcel, but it lacks public utilities, then it probably should at least be considered as an indicator of the subject parcel's present value. If there is some certainty as to when public utilities will be extended to either the subject or the sale parcel, the price of the comparable sale may be discounted or inflated to account for this delay. In adjusting a land sale to account for the cost of extending utilities to the parcel, the appraiser should remember that the closest utility source may be neither the most probable or the least expensive alternative.

Chapter 14, "Location Adjustments for Resort Lots," points out some key trends and value-influencing factors that should be considered when undertaking these appraisal assignments. Interviewing the persons involved in the transaction is probably more important in the appraisal of resort lots and parcels than in valuing other types of real estate. Resort marketing representatives can explain the aberrations in price trends that have resulted from periodic overbuilding, hurricanes, unseasonably warm winters, or a lack of snowfall. The values of resort and recreational lots vary considerably depending on their location.

There are two types of locational influences on site values. First, there are macro location influences that apply to sales located in different parts of a region or in different regions altogether. Generally land sales that require large location adjustments should not be used to estimate the value of an appraised site. The other location influences are micro location factors operating within the same locale and even the same development. In golf communities on the southeastern coast of the United States, for example, the price of lots seems to increase progressively from interior lots to lagoon lots, fairway lots, fairway/lagoon lots, marsh lots, deepwater lots, and ultimately oceanfront lots. In appraising resort lots, the term "view lot" requires clarification. In mountain resort areas, views may be ranked as follows, from most to least desirable: distant view, sunset view, narrow or short distance views, lake view, golf fairway or greens view, stream view, and interior lots.

"Depth Adjustments" is the subject of Chapter 15. The key to determining the need for an adjustment is whether the difference in depth between the comparables and the subject parcel measurably affects their value. Two depth-value relationships generally hold true for parcels of varying depths: 1) the front foot value of a parcel increases as its depth increases, and 2) the square foot (or acre) value decreases as a parcel's depth increases. Early in the twentieth century, many municipal assessors used depth tables to improve the uniformity of appraisals. Today, however, it is inadvisable for appraisers to use published depth tables. Before any adjustment can be made for variations in depth between comparable land sales and a subject parcel, either a value pattern or a common unit of measurement such as price per front foot or per acre must be established. Depth adjustments may be made by graphing the unit value versus depth, using paired sales analysis, or, in some instances, through linear or multiple regression analysis.

Part III examines various land valuation assignments. In Chapter 16, "Sites in Mature Neighborhoods," the site value-to-total property value ratio method, or allocation method, is suggested for use in built-up residential neighborhoods. It is a good alternative when there are few sales of vacant lots. It may serve as a general benchmark of value or a preliminary value estimate, or it may be used simply to corroborate a value estimate derived from a more typical valuation method. The allocation method works best for residential lots of similar size in neighborhoods of homes that are in the same age and price range. The lot value ratio is established in comparable neighborhoods and then applied to recent home sales in the subject neighborhood.

Chapter 17, "Prospective Subdivisions," illustrates how the discounted cash flow technique can be used in valuing prospective residential land as well as nonresidential parcels that can be subdivided into multiple building sites. To apply this method properly, the appraiser must be familiar with the land development process and thoroughly understand the local market for the prospective real estate product, e.g., residential lots of a certain price, size, and amenities. All spreadsheet inputs must be market-derived if the estimated value is to be valid. The chapter presents a detailed discussion of the land development technique.

"Residential Waterfront Property" is the topic of Chapter 18. An elevated lot generally is preferable to a low-lying lot as it affords a superior view and protection from flooding and storm damage. While some people favor marshfront lots, ocean frontage usually brings the highest prices followed by bay or river frontage and, finally, creek frontage. Offshore water depth is important because it affects access to the property. Increased beach width is reflected in higher home and lot prices. A wider beach affords greater recreational benefits and greater protection for the home from storm water surges. The direction of prevailing winds can affect the desirability, maintenance costs, and value of waterfront sites. Appraisers should be familiar with shoreline erosion and accretion trends.

Chapter 19 considers "Office, Retail, and Industrial Land" valuation. It focuses on factors that influence the value of such land, including access, visibility, proximity to transportation modes, freestanding vs. business park locations, the size and shape of sites, and real estate taxes. Units of comparison and the reliability of the comparable sales method are discussed. Comparative analysis of recent, similar land sales is the predominant valuation technique used in appraising industrial land. Great care must be taken to distinguish among different categories of industrial zoning and differences in highest and best use. Wide ranges in property prices may be observed. Sites in master-planned business parks generally will bring higher unit prices than free-standing sites. Since strip retail businesses derive a large amount of their trade from customers traveling in motor vehicles, there is a fairly direct correlation between the amount of street frontage and site sale prices.

Chapter 20, "Agricultural Land," begins with definitions of pertinent terms. Although most appraisers are not prepared to analyze soils, they should be able to interpret soil maps and soil productivity reports. At times it is necessary to allocate value among several categories of land. An algebraic method is presented for estimating the value that crop allotments contribute to land sales. The land value extraction method is most useful in appraising farmland when the sales have old, dilapidated buildings that contribute relatively little to the overall property value. The income capitalization approach can provide evidence as to whether buyers are paying a premium above the amount indicated by the parcel's ability to produce revenue from agricultural productivity. Great care is required in selecting comparable sales when the land to be valued is being converted from agriculture to other uses. A thorough highest and best use analysis is needed to estimate the market value of farmland in transition zones. Both economic trends and government policies may influence the rate of land conversion from farm uses.

Chapter 21, "Forestland," focuses on the appraisal of the land that underlies growing timber, commonly known as *bare land*. Bare land valuation typically is based on an analysis of comparable sales. An appraiser may require the services of a professional forester when undertaking such assignments. Appraising a mixed growth of timber without a breakdown of timber inventory and a separate valuation of the bare land can lead to an erroneous value conclusion.

Key factors influencing timber value include proximity to a forest products mill or log storage yard, soil type, and site index. The three major categories of wood products are pulpwood, chip and saw (CNS), and saw timber. Problems can arise in the estimation of land value prior to the timber having been harvested.

Chapter 22, "Scenic Land Conservation Easements," points out that conservation easements have a negative effect on value because they restrict a fee owner's ability to develop the property. Many property owners voluntarily convey scenic easements on their land to IRS-qualified organizations in order to enjoy lower real estate taxes and receive federal income tax advantages. Estimating the value of a donated easement begins with a careful reading of the easement agreement to determine which uses are allowed and which are prohibited. From this information, the appraiser can compare the prescribed uses to land sales subject to a zoning classification that allows similar uses. The number of sales may be limited, the prices paid may not represent full price, and, if the acquiring agency has the power of eminent domain, the price may be somewhat low if there is the possibility that the agency could obtain the easement through condemnation. Paired sales may be used to estimate the before-and-after value of a parcel, which in turn provides an estimate of the easement value. In estimating conservation easement value, it may sometimes be necessary to use land rentals and land sales of different parcels to develop capitalization rates. Furthermore, the appraiser must realize that the value of the land adjacent to the easement may be enhanced because of the perpetual vista created by the easement.

"Floodplains and Wetlands" are the subject of Chapter 23. A principal difference between the two terms is the frequency and duration of flooding or the height of the water table. Key factors influencing the value of floodplains are access, zoning, the frequency and severity of flooding, and the availability of flood insurance. Frequently, all or some of the comparable sales considered will contain a combination of upland and floodplain. A value extraction methodology that accounts for the value of these land categories is presented in Chapter 23. Appraisers use wetlands, topographic, soil, and floodplain maps to identify wetlands. The U.S. Army Corps of Engineers considers hydrology, vegetation, and soils in determining whether a particular area is a wetland. Generally wetlands may be expected to have a similar or lower value than floodplains since they are more limited from an agricultural, building construction, and regulatory perspective. A valuation methodology is provided to handle appraised parcels that have several land classifications.

Chapter 24 addresses the valuation of "Contaminated Sites." Appraisals may be required for both the parcel from which the environmental impairment emanates as well as for any property whose value has been severely eroded by the release of an environmentally hazardous substance. Ideally, the appraisal is conducted after the appraiser has received a report from a qualified environmental professional. Unfortunately, this information often is not available. This chapter outlines the appraiser's responsibilities in such cases and offers suggested language for the "contingent conditions" section of a report prepared under various scenarios. The nature of Phase I, II, and III environmental site assessments is explained as is the nature of stigma. For an appraiser to analyze the probable adverse impact of contamination thoroughly, he or she would need the expertise of an environmental professional. Measures of impaired value—rent loss, remediation, indemnification costs, and increased marketing time—are addressed.

Chapter 25, "Eminent Domain: Partial Takings," reviews the legal concept of the bundle of rights and explains police power, eminent domain, and condemnation. Distinctions are made between compensable and noncompensable actions and the basis for the payment of just compensation is discussed. The valuation procedure for partial takings is outlined and methods for appraising trees and landscaping are described. The value of rental loss and the value of expected return methods for appraising temporary easements are explained and illustrated. In appraising an affected property remainder, it must be determined whether the benefits accrue to the community as a whole or specifically to the appraised property for which severance damages are claimed. Advice on proper trial preparation and trial procedure for appraisers is offered.

The final part of the book, the "Appendices," contains a glossary, a listing of helpful data sources, references to various maps (including maps of flood zones, topographical features, soil classification, coastal surveys, floodplains, wetlands, and zoning), comprehensive community plans, and assessor's office tax section sheets. Included as well is information on land measurement and conversion tables and aerial photography. Also found in the appendices is a property observation checklist, which includes information on the extent of the appraiser's inspection and possible environmental factors observed by the appraiser and reported by others. Advisory Opinion 9 on the appraiser's responsibility concerning toxic or hazardous substance contamination is included along with Guide Note 8, which covers the consideration of hazardous substances in the appraisal process. Finally, a list of different types of soils and agricultural land values by state is provided.

Economic Significance of Land

It is informative to trace the geographical evolution of the United States, especially in the first century of our independence from Great Britain. As shown in Table 2.1, the federal government acquired lands between 1781 and 1867 that represent 81% of the present U.S. land area. The Louisiana Purchase, the largest acquisition, occurred during the presidency of Thomas Jefferson. Acquired in 1803 from France for $15 million, it doubled the size of the United States. In addition to cessions from the original thirteen colonies, large federal acquisitions included the Alaska Purchase from Russia and the Mexican Cession. It is quite astonishing to note that in the 19-year period between 1848 and 1867, 44% of our present land and water mass was acquired. In nominal dollars, the total purchase price of all this land was $85.1 million, or less than five cents an acre.

According to the U.S. Department of Agriculture, "Land in urban areas totaled 55.9 million acres in 1990, up from 47.3 million acres in

Table 2.1   *Acquisition of the Original Public Domain, 1781–1867*

Acquisition	Year(s)	Land Area	Water Area	Total Area	Percent of Total U.S. Present Domain	Cost in Millions of Dollars*
			Million Acres			
State Cessions	1781–1802	233.4	3.4	236.8	10.5	6.2
Louisiana Purchase[†]	1803	523.4	6.5	529.9	23.4	23.2
Red River Basin	1782–1817	29.1	0.5	29.6	1.3	—
Cession from Spain	1819	43.3	2.8	46.1	2.0	6.7
Oregon Compromise	1846	180.6	2.7	183.4	8.1	—
Mexican Cession	1848	334.5	4.2	338.7	15.0	16.3
Purchase from Texas	1850	78.8	0.1	78.9	3.5	15.5
Gadsden Purchase	1853	19.0	0.0	19.0	0.8	10.0
Alaska Purchase[‡]	1867	365.3	12.9	378.2	16.7	7.2
Total	1781–1867	1,807.5	33.2	1,840.7	81.3	85.1

*   Nominal dollars (actual cost when acquired)

†   Excludes areas eliminated by the treaty of 1819 with Spain.

‡   Adjusted for the re-computation of the United States made for the 1980 decennial census.

Source: USDA, ERS, based on U.S. Department of the Interior, Bureau of Land Management, 1996.

Figure 2.1 *Land Ownership in the United States, 1992*

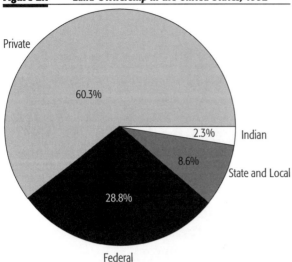

1980." However, the annual rate of land absorption had declined from 1.3 million acres in the 1970s to 900,000 acres in the 1980s.[1] Land in urban areas nevertheless represents a comparatively small part of the nation's total land area. In 1992 urban areas were categorized with other miscellaneous land, including marshes, open swamps, bare rock areas, desert, tundra, and other land generally having low value for agricultural purposes.

The land area of the United States now includes 2.3 billion acres. Of this total, 60.3% is privately owned, up from 58.7% in 1982. Federal lands have shrunk during this period from 32.2% to 28.8% while state and local government holdings rose from 6.8% to 8.6% of total lands. There was no change in the area of Indian lands. (See Figure 2.1 for the latest land ownership distribution.)[2]

Folklore holds that Native Americans were bested by European settlers in the sale of Manhattan Island when Peter Minuit, Director-General of New Netherland, bought Manhattan Island from the Man-a-hat Indians for $24 in trinkets in 1626. In retrospect, it may not have been such a bad deal for the tribe. Suppose that the $24 had been deposited in a savings account that paid an annual interest rate of 6.222%. If so, the $24 investment over the following 364 years (1626–1990) would have grown to a tidy sum of $83,645 billion, which was the estimated land value of Manhattan in 1990. This transaction may have been even better for the tribe than it appears since Native Americans customarily did not view themselves as landowners.[3] Could this transaction have been the precursor of the many future sales of the Brooklyn Bridge?

1. Arthur B. Daugherty, *Major Uses of Land in the United States,* 1992. Agricultural Economic Report, No. 723 (Washington, D.C.: United States Department of Agriculture, 1995), pp. iv and 1.
2. Ibid.
3. James H. Boykin and Richard L. Haney, Jr.,*Financing Real Estate*, 2d ed. (Englewood Cliffs, N.J. :Regents/Prentice Hall, 1993), pp. 28-29. The appraised value of all land in Manhattan borough (excluding streets and other public rights of way) as of April 1990 was reported by the New York City Assessor's Office.

Importance of Real Estate to Top Wealthholders

Real estate, including land and improvements, makes up a substantial share of the investment portfolios of both male and female top wealthholders in the United States. As Figures 2.2 and 2.3 show, in 1995 personal residences and other real estate comprised approximately one-quarter of this group's investment portfolio. This group, with assets of at least $600,000, "…had a combined net worth of almost $5.0 trillion. They represented just over 2.0% of the total U. S. population in 1992, yet their wealth accounted for nearly 28.0% of total U.S. personal wealth."[4] For top male wealthholders under 65, real estate investments and investments in closely held corporations accounted for the largest shares of their portfolios. For females under age 65, investments in all forms of real estate made up the largest portion of their portfolios.[5]

Private Sector Land Holdings

Between 1970 and 1994, as shown in Table 2.2, by far the greatest growth in nongovernment land values has been in the household sector, which grew by a factor of 9.1. Considerable value growth also occurred in the private financial institutions' holdings and to a lesser degree in nonfarm, noncorporate businesses and farm businesses. The only decline in value was among

Figure 2.2   *Top Male Wealthholders, 1995 Portfolio Composition $4.0 Trillion*

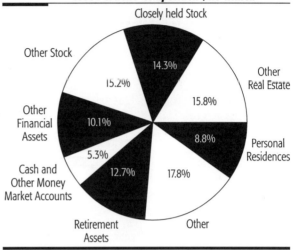

Source: Barry W. Johnson, "Personal Wealth, 1992–1995," *Statistics of Income,* Winter 1997–1998, p. 78.

Figure 2.3   *Top Female Wealthholders, 1995 Portfolio Composition $2.3 Trillion*

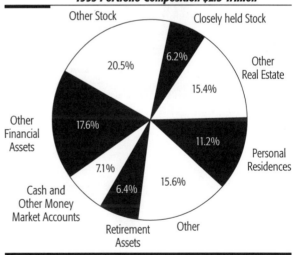

Source: Barry W. Johnson, "Personal Wealth, 1992–1995," *Statistics of Income,* Winter 1997–1998, p. 78.

---

4. Barry W. Johnson, "Personal Wealth, 1992-1995," Statistics of Income (Washington, D.C.: Internal Revenue Service), Winter 1997-1998, p. 70.

5. Ibid., p. 74.

the nonfarm, nonfinance corporate business sector, which had seen steady gains until 1994. In 1994 households and farm businesses controlled 83% of all land value in the United States. Of all farms in the U.S., 86% are owned by sole proprietorships; however, this form of ownership makes up only 64% of all farm acreage, a result of growing farm size, farmland leasing, and partial ownership, especially among larger farms.[6]

Table 2.2   *Market Value of Land in the United States of America (in Billions of Dollars)*

	Year					
Sector	**1970**	**1975**	**1980**	**1985**	**1990**	**1994**
Household	331.8	578.2	1,364.4	2,211.5	2,667.6	3,015.3
Farm business	184.3	354.9	734.0	538.3	566.5	605.3
Nonfarm, noncorp. business	88.6	164.7	377.7	759.9	903.4	550.9
Nonfarm, nonfinance corp. bus.	144.7	275.5	508.0	740.8	752.7	93.3
Private financial institutions	13.1	28.3	55.8	94.3	136.1	99.4
Total	762.5	1,406.7	3,039.9	4,344.8	5,026.8	4,364.2

Source: "Distribution of Tangible Assets by Sector," *Balance Sheets for the U.S. Economy 1945-93* (Washington, D.C.: Board of Governors of the Federal Reserve System, September 20, 1994), Table B.12, pp. 16–19.

Summary

In the 19-year period between 1848 and 1867, 44% of the present land and water mass of the United States was acquired for a per-acre price in nominal dollars of less than five cents. The land area in the United States now includes 2.3 billion acres. Of this total, 60.3% is privately owned. In 1994 households and farm businesses controlled 83% of all land value in the United States. Real estate, including land and improvements, makes up a substantial share of the investment portfolios of top American wealthholders in the United States. In 1995 personal residences and other real estate comprised approximately one-quarter of this group's investment portfolio.

---

6.   "Farms, land in farms, and value of production by type of business organization, 1992,"AREI/Land, Table 1.2.10 p. 34.

Locating Properties in the Field

A rudimentary rule in appraising land is to be certain to appraise the property that the client desires to have appraised. For some readers this may seem too obvious to even mention. Yet, by failing to locate a property or its boundaries accurately, time is wasted in the field and the deadline is missed. It may become necessary to return to the appraiser's office or municipal offices to determine this essential information before making another trip to the property. For example, a party misidentified a residential property several years ago after a hurricane toppled several chimneys in a neighborhood. After waiting two weeks for his chimney to be rebuilt, a home owner berated his insurance agent for his failure to send a brick mason to his home. He was exasperated because his neighbor's chimney had already been rebuilt. As you may have guessed, the repair was made to the wrong property. Similar tales involve real estate appraisers. The following suggestions should improve practioners' proficiency and confidence in identifying the location of an appraised property and comparable sale properties.

Assessor's Section Sheet

In conducting pre-inspection research, either in your own office or perhaps in the assessor's office in the jurisdiction where the appraised property is situated, identify the property by its section sheet or page and parcel number. For example, see parcel 95 in Figure 3.1 (fully identified as 24-95). Having spotted the parcel in the assessor's (or zoning office's) map book, relate it to a prominent structure, road, or natural feature such as a stream or creek. In this example, you could scale the distance from the intersection of Routes 360 and 628 to the northeast corner of the parcel, a distance of approximately 3,100 feet, or 0.59 mile.

Scaled Distances and Odometer

After having referenced a property on a county or city map or section sheet from the municipal zoning or assessor's office, determine the scale of

Figure 3.1   Tax Map Section Sheet

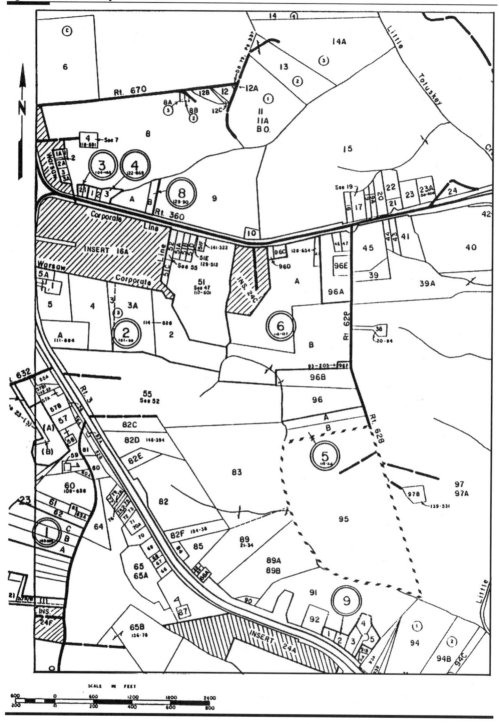

the map. Use an engineering scale to convert the mileage, keeping in mind that there are 5,280 feet in a mile. Then use the ratio of distance on the scale to one mile to scale the distance from a landmark to the nearest corner of the appraised property. Other street maps will give a scale, perhaps in quarter-mile increments, that can be used to gauge the distance to a property.

Greater accuracy will be achieved if an appraiser works from a tax map section sheet where the individual parcels are shown. Because less area is shown than on a municipal street map, more detail and landmarks can be identified. The scale on such maps may be in the range of one inch equals 400 feet. For example, if the distance from a road intersection to the nearest corner of the subject property is scaled to be 2,450 feet, a calculator can be used to convert this into miles, which the appraiser can read on his or her vehicle's odometer. In this case, the 2,450 foot distance converts to 0.464 mile. An appraiser would expect to have approached the nearest corner of the property as the odometer reaches halfway between 0.40 and 0.50 mile. If there is extensive road frontage, this distance could be measured similarly.

Computer-Generated Maps

A wide range of maps are available via computers. Some may be generated from Internet sites. These generally provide insufficient detail for locating a specific property. Other detailed maps may be obtained from available software (see Appendix B). Some of these map programs allow the user to locate a neighborhood and particular property by telephone number, zip code, place name, and street address. After locating a particular neighborhood, it is possible to adjust the scale (zoom in) to magnify the area of interest. In addition to identifying a property, these programs may be customized to produced a location map or a comparable sales map to be used in an appraisal report.

U. S. Geological Survey Maps

These maps are readily available from drafting and technical supply stores and from the U. S. Geological Survey (USGS) in Denver, Colorado and Reston, Virginia. (More detailed information on obtaining products from the USGS may be found in Appendix C.) These maps, measuring 22 inches by 26 inches, provide valuable information in addition to enabling an appraiser to locate a tract. These other uses will be discussed in Chapters 4 and 18. For example, the maps display in color streams, developed areas, open fields, woods, contour in 10-ft. intervals, and houses. Buildings and major structures such as hospitals and schools are named. Shown as well are roads classified by type of route, e.g., U. S. Route 60, and type of road, ranging from unimproved dirt roads to heavy-duty roads. By viewing two or more of these maps prepared at different times for the same quadrangle, an appraiser can readily detect the magnitude and direction of growth. These maps may be used to help appraisers find a property by referencing it to a landmark, street, or natural feature. The scale is given in feet, miles, and kilometers. Part of one of these quadrangle maps is shown in Figure 3.2. A variation of these maps is the statewide

Figure 3.2   *Topographical Map*

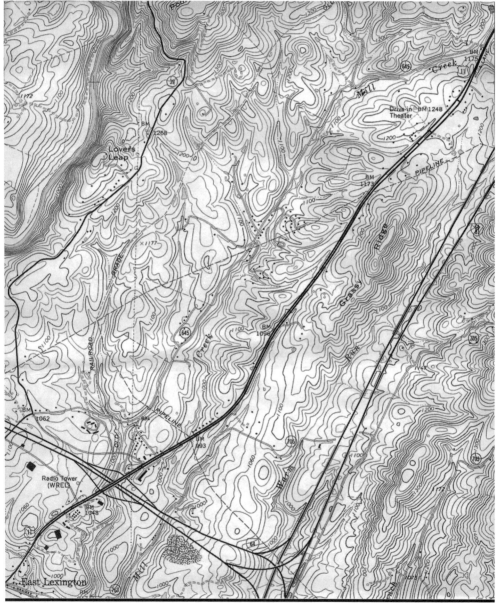

Source: U.S. Department of the Interior, Geological Survey "Lexington, Virginia," photo revised 1978.

Land Valuation: Adjustment Procedures and Assignments

atlas and gazetteer published by DeLorme; these topographic maps show marshes, open fields and woods, floodplains, and urban areas.

Utility Pole Markers

When an appraiser has been retained to appraise a property that a proposed right of way will affect, such as a relocated highway or new road, plans provided by the highway department often will show the location of existing utility poles and their identification numbers. If the pole is situated adjacent to an existing right of way, it is possible to check the number on a metal plate on the pole and then scale the distance to a corner of the property. Alternatively, you can often spot survey stakes that give station numbers, such as 108 +00. From this station, the distance to a property line of the subject property can be measured. It is advisable to carry an engineering scale, compass, and construction plan sheets when attempting to relate these survey stations and property lines on highway plans to actual landmarks. These plan sheets also may be used to locate a property line if the centerline survey station stakes are in place on the ground.

Aerial Photography

Depending on the scale of the photos, aerial photography can be an excellent means of locating a property, especially if used in conjunction with a property survey. The source may be able to provide the date the photo was taken and its scale, such as one inch equals 400 feet. Sources of aerial photography are noted in Appendix D.

Using Visible Corner Markers

Sometimes it is necessary to view an appraised property from the air to comprehend clearly its physical features, access, and relationship to adjacent properties and road systems. Similarly, it is desirable to gain an overview of comparable sale properties from aloft as well. However, the appearance of a property is quite different from the ground and from an aircraft. For instance, one can readily spot the corners of a property from 50 feet when stationary on the ground, but you may not even be certain that the property itself has been found when peering out the window of a small aircraft traveling at a speed of 80 to 100 miles per hour some 500 feet or more above the ground. White corner markers or ground controls may be away from the corners in accessible areas such as along power line easements or roads. These locations generally are visible from an airplane. One type of marker that may be used is a six-foot L-shaped corner marker. These may need to be off the actual corners to be visible. Marking corners in wooded areas that will be visible aerially is difficult.

Prominent Landmarks and Changes in Ground Cover

The advantage of using aerial photography is that it can depict structural and natural features, such as driveways, roads, buildings, and ponds. Also, the appraiser can often use it in connection with municipal planning office section sheets or U. S. Geological Survey quadrangle maps to pinpoint a property line that may coincide with the juncture of an open field and wooded lot. An increasing number of municipal planning offices have installed geographic information system (GIS) computer software, which can provide aerial photo-based views of land.

Deed Book References

When researching the last transfer of the appraised parcel in the city or county record files, the appraiser customarily will read the deed pertaining to the sale. Often a deed will contain a plat book reference for the survey made in connection with the land sale. This survey may give the distance from one corner of the parcel's road frontage to the nearest road intersection. Also, plats frequently contain a small vicinity map which may be used to locate the parcel.

Using a Compass

Compasses, particularly those mounted on the dashboard or above the windshield of a motor vehicle, can be coordinated with road maps to locate properties. When an appraiser is searching for a remote property, it may be helpful to choose a county map over a state road map. The county map not only shows interstate highways and major primary highways, but depicts secondary roads and roads varying from hard surface, to light surface, to unsurfaced. The scale of these county maps may be one inch equals two miles, which is sufficiently detailed so that it is relatively easy to locate a property on the map before driving to it.

Most appraisers have a working knowledge of how to use a compass. To determine a given direction in the field using a compass, you first should face in the direction you wish to proceed, such as toward the corner of a timber tract. It is possible that the parcel is some distance from a paved road. You can use a map (with a north arrow) and compass together to find the property by using a Silva-system compass, which is a combination compass-protractor. (The parts of a Silva compass are identified in Figure 3.3.) The three-step process is described below.

Step 1. On the map, line up the edge of the compass with the route. Place the clear plastic compass on the map so that the edge of its base plate is at the beginning point and along the desired line of travel to the destination, with the base plate's direction-of-travel arrow pointing in the desired direction.

Step 2. Set the compass heading to the route. Hold the base plate firmly on the map. Paying no attention to the needle, turn the compass dial until the north arrow on the bottom of it points to north on the map. (North generally will be at the top of the map.) The direction to your destination is read at the index line on the dial.

Step 3. In the field, follow the direction set on the compass. Hold the compass level in front of you with the direction-of-travel arrow pointing straight ahead. Turn until the north part of the compass needle (red) covers the north arrow on the bottom of the compass housing and points to "N" on the dial. The direction-of-travel now points at the destination. Pick a landmark in that direction and walk toward it. Repeat this process until you reach your destination.[1] Each of these three steps is described in Figure 3.4.

Continuing with the explanation in Step 3, look in the direction-of-travel arrow, say 40 degrees. Look ahead some distance to a landmark such

Figure 3.3 *Parts of a Silva Compass*

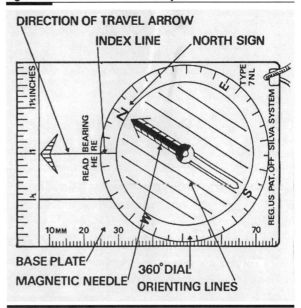

Source: "How To Find Your Way With The Silva Compass," Binghamton, NY: Silva Company.

Figure 3.4 *Plotting a Course With a Compass*

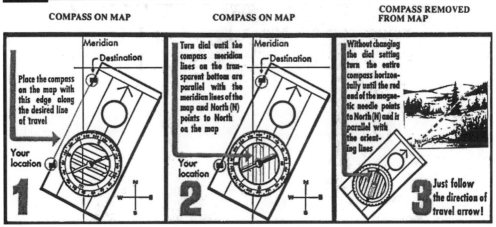

Source: "How To Find Your Way With The Silva Compass," (Binghamton, N.Y.: Silva Company.)

1. Boy Scouts of America, *How To Find Your Way With The Silva Compass* (Binghamton, N.Y.: Silva Co.),1996.

as a tall tree or a structure. Ignore the compass until you have reached your destination. If it is an intermediate point, then repeat the previous procedure to use the compass to find the next landmark and continue walking in that direction (e.g., 40 degrees). You should be able to reference your path of travel with a prominent feature on your map as a check that you are traveling in the correct direction.

Global Positioning System

Global Positioning System (GPS) is a satellite-based radio navigation system that the U.S. Department of Defense developed. A principal application for this system is to provide crucial travel information, including speed, time, and distance to a destination and precise position. It also will display land elevation at a given point. Appraisers may use handheld devices to reach any city address using an electronic map. A handheld personal navigator may be used to find a position (as defined by latitude and longitude). The practical use of GPS is somewhat limited because city properties are already relatively easy to find and it is rare that the precise longitude and latitude of an outlying property are available. However, GPS may be used with the U.S. Department of Interior quadrangle maps, which show longitude and latitude.

Summary

An obvious rule in appraising land is to be certain to appraise the correct property. The following suggestions may assist in accurately identifying the location of appraised and comparable properties.

- Spot the appraised parcel on an assessor's section sheet in reference to a prominent structure, road, or natural feature such as a stream or creek.

- Scale distances from a reference point on a section sheet and convert to mileage using a motor vehicle odometer reading to the nearest corner of an appraised property.

- Use computer-generated maps to identify a property and to create customized location or comparable sales maps for an appraisal report.

- Use U. S. Geological Survey maps for locating parcels and to depict land contours, significant land and structural features, and wooded versus open fields.

Utility pole markers can be used to identify property corners on construction plans for proposed right of way projects. Aerial photography can be an excellent means of locating a property, especially in conjunction with a property survey. White corner markers or ground controls may also be used with aerial photography to pinpoint property corners. Deed book references for land sales often refer to a plat book and page that describes a parcel. These plats often contain a small vicinity map, which may be used to locate a parcel. Dashboard-mounted compasses can be coordinated with road maps to locate properties. Once on a parcel, a compass may be used to tract property lines and significant features of the property. Handheld GPS devices can also be used to locate parcels if their precise longitude and latitude are known.

Site Analysis

Purpose of Site Analysis

In appraising a parcel, the appraiser must investigate in sufficient detail regional, community, and neighborhood influences on the market appeal, utility, highest and best use, and, finally, value of the parcel. Each stage of analysis must relate to the ultimate goal of ascertaining the appraised property's highest and best use and value. In the most basic sense, a site analysis involves determining the site's usefulness. This includes an analysis of the site's ownership rights, mineral rights, riparian rights, zoning, private restrictions, boundary lines, easements, terrain, soil conditions, and flood hazards to reveal the optimum use(s) of the site.

Identifying Rights to be Appraised

Ownership Rights

Obviously, it is important to identify and analyze accurately the physical characteristics of an appraised property. Likewise, it is crucial to determine precisely the ownership rights that are to be appraised. Although the terms *real estate* and *real property* frequently are used interchangeably, there is a significant difference between them. *Real estate* relates to the physical aspects of land while *real property* is defined as the rights and interests connected with ownership of the physical real estate. Most appraisal assignments obligate appraisers to ascertain the value of an owner's legal interest in real property. In doing so, it is necessary to identify the rights that are embraced in the largest possible estate, which is called the *fee simple estate*. Both governmental and private limitations may constrict this unimpaired estate and restrict the full use and enjoyment of a parcel. The governmental limitations are police power, escheat, eminent domain, and taxation. Private constraints include leases, easements, mortgages, and restrictive covenants.

Mineral Rights

A brief explanation of the term *mineral,* which has many interpretations, is appropriate before discussing mineral rights. Terms must be defined precisely before interests and rights in real property are valued. Terry Maley states, "The controlling factor is how 'minerals' are defined in the statute or the conveyance instrument." Further, "...to determine what is included in the 'minerals' definition, one must determine the intent of the parties involved."[1] Typically, real estate appraisers lack the geophysical and geochemical expertise to analyze the nature, scope, or value of minerals that usually are beneath the earth's surface. They customarily focus their valuation on the rights of the surface owner. Nevertheless, it is prudent for the appraiser to include as much available information on mineral rights as is relevant to a particular valuation assignment.

Land ownership may include both mineral interests and royalty interests. *Mineral interests* relate to the ownership of minerals in place as well as access, exploration, extraction, processing, and transport rights. *Royalty interests* are concerned with the right to receive revenue from the extraction of minerals with neither the right to extract nor the financial burden to do so. Examples of potentially valuable minerals include oil, gas, and coal as well as construction materials such as clay, rock, gravel, sand, and slate. Crushed rock may come from a quarry and be used with cement to form concrete; sand from a pit or a river may be used for plaster; and slate from a quarry can be used for roof covering.

The important factors of location and zoning affect the value of mineral rights. Additionally, the size of the deposit and the quality of the material influence value. Because rock, gravel, and sand are heavy, low-value products, their value is enhanced if they are conveniently located near urban centers.

Location is crucial because products made from stone and gravel, such as concrete pipes and septic tanks, do not justify long truck hauls. The same weight, value, and distance economics apply to these materials, which must be situated close to road construction projects. In fact, the value of mineral deposits increases directly with their proximity to their markets. Sometimes an apparently favorable location is negated because the zoning ordinance prohibits production or processing of these natural products. Typically, mineral processing is allowed in agricultural or heavy industrial districts.

The value of a deposit increases with parcel size and if the parcel approximates a square shape. A smaller, narrower parcel has proportionately less recoverable material due to borrow pit slopes and the inability to generate the minimum quantity of material necessary to amortize a processing plant's capital investment profitably.

---

1.   Terry S. Maley, "Mineral Rights for Land Appraisers," *Journal of the American Society of Farm Managers and Rural Appraisers* (April 1982), pp. 12–13.

The value of a deposit increases in proportion to its depth. The feasible extraction depth may be reduced sharply in low-lying areas with high water tables or in areas where there is a substantial strata of noncommercial materials. The quality or purity of the mineable material also affects a parcel's value. For example, a tract that produces a rock-gravel ratio that customers desire will have the maximum value. Also, a source producing rock that meets the required hardness standards of an agency, such as a municipal or state transportation department, will enjoy the highest value.

Valuation of Minerals. The two most reliable valuation techniques for appraising land with mineral deposits are the royalty income and production methods. The comparative land sales method usually is not satisfactory in valuing land with mineral deposits because of the dissimilarities in the factors discussed previously: location, size, shape, and depth and quality of mineable material. Also, there are usually few current sales of these parcels within a given market.

The *royalty income method* is similar to estimating the present worth of an annuity plus the present worth of the residual at the end of the projection period. It probably is best to project the royalty income for the time frame over which the material will be fully depleted. Assistance from a geologist or engineer is required to determine the quantity of materials that can be mined. The depth of overburden to be removed is a factor in determining the feasibility of a prospective site. Generally, the overburden should be less than the depth of the sand or gravel deposit.

To amortize the plant, there may need to be a foreseeable 20- to 30-year mining operation. Consultation with mining staff and others familiar with historic and probable market demand and the characteristics of the mineral is necessary to forecast the annual level of sales and absorption period accurately. The compilation and investigation of sales of other mined-out pits will be required to ascertain the residual value, if any, once the extraction process has been completed. Also, yield rates for similar mining operations must be determined. Once the necessary background data have been compiled, the following format may be used to derive the value of the royalty income plus pit reversion. It is possible that some restoration costs will be necessary once the operation is completed. This cost may equal or outweigh the residual value of the land. Depending on the location and height of the water table, the pit may have value as a lake for an adjoining residential subdivision, suburban office park, or recreational activities. Most jurisdictions impose reclamation requirements, such as a slope ratio of no more than 1:5, retention and spreading of topsoil, and seeding.

For simplicity, assume that the annual quantity of gravel/sand removed from a 50-acre parcel is 500,000 tons at a net royalty of $0.50 per ton, increasing by 3% each 5-year period for 25 years (taxes will be paid by the lessee.) The residual value of the pit is judged to be zero. Due to uncertainty of demand and other market variables, an investor would expect a 12% annual yield. Thus, the present value of the royalty income can be calculated as follows:

Years	Value
1–5	$250,000
5–10	$257,500
11–15	$265,225
16–20	$273,182
21–25	$281,377
Total present value	$2,020,790, or $40,416 per acre

If the pit had a reversionary value of $25,000, this value would be based on the present value of one premise, or $25,000 × 0.059 = $1,470, an insignificant value.

The following illustration of the *production valuation method* relates to an oil well operation:[2]

1.	Annual production, in gross barrels	$_____
2.	Less royalties, in net barrels	$_____
3.	Annual net production (Item 1 – 2)	$_____
4.	Annual gross receipts (Item 3 × sale price/barrel)	$_____
5.	Annual expenses	
	(a) production cost	
	(b) taxes and overhead cost	
	(c) misc. (land, geophysical, environmental studies)	
6.	Total annual expenses	$_____
7.	Annual operating income (Item 4 – 6)	$_____
8.	Value of operation:	$_____
	Present worth of Item 7 for projected operations period*	$_____

*   Usually computations are made for each separate year.

John S. Baen offers several well-founded caveats to real estate appraisers when appraising surface rights in areas where there are established oil or gas drilling operations.

- Allow for damages that the land may suffer due to the drilling.

- A surface owner without mineral rights is entitled only to one-time surface damages at the time that the well is drilled and has no interest in the well or future wells whatsoever.

---

2.   George L. Schmutz, *Condemnation Appraisal Book,* revised by Edwin M. Rams, (Englewood Cliffs, N.J. : Prentice Hall, 1963), p. 253; also see other income examples on pages 247–253. Example revised by author.

- To value the surface rights, the appraiser must find comparable sales without mineral rights or discount each comparable sale by an appropriate amount.

- The appraiser must consider what percentage of the mineral rights passed with the sale of each comparable.

- A lease may allow for drilling of multiple wells based on a drilling and spacing grid.

- A geologist or petroleum engineer needs to be consulted in projecting the future cash flow of a well with regard to the price of oil, size of the reservoir, pressure of the reservoir, and projected decline curve of the well.[3]

Riparian Rights

Riparian rights are a form of water rights. Property owners whose land abuts a body of water such as a stream or river enjoy riparian rights. The general right is to use the water as long as the use does not harm other downstream riparian owners. An example of harmful action would be an upstream landowner who dams up a stream to create a pond, thus depriving downstream owners of an uninterrupted flow of water. Unreasonable diversion of water is not acceptable. Included in the rights are such activities as building boathouses and piers and using a waterway for boating, swimming, and fishing. These rights are not absolute if the waters are navigable because boaters must be able to navigate within the channels and not have their passage endangered by structures erected by abutting land owners. Waterfront properties are discussed in Chapter 18.

Water Law

When valuing land suited for recreational subdivision purposes in the western part of the United States, it is important to understand water law. In most western states that are considered arid, the principle is that water must have been put to a beneficial use under the theory of first in time, first in use. Many western states operate on an appropriation basis, as compared to eastern or midwestern states, which generally subscribe to riparian water rights theory. For example, Colorado lands may be subdivided into small acreage plots and water wells drilled for domestic purposes only, limiting their pumping capacity to 15 gallons per hour. It is presumed that imposing this pumping limitation will not impinge upon the owners of other water rights that have been previously appropriated and adjudicated.

---

3.   John S. Baen, "Oil and Gas Mineral Rights in Land Appraisal," *The Appraisal Journal* (April 1988), pp. 205, 208, 210, and 212–213.

Zoning

An analysis of an appraised property's zoning will reveal the several land use activities that can be constructed legally on the site. In addition to listing a variety of uses, the zoning ordinance will specify building setbacks, including front, rear, and side yards. Building height limitations also are specified. Beyond ascertaining the allowable uses set forth in a zoning ordinance for the appraised parcel, the appraiser should determine the value impact of the zoning of adjacent parcels on the subject parcel. The subject parcel's zoning may be incompatible with that of nearby properties and vice versa.

In addition to considering the permitted and prohibited uses under the section of the zoning ordinance that affects the subject property, the likelihood of rezoning the parcel also must be considered. If there is the prospect of rezoning the appraised site based on the case history of other, similar parcels, the appraiser probably will bracket the appraised value of the subject by adjusting the sale prices of comparable land sales with the same zoning upward, and adjusting the sale prices of parcels already subject to the zoning anticipated for the subject downward—assuming it will be for a more valuable use. Two other factors that should be built into the zoning adjustment are the time lag in securing the rezoning and the risk of not achieving the more valuable zoning.

Private Restrictions

Restrictive covenants are private land use controls prepared on behalf of a developer to protect and preserve the physical, social, and economic integrity of the development. Covenants are written agreements between the developer and the property buyers and may be recorded at the time of the first lot sale. The developer has the initial responsibility for enforcement but, at a specified time in the sale program, the administration of the covenants (sometimes called *deed restrictions*) is usually assumed by a property owners' association. An important function of the covenants is to provide for compliance with proposed building plans. The following types of provisions for architectural controls may be contained in residential subdivision restrictive covenants.

1. Before any improvement is built, the building plans, specifications of materials including exterior paint color, and plat plan showing locations of said structure, driveway and parking, fuel storage, refuse storage containers, and fences must be approved in writing by the Declarant, its successors or assigns. No additions, such as carports, porches, radio towers, antennas, satellite dishes, clothes lines, or any substantial architectural changes to any dwelling or accessory buildings, shall be erected on any lot unless such

additional changes have been approved in writing by the Declarant, its successors or assigns.

2. Minimum total living space for dwellings, exclusive of basement, porches, decks, breeze-way, garage, tool room, and storage space, shall be 1,300 square feet for a one-story dwelling, or 1,400 square feet for a two-story dwelling. Block and brick foundation walls and brick front stoops, including steps, are required. Roof pitch, except for covered porches, shall have a minimum of a six-inch rise per horizontal foot (6/12). The undersides of all decks and porches that are visible from the street shall be screened by landscaping or lattice material. Approval in writing from the Declarant must be obtained prior to the removal of any tree with a diameter in excess of nine inches that is outside of the dwelling footprint or driveway.

Importantly, restrictive covenants generally are more stringent than municipal zoning ordinances. In addition to containing architectural controls, they may regulate signage and maximum completion time once a building has been started, and prohibit the raising of animals for commercial purposes. The covenants usually run with the land for a set period, perhaps 20 or 30 years; changes require the consent of a certain number of property owners. The covenants tend to cover an entire development rather than an individual lot.

Determining Boundary Lines

It is wise to request a copy of a boundary survey of the appraised parcel at the outset of an assignment. If possible, a current title report should be obtained to determine whether any acquisitions or out-conveyances from the parcel have occurred since the latest survey was made. The property's parcel number should be determined so that it may be identified on the appropriate municipal real estate assessor's office section sheet. The size and shape of the parcel in these records may be more current than the survey the property owner provides. Also, the assessor's office property record for the appraised parcel may show any changes in the property boundaries, including references to such conveyances on specific pages in deed books. Checking the deed books should also reveal references to any accompanying plats.

Before inspecting the appraised parcel, it may be helpful to invite the property owner or his agent to join the appraiser. This effort may not only save the appraiser time, but the property boundaries can be determined with greater certainty. It is helpful to take a plat, a compass, and an aerial photograph onto large properties to detect open versus wooded areas or streams that may form property boundaries. (For more detail, see Chapter 3,

"Locating Properties in the Field" and Appendix E "Land Measurement and ConversionTables.") When inspecting wooded tracts, property lines sometimes can be identified by changes in the age of timber as well as by blazing or painted markings on trees that show different timber company's ownership.

A useful skill to develop is an accurate three-foot stride. This can be practiced by marking off a set distance, such as 60 feet, and counting paces until they exactly equal the measured distance. Then, using a compass, plat, and engineer's scale, an appraiser can generally locate a property corner, monument, or other land feature. Of course, a recently surveyed parcel should have survey stakes in place and underbrush and low-growing tree limbs may have been cut to provide the surveyors an unobstructed view of the property lines being surveyed.

Easements

An easement is a nonpossessory interest in another party's real property that benefits the second party. The two principal types of easements are *affirmative easements* and *negative easements*. An *affirmative easement* grants a nonowner the right to perform a specific action on a specific parcel or part of a parcel. The fee owner gives up some of his or her rights as a result of the easement. The right may or may not be an exclusive right. A *negative easement* prohibits a land owner from using his or her land for zoned uses. Types of easements include power line distribution (generally along the front or rear of a property and used to provide electricity to buildings), transmission line (for gas or electricity and generally not to provide service to adjoining properties), sewer and storm water (trunk lines that provide no service to abutting property or may require expensive pumping stations to service a particular parcel), and avigation (restricts the use of airspace by limiting building type and height). Easements may be subsurface (water and sewer lines and tunnels), surface (drainage and flowage), or overhead (avigation and line-of-sight).

Plats and title reports should be studied to determine the presence of all easements. Upon discovering an easement on an appraised parcel, the easement agreement must be read to reveal the use limitations that it imposes on the parcel and the duration of such limitations. Of concern to the appraiser is the degree to which an easement adversely affects a parcel's highest and best use. Underground easements may not be as severe impediments as above-ground easements. Easements within the front, rear, or side yard setback area tend to have a less severe value impact than those within potential areas of development. Wide overhead electric transmission line easements traversing the open, interior of a parcel may cause a substantial loss in value not only to the easement area, but also to the adjacent land. Site design and lot yields become a problem, which in turn may reduce the land value. All possible easements must be located, their restrictions noted, and the parcel appraised with these encroachments fully recognized. An example of an electric transmission easement is shown in Figure 4.1.

Terrain

Terrain features affect the appeal, utility, highest and best use, development and construction costs, and value of a parcel. Variations in terrain do not affect the desirability of land for all prospective land use activities uniformly. A steep, mountainous site with a commanding vista may bring a premium price as a second home site, while a manufacturer would immediately disregard this site because of its remoteness and huge site preparation expenses. Generally, tracts with a moderate degree of variation in topography are attractive for residential development as it adds interest to a subdivision.

Some topographical relief is beneficial in facilitating surface water runoff and for minimizing

Figure 4.1   *Electric Transmission Line Easement*

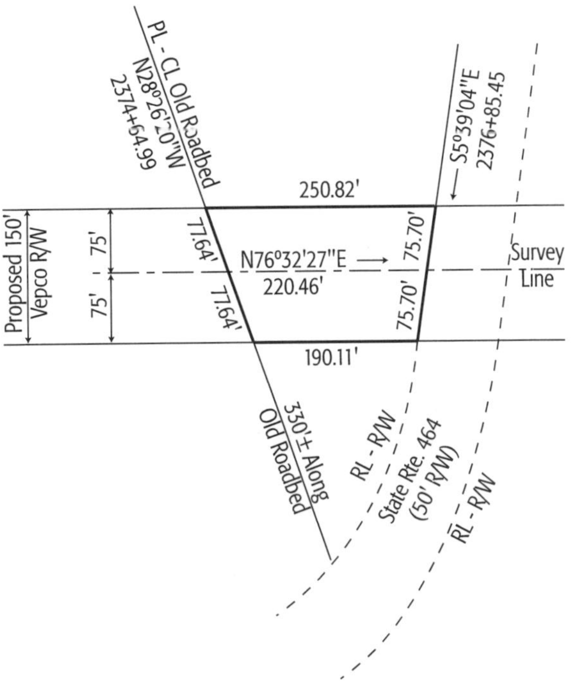

Source: Virginia Power, Richmond, Virginia.

the installation cost of sanitary sewers. Topographical variation can prevent water from standing in streets and under homes, which will lead eventually to deterioration of wood structural members and, in some regions of the country, encourage termite infestation. Contrarily, severe slopes can cause erosion, high foundation construction costs, and expensive storm water countermeasures, including the acquisition of offsite drainage easements and construction of storm water sewer systems. In fact, larger diameter storm water systems may be required on steep slopes because sewer lines may not carry as much water as moderately sloped systems due to high water velocities causing turbulence. Generally, a 10% to 15% grade is the maximum allowable slope for subdivision streets. Higher slopes are allowed in mountainous areas and where vehicular traffic is modest.

An initial impression of a parcel's terrain features can be obtained by analyzing a topographical map. Ideally, one will be available for the subject property, but certainly not for each of the comparable land sales. It is possible to use a topographical map prepared by the U.S. Geological Survey (USGS) to understand a parcel's relief, especially if it is a large tract. Many state and local governmental agencies can provide more detailed topographical maps than USGS. That is, contour lines may be shown in two- to five-foot intervals rather than 10-foot intervals.

A topographical map depicts the shape of the surface of land through contour lines. These imaginary contour lines connect surfaces of equal elevation. The elevations generally are identified as so many feet above or below sea level. In reading these maps (see Figure 3.2 on page 18), topographical contours for steep terrain are shown close together, while level ground will either show no contour lines or they will be spaced widely. In reading a topographical map, observe the number of lines between the bold lines for which elevations are stated. For example, in Figure 3.2 there are five narrow or intermediate lines between each 50-foot main contour line; therefore, the terrain changes 10 feet per contour line. A rough computation of the topographical slope can be made by comparing the vertical rise to horizontal distance much like the pitch of a roof. For example, if the land rises 10 feet for every 100 feet of horizontal distance, the slope is 10%.

Another relatively simple way to measure slopes in the field is by use of a Locke hand level.[4] This handheld device is used for rough leveling. It is a metal tube about six inches long. At the eye end there is a peephole through which the appraiser can view a reference point. The circle at the other end of the tube is bisected. The level should be held so that the viewer can see the reference point directly without magnification on one half. The other half contains a bubble that will be aligned with a cross wire when the tube is held in a level position. To measure the slope, the appraiser places the level at a given height, such as the appraiser's eye level. Next he or she views horizontally on a level plane to a point on a slope. (See Figure 4.2.) An approximation of the slope can be made by comparing the distance along the ground (the hypothenuse) from the viewing position to the viewed point. This method is sufficiently accurate because the slope of an incline will vary from different points along the hill anyway.

Suppose the distance along the ground (c) is 50 feet and the vertical distance (a) is five feet; the slope (b) then is approximately 10%. A more precise computation method is to divide the base of the right triangle (height taken at the Locke hand level) by the horizontal leg of the

---

4. Another instrument is the Abney level, which is calibrated to display the slope in degrees. The appraiser can even use a simple carpenter's level, but its use presents some difficulty since the user cannot simultaneously look at the level bubble and a distant point on the terrain.

triangle. This latter distance is calculated by solving the equation $b^2 = c^2 - a^2$. The slope calculation then is $b^2 = 2,500 - 25$, or $b = 49.75$ feet, with the slope equal to 10.05% (5 ft./49.75 ft.). The slope of a parcel will vary at different points. Thus, by taking several readings the appraiser can find one that typifies the overall slope of the incline.

Figure 4.2   *Using Locke Hand Level*

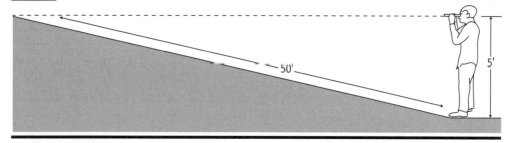

Soil Conditions

An understanding of soil conditions can be valuable to an appraiser in determining a parcel's highest and best use, its market appeal, and ultimately its value. In most parts of the country, soil surveys are available—either from municipal planning offices, the Soil Conservation Service of the United States Department of Agriculture, or universities. A site inspection, coupled with analysis of a topographical map and a soil survey map, can give a fairly clear idea about the soil conditions of a tract.

Figure 4.3 identifies the various soils in a limited area. Suppose, for instance, that the cultivated fields on the parcel at the top right corner of this map are zoned for single-family, detached residential use; public water is available to the parcel, but there is no sewer. A review of this map shows that the prominent soil classifications are Ro, Le, and AgA. Ro soil, Roanoke silt loam, is not well-suited either for septic tank absorption fields or basements because it is poorly drained, has slow permeability, is susceptible to flooding and a seasonal high water table, and has high shrink-swell potential. The Le soil, Lenoir, exhibits the same unsatisfactory conditions as the Roanoke soil, plus it has a clayey subsoil. Finally, the AgA soil, Angie, is somewhat better than the other two classifications. This soil is moderately well-drained and has slow permeability and moderate shrink-swell characteristics. Initially, this site would not appear to have a highest and best use for single-family houses that require septic tanks or basements. Of course, the appraiser will want to note in the limiting conditions of the report the basis for this conclusion and further state that no soils test were made for the appraisal assignment.

Figure 4.3 *Soils Map*

Source: *Soil Survey of Henrico County, Virginia* United States Department of Agriculture Soil Conservation Service in cooperation with Virginia Polytechnic Institute and State University (October 1975).

Flood Hazards

Flood damage occurs along the banks of streams, creeks, rivers, bays, and oceans. The zone in which most flooding occurs is known as a floodplain. An appraiser should take steps to detect the presence of areas that are periodically subject to flooding. (See Chapter 18 "Residential Waterfront Property" and Chapter 23 "Floodplains and Wetlands" for a detailed discussion on the detection of floodplains, appraisal methodology, and shoreline erosion.) A good source for information on flood-prone areas are FEMA (Federal Emergency Management Agency) flood hazard and rate maps. (See Figure 23.2 for a sample map.) The FEMA map shows zones rated according to their severity of flooding, ranging from those expected to flood every 100 years, those forecast to flood every 100 to 500 years, and those where flooding is not expected to occur more often than every 500 years. These maps are helpful during dry seasons when evidence of flooding is not always apparent.

Summary

A site analysis involves determining a site's usefulness. This includes an analysis of the site's ownership rights, mineral rights, riparian rights, zoning, private restrictions, boundary lines, easements, terrain, soil conditions, and flood hazards to reveal the optimum property use(s). Most appraisal assignments obligate appraisers to ascertain the value of an owner's legal interest in real property. It is prudent for the appraiser to include as much available information on mineral rights as is relevant to a particular valuation assignment. Land ownership may include both mineral interests and royalty interests. Mineral interests relate to the ownership of minerals in place as well as access, exploration, extraction, processing, and transport rights. Royalty interests are concerned with the right to receive revenue from the extraction of minerals with neither the right to extract nor the financial burden to do so. The two most reliable valuation techniques for appraising land with mineral deposits are the royalty income and production methods.

Riparian rights are a form of water rights. Property owners whose land abuts a body of water such as a stream or river enjoy riparian rights. When valuing land suited for recreational subdivision purposes in the western part of the United States, it is important to understand water law.

An analysis of an appraised property's zoning will reveal the land use activities that can legally be conducted on the site. In addition, the likelihood of rezoning a parcel must be considered. Restrictive covenants are private land use controls that are prepared on behalf of a developer to protect and preserve the physical, social, and economic integrity of a development. An important function of the covenants is to provide for the compliance of proposed building plans.

The assessor's office property records for the appraised parcel may show any changes in the property boundaries, including references to conveyances as specified in particular deed books and pages. It generally is a good idea to invite the property owner to accompany the appraiser on the site inspection to identify property lines and other value-related features accurately. An easement basically is a nonpossessory interest in another party's real property that benefits the second party. The two principal types of easements are affirmative easements and negative easements. An affirmative easement grants a right to a nonowner to perform a specific action on a specific parcel, or part of a parcel. The fee owner gives up some rights as a result of the easement. The right may or may not be an exclusive right. A negative easement such as an avigation easement prohibits a landowner from using land for zoned uses.

Terrain features affect the appeal, utility, highest and best use, development and construction costs, and value of a parcel. Variations in terrain do not affect the desirability of land for all prospective land use in the same way. An initial impression of a parcel's terrain can be obtained by analyzing a topographical map. In the field, a relatively simple way to measure slopes is by use of a Locke hand level.

An understanding of soil conditions can be valuable to an appraiser in comprehending a parcel's highest and best use, market appeal, and value. A site inspection, coupled with analysis of a topographical map and a soil survey map, can provide a fairly clear picture of the soil conditions of a tract.

Flood damage occurs along the banks of streams, creeks, rivers, bays, and oceans. The zones in which most flooding occurs are known as floodplains. An appraiser should detect the presence of areas that are periodically subject to flooding using FEMA flood hazard and rate maps.

Judging Highest and Best Use

The purpose of ascertaining a parcel's highest and best use is to provide a basis for accurately estimating market value. This analytical process should be straightforward and solidly reflect the real estate market. *Highest and best use* for appraisal purposes is defined as that use or succession of available, legal, and physically permitted uses for which there is sufficient demand that produces the most probable present site value. The Appraisal Institute provides a variation of this definition, which states that highest and best use is "the reasonably probable and legal use of vacant land or an improved property, which is physically possible, appropriately supported, financially feasible, and that results in the highest value."[1]

Available Uses

Available uses refer to those land uses to which the parcel would likely be put with a reasonably high degree of certainty in the near term. Excluded from available uses are those that are remote in time, conjectural, or unlikely to be developed in the foreseeable future. A careful analysis of community growth trends, especially in the immediate neighborhood, should either confirm or refute the likelihood of a prospective use actually being achieved on the appraised parcel within the next three to five years.

Legal Uses

Legal uses should be considered early in the highest and best use analysis. They are relatively easy to identify and can eliminate many probable uses. The primary indication of legality is provided by the municipal zoning ordinance. Never to be overlooked is the locality's comprehensive or master plan. This long-range plan specifies the local government's broad intent for land use activities. For instance, the highest and best use of an appraised parcel might be greatly overstated as a single-family residential

---

1. Appraisal Institute, *The Appraisal of Real Estate,* 11th ed. (Chicago: Appraisal Institute, 1996), p. 297.

subdivision when the present zoning allows this use, but the comprehensive plan designates the land as a future public park. The client should be informed in the appraisal report of this future public land use prospect.

A long-term ground lease that restricts a parcel's use must be considered in the analysis of highest and best use. Likewise, an appraiser must be familiar with blanket subdivision restrictive covenants that may regulate a site's use. (See the discussion of this topic in Chapter 4.) Other legal constraints on use include municipal building codes, easements, and environmental restrictions. Building codes regulate the design, materials, occupancy, and construction of buildings under state or local ordinances. If a particular community's building code is obsolete or greatly increases the cost of construction, then the highest and best use of parcels in that community is affected adversely.

A variety of different easements can limit the future use of a parcel. These include gas and electric transmission line, sewer and storm water, avigation, and scenic land conservation easements (see Chapter 22). Conservation easements may prohibit future development or restrict a property owner from cutting timber or demolishing historic structures. Environmentally protected lands such as wetlands may be unavailable for many forms of development. These lands may be protected from development by state and federal agencies such as the U. S. Army Corps of Engineers.

Probability of Rezoning

A parcel may not currently be zoned for an activity that satisfies all the other criteria for a prospective highest and best use. Yet, the prospect for rezoning should not automatically be dismissed. That is, the presumed highest and best use should not fail on this one point without additional research. A pivotal point in determining whether the likely highest and best use is valid is the probability of rezoning.[2]

In determining whether the rezoning necessary to achieve a particular highest and best use is likely to occur, an appraiser should consider neighborhood land use trends; the history, especially recent history, of parcels having the same or similar zoning as the subject parcel being

---

2. In his article "Valuing the Probability of Rezoning," *The Appraisal Journal* (April 1988), p. 221, William B. Knipe, III, quotes J. D. Eaton, *Real Estate Valuation in Litigation* (Chicago: Appraisal Institute, 1982), on how to decide which zoning classification should be compared to the subject property when there is a possibility of rezoning: "If there is little doubt that the property will be rezoned, and the discount applicable to the higher-zoned sales would be comparatively minimal, it may be advisable to use sales of higher-zoned property. On the other hand, if there is only a marginal increment in value attributable to the probability of rezoning, it is generally best to utilize sale properties that have the same zoning as the property being appraised and adjust the values upward."

rezoned to allow the prospective use; and the probability of the appraised site being rezoned as indicated by the municipal zoning/planning staff. This line of inquiry should substantiate the likelihood of the subject parcel obtaining the required rezoning. Finally, an informed estimate should be made concerning the cost of expert assistance, such as civil and traffic engineering, legal expenses, and delays incurred to obtain the rezoning. Sometimes the local government requires substantial proffers as a prerequisite for rezoning. These various costs, delays, and uncertainty may largely negate the perceived financial benefit of obtaining the rezoning necessary for a higher and better use.

Physically Permitted Uses

Physically permitted uses are those activities that a parcel's physical features will allow. Physical constraints are detailed in Chapter 4 and include such considerations as size, shape, surface and subsurface soil conditions, height of water table, flood hazards, wetlands, terrain, access, and availability of public utilities. These physical limitations on a parcel's highest and best use are covered in detail in Chapters 8 through 14, 22, and 23. A parcel may be of an appropriate size for certain activities or it may be too small or large to achieve its optimum use. Likewise, it may be too narrow to justify construction or its shape may severely constrain on-site vehicle circulation and parking. Its soils may be highly erosive, contain excessive rock, or be so impermeable as to prohibit the operation of individual septic systems. The height of a parcel's water table, presence of wetlands, and seasonal flooding may prohibit the full utilization of a parcel. A site's terrain either may enhance its appeal and value or increase development and construction expenses to the point that it is unacceptable for many uses. Without adequate access and public utility capacity, a parcel seldom can achieve its optimum use and value potential.

Sufficiency of Demand

The level of demand for a specific land use activity is a crucial test of a site's highest and best use. Even if all of the other requisites for a given highest and best use have been met, without sufficient tenant or purchaser interest that highest and best use cannot be realized. In gauging the strength of demand for prospective uses, the appraiser should consider the comparative supply and demand for competitive sites as well as demand in the market for the apparent highest and best use. For example, in a particular office sector, surveyed office parks containing 219,120 square feet had a 90% occupancy level (197,208 sq. ft.). Six months later, the office park inventory increased to 259,600 square feet while the occupancy rate declined to 87% (225,852 sq. ft.) Thus, an additional 40,480 square feet of space was delivered while just 28,644 square feet of space was absorbed, resulting in a negative absorption rate.

Duration and Intensity of Parcel Uses

To note that the highest and best use of an appraised parcel is residential, for example, may be both insufficient and confusing. The difficulty with such a cursory statement is that the client has to substitute his or her judgment when the appraiser does not supply the desired specifics of how long a given use or uses likely will continue and specifically what use is forecast to occur. As an example, the following land uses are forecast for the subject parcel:

Years 0–3	Years 4–10	Years 11–40
sod farm	golf driving range	garden apartments

A short-term existing or future use is known as an *interim use*. Sometimes an interim use provides just enough revenue to pay the real estate taxes. Hence, a short-term lease such as a ground lease for a graveled surface parking lot sometimes is referred to as a "tax payer." That is, the use produces income just sufficient to offset the real estate taxes and possibly public liability insurance premiums. Based on an understanding of the elements of a parcel's highest and best use, in this example an appraiser may conclude that the highest and best use of the parcel in 11 years will be for garden apartments at a density of 14 dwelling units per gross acre.

Most Probable Site Value

The highest degree of reliability for an estimate of value occurs when a rigorous regional, community, neighborhood, and site analysis leads to a sound highest and best use conclusion. There is an undeniable and essential linkage between a site's highest and best use analysis and its estimated market value. If the highest and best use analysis accurately identifies a parcel's use or succession of available legal and physically permitted uses for which there is sufficient demand, then the subsequent data compilation and analysis should result in a well-reasoned and convincing estimate of value.

The tendency for some appraisers to either ignore or greatly abbreviate a thorough highest and best use analysis in an appraisal assignment will produce a poor outcome, like the impulsive person whose decision-making process may be characterized as "ready, aim, fire." Conversely, an orderly, sequential review and consideration of all influences on a property's highest and best use invariably leads to a defensible estimate of its most probable value.

Excess and Surplus Land

At times, an appraiser is called on to appraise improved properties that have an above-average amount of land. These assignments may either be for single-family residential or commercial and industrial parcels. Two questions arise in such assignments. What is excess land and how should it be appraised? *Excess land* is land that is not needed to support the use of existing or probable future improvements. There are two variations of excess land. Some housing agencies and residential mortgage lenders will not lend on an additional lot or acreage that is judged to be beyond the needs of a typical borrower (or common and customary for a particular area). That is, if a half-acre lot is typical for homes of a particular price in a suburban neighborhood, then an extra lot would be excluded from the transaction and the borrower would have to acquire it with cash. The appraiser would only appraise the underlying home site and building. However, if it were necessary to appraise the additional lot or land, it could be done readily and without any discount in unit value because it has value as a separate economic entity.

Similarly, income-producing properties have an optimum size and excess land may be excluded from an appraisal of the economic entity. To produce similar value indications using the depreciated cost and income approaches, the additional land would be set aside in the income approach and later added to the subtotal, as shown below.

Value indicated by depreciated cost approach	$1,200,000
Value indicated by income approach	$1,000,000

The $200,000 difference is the result of the capitalized building income excluding rental income from the excess land, but its value is included in the depreciated cost approach. The difference can be reconciled by adding in the estimated value of the excess land, which in this case is $200,000. The same land unit value developed in the depreciated cost approach would be applied for the nonproductive land in the income approach.

Land that is in excess of typical parcel size may not be excessive if it supports the primary land use activity on the parcel. For example, parking lots and reserve septic system drain fields are necessary for a primary use. These areas are not excess land because they support the major activity.

Surplus land relates only to existing improvements, not proposed or hypothetical structures. It exists when a structure(s) is so situated on a parcel that it encumbers the entire site. Surplus land does not support or is not necessary for the highest and best use of an existing improvement, but due to its location relative to the building, it cannot be marketed as a separate entity. For example, a dwelling is placed in the middle of two lots. Suppose that lots in this neighborhood are selling for about $125,000. Would the combined two lots be worth $250,000? It is unlikely that the two lots would be worth the full value because in the combined state they comprise just one lot, albeit twice the size of a typical lot. Moreover, neither of the subject's two lots can be sold separately because part of the house rests on each lot.

Most Probable Use

Some appraisers prefer the most probable use concept over the highest and best use of a parcel because it is rooted in the marketplace and is neither theoretical, an idealized notion of value maximization, nor an "abstracted set of conditions unlikely and probably impossible to be achieved."[3] *Most probable use* is defined as the use to which a site will most likely be placed. Further, it is based on actual behavioral patterns of active market participants.

Often, most probable use serves a client's needs better than highest and best use for appraisal purposes. It logically leads the appraiser to the expected use of an appraised parcel and, in turn, to similar comparable land sales. This valuation concept departs from the idea of valuing a parcel on the basis of the use(s) that will maximize value. Instead of seeking a use that will maximize value, which usually is the seller's objective (while the purchaser is motivated to pay the lowest possible price), this alternative line of reasoning seeks to identify the most likely use that will produce the most probable price that a purchaser will pay.

Highest and Best Use Studies

The purpose of highest and best use studies is to determine the optimal use for a site. An investor may be interested in acquiring a parcel for one of several possible uses. He or she wants to choose that use which will maximize the parcel's present value. The analytical process used in seeking the maximum parcel value is similar to that used in estimating highest and best use in an appraisal report, but it is more comprehensive. Highest and best use analysis is a section of an appraisal report, while a highest and best use study is an entire report. A highest and best use report often is used to guide future development of a parcel to build the most profitable set of improvements. The highest present value may be estimated either through the discounted cash flow or land residual methods. The discounted cash flow method is illustrated in Table 17.2 in Chapter 17. The land residual method of finding a parcel's highest present site value is illustrated in

---

3.   William N. Kinnard, Jr., "New Thinking in Appraisal Theory," *The Real Estate Appraiser* (August 1966), p. 8.

Table 5.1. In this example, construction of the four-unit apartment building is the highest and best use of the vacant lot because it produces the highest site value.

Summary

The purpose of determining a parcel's highest and best use is to provide the basis for accurately estimating its market value. Highest and best use is that use or succession of available, legal, and physically permitted uses for which there is sufficient demand that produces the most probable present site value. Available use refers to those land uses to which the parcel would likely be placed with a reasonably high degree of certainty in the near future.

Legal uses should be considered early in the highest and best use analysis. The municipal zoning ordinance and its comprehensive plan provide the primary indication. Other legal constraints on utilizing a parcel are municipal building codes, easements, and environmental restrictions. A parcel currently may not be zoned for an activity that satisfies all of the other criteria for a prospective highest and best use. A pivotal point as to whether the likely highest and best use is valid is the probability of rezoning.

Physically permitted uses are those activities that a parcel's physical features will allow. Physical constraints include such considerations as size, shape, surface and subsurface soil conditions, height of water table, flood hazards, wetlands, terrain, access, and the availability of public utilities. The level of demand for a specific land use activity is a crucial test of a site's highest and best use. Even if all of the other requisites for a given highest

Table 5.1   *Highest and Best Use Analysis Via Land Residual Method*

	Residential Duplex	Residential Quadruplex
Potential gross annual income		
Duplex units $750 × 2 × 12 (months)	$18,000	
Quadruplex $700 × 4 × 12		$33,600
Less vacancy and collection losses @ 8%	1,440	2,688
Effective gross annual income	$16,560	$30,912
Less operating expenses		
Management fee (7%)	$1,159	$2,164
Real estate taxes (1.8% × bldg. cost*)	1,287	2,268
Maintenance and repairs (incl. turnover prep.)	700	1,250
Hazard insurance	250	425
Utilities (water and sewer)	800	1,500
Janitorial service	300	450
Reserves for roof, HVAC and appliances	600	1,150
Total operating expenses	$5,096	$9,207
Net operating expenses	$11,464	$21,705
Less income attributable to proposed buildings		
Duplex ($65 × 1,100 sq. ft.)(0.138†)	$9,867	
Quadruplex ($60 × 2,100 sq. ft.)(0.138)		17,388
Net income residual to site	$1,597	$4,317
Value of land:		
Duplex ($1,597 ÷ 11.8%‡)	$13,534	
Quadruplex ($4,317 ÷ 11.8%)		$36,585

*   Because the building has not been constructed, no tax levy has been imposed on the appraised property's improvements. Nevertheless, the dollar amount of the probable tax levy can be estimated by applying the effective tax rate against the current construction cost of a proposed building. In this case, property is assessed at full market value. Otherwise, the nominal tax rate would have been multiplied by the assessment ratio (assessed value ÷ market value).

†   Building capitalization rate = interest rate   0.100
                          + recapture rate 100% ÷ 50 years   0.020
                          + real estate effective tax rate   0.018
                                                    0.138

‡   Interest rate (0.100) + effective tax rate (0.018) = 0.118; that is, 10% land capitalization rate + 1.8% real estate tax rate.

and best use have been met, without sufficient purchaser or tenant interest, that highest and best use cannot be realized.

A highest and best use analysis should specify how long a given use or uses likely will continue and specifically what use is forecast to occur. An orderly, sequential review and consideration of all influences on a property's highest and best use invariably leads to a defensible estimate of its most probable value. At times, an appraiser is called on to appraise improved properties that have an above-average amount of land. Excess land is land that is not needed to support the use of existing or probable future improvements. Most probable use is the use to which a site will most likely be placed. It is based on actual behavioral patterns of active market participants. The purpose of highest and best use studies is to determine the optimal use for a site. A highest and best use report often is used to guide future development of a parcel to build the most profitable set of improvements.

PART

II

Adjustment Procedures

Adjusting for Size Differences

To be used as a comparable, a land sale should have the same or similar zoning as the appraised parcel; have similar terrain, access, and public utilities; and be situated a relatively short distance from the subject property. If there are unadjusted differences for any of these features after a size adjustment has been made, the client will be left with a nonsensical conclusion of value. Additionally, the two parcels should have the same specific highest and best use, not simply a residential or commercial use. For example, each should have a highest and best use for a single-family, detached dwelling with similar square footage requirements; for a commercial site, the use should be specified for a service station site, for example, rather than for retail use in general. In short, the sale site should be a reasonably close substitute for the subject site, so that a prospective buyer would be indifferent about choosing one site over the other.

Avoid Sales That Differ Widely in Size

Whenever possible, an appraiser should avoid using sales that differ substantially in size from the appraised parcel. Parcels of greatly different size appeal to different sectors of the market and command much different unit prices. Even when using the size adjustment techniques discussed in this chapter, a more convincing case for an estimated value can be made from the comparison of like-size comparable land sales and appraised property. It is unacceptable for an appraiser to provide no support or explanation of his or her reasoning for size adjustments of 25% to 50%. Generally, there are more small land sales than large sales. As a rule, small land sales (at high unit prices) are misused in the appraisal of large tracts. This valuation approach is flawed unless proper analysis and market-based substantiation accompany such size adjustments.

In highly desirable resort areas, lot size versus value can sometimes be misleading. For example, in one of Colorado's most renown ski areas, residential lots may sell for nearly the same price even though their sizes may range from 0.25 acre to 35 acres. In these situations, it is important for the appraiser to determine how much, if any, the additional land mass contributes to the larger site's value. There is some evidence that in popular resorts the total square feet of buildable area allowed under existing zoning influences the price paid.

Court Rulings

A review of various judicial rulings on the subject of land size adjustments is instructive. A distortion in appraised value is likely to result when small site sales are used to value a large parcel. For instance, a North Carolina court ruled: "A large piece of land cannot usually be applied profitably to the same uses as a small piece." In another North Carolina case, a land owner introduced comparable sales of 75 and 80 acres to support the value of his 495-acre tract. "After having heard arguments of the parties, the court found that neither sale tract was sufficiently similar to the owner's property to be considered a comparable sale . . . ." In an Iowa case, the owner of a 242-acre farm appealed a ruling where ". . . the court refused him an opportunity to admit into evidence the sale prices of seven separate tracts, all small parcels taken from larger acreages. The small parcels varied in size from 10 to 25 acres. On appeal, the owner's motion was denied with the court stating that land sales should have been similar in size to the subject farm and not sales of a portion of farms which were sold for development purposes."[1]

Supported Size Adjustments

Generally, it is expected that as the size of a parcel increases, the unit value declines. However, this decline tends to occur at an exponential rate rather than on a linear basis. That is, the unit value change corresponds to the rate of change rather than the dollar amount of change per unit (e.g., acre). A size adjustment can be made using the methods described below, keeping in mind that some error will be introduced by using a linear adjustment rather than an exponential adjustment. The estimated value of the appraised property based on linear computations will be sufficiently accurate if the comparables are not markedly different in size.

Calculating Unit Price Rate of Change

In this example, the subject parcel contains 10 acres and is similar to the recent comparable land sales in zoning and location attributes. The steps in this land valuation method follow.

---

1.   James H. Boykin, "Impropriety of Using Dissimilar-Size Comparable Land Sales ," *The Appraisal Journal* (July 1996), pp. 313–314.

Average size of outparcel sales compiled	1.11 acres
Average per-square-foot price of outparcel sales	$8.36
Average size of shopping center land sales	15.27 acres
Average per-square-foot price of shopping center land sales	$5.79

Derived per-unit adjustment	
1.11 acre	$8.36/sq. ft.
− 15.27 acres	− 5.79/sq. ft.
14.16 acres	$2.57/sq. ft.

The average rate of price change per square foot is $0.0000042, computed as follows:

$$\frac{\$2.57/\text{sq. ft.}}{14.16 \text{ acres} \times 43{,}560 \text{ sq. ft.}}$$

When this rate of change is applied to the subject 10-acre parcel, the following value is indicated:

15.27 acres	$5.79/ sq. ft.
− 10.00 acres	
5.27 acres × 43,560 × $0.0000042 =	+ 0.96/sq. ft.
	$6.75/sq. ft.

The estimated value of the 10-acre parcel is $6.75 × (10 ac. × 43,560 sq. ft.) = $2,940,300.[2]

Interpolation Method

Using the interpolation method, the same result is achieved. All assumptions and values used in the previous example apply.

$8.36/sq. ft.	1.11 acre	1.11 acre
?	10.00 acres	
− 5.79/sq. ft.		− 15.27 acres
$2.57/sq. ft.	8.89 acres	14.16 acres

The computed per-square-foot value of the 10-acre parcel and its total value equal:

$$\$8.36 - [\$2.57(8.89 \text{ acres}/14.16 \text{ acres})]$$
$$\$8.36 - [\$2.57 \times 0.62781]$$
$$\$8.36 - \$1.61 =$$
$$\$6.75/ \text{ square foot} \times 435{,}600 \text{ square feet} = \$2{,}940{,}300$$

---

2.   Ibid. , pp. 315, 317.

Alternative Methods

In addition to the two methods discussed above, the following methods (explained fully in Chapters 8 and 9) may prove helpful when comparable size land sales are unavailable or the sales are not sufficiently similar to the appraised parcel to produce a reliable indication of its market value. The first of these methods makes use of land sale listings. By determining the ratio of sale prices to listing prices of a large number of similar listings that have sold, this method becomes even more useful. The second method is the land value extraction method and is especially applicable to sales of land with minimal-value improvements. The methodology of handling improvements with a net positive and net negative value is explained. Significantly, these latter two methods may be used for virtually any type of land valuation assignment.

Still another method of analyzing and depicting the relationship between parcel size and unit price is graphing and curve plotting. Figure 6.1 shows a curvilinear relationship that may be referred to as a "hockey stick" curve. The graph depicts a sharp unit price decline initially for smaller sale parcels, which flattens out for larger parcels. In regard to commercially zoned sale parcels in Florida, for example, there is considerably more similarity in the per-acre price of parcels in the 8- to 37-acre range than sales of under 1 to 5 acres. This graphic depiction of land sales can help the client understand size adjustments.

Figure 6.1   *Size vs. Price Per Acre*

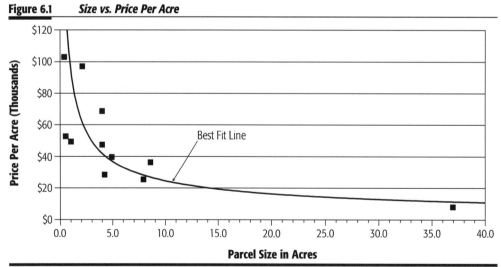

Courtesy of Emerson Appraisal Company, Gainesville, Florida

Summary

A comparable land sale should have the same or similar zoning as the appraised parcel; have similar terrain, access, and public utilities; and be within a relatively short distance from the appraised parcel. A buyer should view it as a substitute site for the subject site. Comparable land sales that differ substantially in size from the subject parcel usually should be avoided because they appeal to different buyers and bring much different unit prices. A distorted appraised value is likely to occur if a small site sale is used to value a large parcel. As the size of a parcel increases, the unit value declines at an exponential rate. Yet, the estimated value of an appraised parcel based on linear computations will be sufficiently accurate if the comparables are not markedly different in size from the appraised parcel.

Adjusting for Changing Market Conditions

This chapter explores when adjustments for changing market conditions should be made and how to improve the accuracy of time adjustments when governmental and physical changes have occurred. Appraisers should keep these rudiments in mind when adjusting the prices of comparable land sales:

- Adjust for changing market conditions before making adjustments for physical and legal differences or conditions of sale. That is, first answer the question, "What price would this sale property have brought in today's market, assuming the effective date of appraisal for the subject property is the current date?"

- Improve the accuracy of time adjustments by using a series of periods rather than a single, long period. Of course, this technique will necessitate more sales, but will produce more accurate results. For example, Table 7.1 on page 58 shows a considerable variance in value from year to year (ranging from -10.27% to +8.05%) but little overall value change (-2.62%).

- Be familiar with the zoning, utilities, and physical state of each sale when it was transferred.

Analyze Resale of the Same Sites

Whenever possible, it is advisable to identify and analyze several sets of sales and resales of the same parcel. The logic behind using several sets of sales is to assure both the direction (plus or minus) and the magnitude of the change in market prices of similar parcels and, in turn, the appraised parcel. In analyzing more than one sale transaction of a comparable sale, it is important to determine if any physical or neighborhood conditions changed between the time of the sales. For instance, has the parcel been rezoned; have public utilities been made available; has any site work been performed; has the site's access changed; have off-site public improvements, such as street paving, sidewalks, or storm water retention ponds, been built; or have neighborhood businesses been upgraded? If none of these conditions changed, then any change in price would appear to have resulted from changes in general market conditions. Before reaching this conclusion, however, the appraiser should interview a person familiar with the motivation of the buyers involved in each transaction. Depending on the potential influence of this motivation on the sale prices, the appraiser can either discard the sale or make an adjustment for market conditions. At this point, the appraiser should determine if either the earlier or later sale price was above or below market value. An example of a time adjustment made using this method follows.

Land Sale 5

Location:	On south line of Freeboard Boulevard in South Wind County, approximately one mile northeast of Iron Gate Road.
Zoning:	R-16 Garden Apartments
Grantor:	Land Ventures, Inc.
Grantee:	Zenith Limited Partnership
Deed Book/Page:	788/46
Date of Sale:	March 22, 1997
Site Size:	18 acres
Sale Price:	$810,000
Price/Acre	$45,000
Public Utilities:	Water and sewer
Comments:	No unusual conditions influenced the sale price; parcel has gently rolling terrain and is situated in an area developing for garden apartments and detached, single-family homes.

Land Sale 6

Location:	On south line of Freeboard Boulevard in South Wind County, approximately one mile northeast of Iron Gate Road.
Zoning:	R-16 Garden Apartments
Grantor:	Zenith Limited Partnership
Grantee:	Life Style Construction Corp.
Deed Book/Page:	790/23
Date of Sale:	June 19, 1999
Site Size:	18 acres
Sale Price:	$891,000
Price/Acre	$49,500
Public Utilities:	Water and sewer
Comments:	This is a subsequent sale of Land Sale 5. No changes have occurred to the site since its purchase in 1997.

An upward adjustment is indicated for changes in market conditions since Sale 5 occurred in 1997. (It may be computed monthly, quarterly, or annually.) In this example, an annual price adjustment is made.

Land Sale 6	$891,000	6/19/99
Land Sale 5	$810,000	3/22/97
Difference	$81,000	2 $1/4$ years
Total percentage change	$81,000/$810,000 =	10.00%
Annual rate of change	10.00%/2.25 years =	+4.44%

Analyze Sales of Similar Sites at Different Times

It is not always possible to locate resales of the same site, but often an appraiser can find several similar sales in the immediate area that have sold at different times. An analysis of such sales may produce an adjustment for changing market conditions. As in the analysis of resales, care must be taken to determine the comparability of the properties when each sale occurred, not when the appraisal is prepared. For example, public utilities may have been extended to a sale parcel between the time it sold and the appraisal date. The appraiser needs to account for any differences among the land sales. One method for identifying differences in the prices paid is paired sales analysis, which is covered in Chapter 10.

Assume for this example that there are no significant differences in the following land sales and the adjustment is made on a monthly basis.

Land Sale 4

Location:	At southwest corner of High Tower and Express Roads in Dabney Industrial Park
Zoning:	M-2 Industrial
Grantor:	Glen Bay Partnership
Grantee:	Matterfact Corp.
Deed Book/Page:	1056/273
Date of Sale:	October 6, 1998
Site Size:	47,000 square feet
Sale Price:	$180,000
Price/Sq. Ft.	$3.83
Public Utilities:	Water, sewer, and gas
Comments:	This parcel is level and is readily accessible from a nearby interchange of the Crosstown Expressway.

Land Sale 7

Location:	7229 High Tower Road in Dabney Industrial Park
Zoning:	M-2 Industrial
Grantor:	Bookbinder, Ltd.
Grantee:	Fabricators, Inc.
Deed Book/Page:	1062/339
Date of Sale:	March 11, 2000
Site Size:	45,200 square feet
Sale Price:	$210,000
Price/Sq. Ft.	$4.65
Public Utilities:	Water, sewer, and gas
Comments:	This sale parcel is located in the same industrial park as Sale 4 and is similar in nearly all respects.

A monthly market conditions adjustment is made as follows:

Land Sale 7	$4.65/sq. ft.	3/11/00
Land Sale 4	$3.83/sq. ft.	10/6/98
Difference	$0.82/sq. ft.	17 months
Total percentage change	$0.82/$3.83 =	21.41%
Monthly rate of change	21.41%/17 months =	+1.26%

Indexed Time/Price Changes

One of the first lessons learned in real investing and valuation is that land is local in nature. This truism reflects the fact that local economic influences cause demand to vary from locale to locale as well as within local jurisdictions and even within the same developments. Often this lesson is learned in a relatively painless classroom or office environment, but sometimes it is learned more forcefully through experience (or "the school of hard knocks"). There are some indices of land value that can supplement local land sales price trends. When such indices are localized and representative of the appraised property's highest and best use, zoning, and size, they are useful for estimating market price trends (time adjustments).

Table 7.1 shows annual land value changes in the United States on a gross basis. Useful trend information can be drawn from national data such as this. The table describes a six-year real estate cycle that was traumatic for many real estate investors and appraisers. Many institutional investors

Table 7.1 *Land at Market Value, USA (in Billions of Dollars) 1988–1994*

1988	1989	1990	1991	1992	1993	1994
5184.7	5602.2	5026.8	4821.1	4351.7	4286.2	4364.2
–	+8.05%	-10.27%	-4.09%	-9.74%	-1.51%	+1.82

Source: Table 8.12 "Distribution of Tangible Assets by Sector," *Balance Sheets for the U.S. Economy 1945–93* (Washington, D.C.: Board of Governors of the Federal Reserve System, 1994), pp. 18–19.

Land Valuation: Adjustment Procedures and Assignments

and mortgage lenders lost their appetite for acquiring, developing and funding real estate ventures and land in the United States as a whole passed through a period of declining values. This table illustrates the fallacy of assuming that land values will rise continually. It is true that, nationwide, land values rose between 1945 and 1989—a period of 44 years—but this trend has not been steady. This underscores the error of some appraisers who mechanically make positive time adjustments, frequently without any market-based evidence, because they believe that the market can only continue to go up.

Straight-Line or Exponential Rate of Change

If appraisers use several, similar comparable sales to measure the periodic change in value for a series of relatively short periods, accurate results can be obtained. Some observers hold that to use an arithmetic mean results in an overestimation of average growth rates.[1] A more accurate method is to use a compound monthly rate of growth similar to that of a financial instrument. In the example developed from Land Sales 4 and 7, a compound monthly rate of change of +1.15% is calculated; an average monthly rate of change of +1.26% was computed previously. Using a Hewlett-Packard 12C financial calculator, the compound monthly rate of land value change is computed as follows.

17n 3.83 chs PV 4.65 FV Solve for i Read 1.15

Summary

When adjusting the prices of comparable land sales: 1) adjust for changing market conditions prior to making adjustments for physical and legal factors or conditions of sale; 2) improve the accuracy of time adjustments by using a series of periods rather than one long period; and 3) be familiar with the zoning, utilities, and physical state of each sale when its was transferred. Whenever possible, try to identify and analyze several sets of sales and resales of the same parcel. It is not always possible to locate resales of the same site, but often an appraiser can find several, similar sales in the immediate area that have sold at different times. An analysis of such sales may produce an adjustment for changing market conditions. A preferred method of computing value changes over a longer period is to use compound monthly rates of growth instead of straight-line change, which may overstate growth rates.

---

1. See, for example, Julian Diaz, III, "Estimation of a Monthly Adjustment for Market Conditions," *The Appraisal Journal* (April 1994), pp. 251–255.

Using Property Listings

Some appraisers may dislike using land listings as a gauge of the market value of an appraised parcel because they are not consummated sales. Certainly, listings for sale should not be the sole indicator of value. Yet, there often are periods when there is little sales activity or the available land sales are not truly similar to the appraised parcel. In such instances, the appraiser is left with a high degree of discomfort in estimating the value of a particular parcel. Including an analysis of parcels listed for sale may provide additional value corroboration to assure that a reliable estimate of value has been made. As with comparable land sales, the listings should be as similar as possible to the subject parcel in all respects. Options to purchase are another measure of a parcel's value. In fact, the price set forth in an option agreement is a better indicator of value than a listing price because both the buyer and seller have agreed to the option price.

Benefits of Using Listings for Sale

In addition to serving as an indicator of the value of an appraised parcel, land listings can benefit an appraiser in two other ways. First, they can be used to set a value ceiling. That is, if several similar parcels were listed for $10,000 to $13,000 an acre, then the appraised parcel's upper limit of value would be established within this range. Second, an analysis of several listings will show how long each listed property has been on the market and whether the price has been adjusted down during this or prior listing periods. This will give a sense of how strong or soft the market is for this class of land as well as the estimated exposure time for the appraised property.[1]

---

1. *Exposure time* is defined in USPAP Advisory Opinion AO-7 "...as always presumed to precede the effective date of an appraisal." Additionally, this analysis can assist the appraiser in estimating reasonable marketing time. *Reasonable marketing time* is defined as ". . .an estimate of the amount of time it might take to sell a property interest in real estate at the estimated market value level during the period immediately after the effective date of an appraisal." *Standards of Professional Appraisal Practice of the Appraisal Institute*, p. 109.

Compare Pattern of Sale Prices to Listing Prices

The land sale listing analysis can be extended to provide even more assistance in appraising a property if the appraiser can relate the listing prices to the sale prices of a number of parcels. For example, if there is sufficient information that residential lots sold for 97% of their listing prices during the past 12 months, then this refined information could be combined with other market value analysis of the appraised parcel to produce a strong estimate of its value. Such a sale price-listing price ratio was determined for the Richmond, Virginia, metropolitan area during 1997. It was found that among nearly 500 land sale transactions, the following ratio of sale prices to listing prices was indicated.

Property Type	Sale Price/Listing Price
Home sites	95.67
Residential land	94.59
Commercial land	92.94
Farmland	93.35

Apply Findings to Appraised Parcel

Applying such ratios to current listing prices would provide more accurate indicators of the probable sale prices of these comparable sales. This method always should be tempered by the use of other land valuation methods.

Summary

Listings for sale should not be the sole indicator of value. However, they do provide another means of judging the value of land—especially when there is limited sales activity of tracts similar to the subject parcel. Options to purchase are another measure of a parcel's value. In fact, the price set forth in an option agreement is a better indicator of value than a listing price because both the buyer and seller agreed to the price. Land listings can be used to set a ceiling of value. Also, an analysis of several listings will show how long each listed parcel has been on the market and whether the price has been adjusted down during the listing period. This information provides a sense of the strength of the market for a class of land as well as the estimated exposure time for an appraised property.

Handling Improved Property Sales

Frequently when working on land appraisal assignments, appraisers turn up sales of improved properties that can provide valid indicators of value for an appraised parcel. The best results are achieved when the improvements on these sales have only a nominal value. Such sales include land with dilapidated buildings or buildings that no longer serve a useful purpose. For instance, the site may be encumbered with a deteriorated loft industrial building or perhaps an old residence on commercially zoned land.

Land Value Extraction Method

Two possibilities arise when extracting the underlying land value from marginally improved sale properties: the improvements add to the value of the sale parcel and, in turn, their value must be deducted from the overall sale price to derive the price paid for the land; or the buyer will incur a demolition cost to remove the structures to put the underlying site to its intended use. Thus, a positive adjustment must be made to reflect the full amount of the purchase price. Each of these two possibilities in the land value extraction method are discussed later. In applying this valuation technique, the following steps are recommended.

1. *Confirm the sale price of each comparable sale.* This step is standard appraisal practice and is necessary to determine whether it is a valid comparable sale. If possible, at this time it should be ascertained how much value the purchaser assigned to the improvements.

2. *Determine the intended use of the improvements.* While confirming the sale price, ask the buyer what, if any, use he or she had planned for the improvements when purchasing the property. The response will determine whether the improvements make a positive or negative contribution to the land.

3. *Estimate the salvage value of the improvements less demolition expenses.* The appraiser may be able to do this, but it is preferable

if the purchaser can furnish this information. It is likely that he or she either has obtained a bid to perform the demolition work or it already has been done before the appraiser speaks to the owner. The appraiser should inspect the improvements if they still exist to determine their condition.

4. *Deduct the net salvage value of the improvements from the sale price.*[1] If the improvements have a positive value after having allowed for demolition expenses, the land value for a sale may be computed as shown in this example. A 10-acre parcel sold last month for $250,000. This apartment-zoned tract had an old equipment building near the rear property line that will not interfere with the construction of the new apartments. After some remodeling, it will be used as a maintenance building for the apartment complex. The purchaser attributed $20,000 of the total purchase price to this building. Thus, the price paid for the land was:

Sale price	$250,000
Less equipment building	− 20,000
Indicated land value	$230,000,
	or $23,000 per acre

5. *Add the demolition costs in excess of salvage value.* A comparable land sale is improved with a dilapidated barn, dwelling, and underground fuel tank. None of these items have any salvage value. The buyer will pay $10,000 for building demolition and scrap and tank removal cost. The purchase price for this 25-acre tract was $380,000. However, the total price paid for the land was $390,000.

Sale price	$380,000
Plus demolition and removal cost	+ 10,000
Land price	$390,000,
	or $15,600 per acre

Summary

Sales of improved properties can provide valid indicators of value for an appraised parcel. The best results are achieved when the improvements on these sales have only a nominal value. Such sales include land with dilapidated buildings or buildings that no longer serve a useful purpose. Either the improvements add to the value of the sale parcel and their value must be deducted from the overall sale price to derive the price paid for

---

1. James H. Boykin and Alfred A. Ring, *The Valuation of Real Estate,* 4th ed. (Englewood Cliffs, New Jersey: Regents/Prentice Hall, 1993), p. 162.

the land, or the buyer will incur a demolition cost to remove the structures which must be added to the sale price.

The recommended steps in the land value extraction method are to confirm the sale price of each comparable sale; determine the intended use of the improvements; estimate the salvage value of the improvements less demolition expenses; and deduct the net salvage value of the improvements from the sale price or add the negative value of the demolition costs in excess of salvage value.

10

Paired Sales Analysis

The paired sales analysis valuation technique, also known as the *matched pairs method*, is an unquestionably sound concept. Essentially, an appraiser locates several pairs of sales that are similar in all respects except one. By comparing each pair of land sales on a unit basis, such as price per acre, the difference in price indicates the value contribution of a particular feature.

Unfortunately, the real estate market is not always cooperative in supplying appraisers with clear-cut value attribute data. Some critics of this method suspect that this price adjustment technique has been applied more often in classrooms than in appraisal offices. Certainly it is easier to demonstrate how to isolate the value contribution of different components in instructional material and courses than in actual practice. In these controlled environments, emphasis is devoted to conveying the proper valuation methodology. Similarly, proper life-saving techniques are taught to emergency rescue professionals in a simulated real-life environment rather than in a life-endangering situation.

Rarely will appraisers discover sets of land sales that can be analyzed in a manner that clearly reveals the value of different value-influencing components such as size, shape, access, public utilities, date of sale, and topography. Yet, when used with an awareness of its imprecision, this method can provide corroborating support for an appraised parcel's value. In using this method (and all other valuation methods), it is important to introduce supporting evidence for each adjustment. It may be misleading to rely on one set of sales to support, for example, a time adjustment. Nevertheless, paired sales analysis, when used with proper caution, offers another valuable analytical tool for the appraiser's tool kit.[1] The steps used in the method are described here along with an example of how adjustments may be made for different value attributes.

---

1. A variation of this method is multiple regression analysis. This statistical technique involves correlating each value determinant (called *independent variable*) with the estimated value (known as the *dependent variable*). During this process the rest of the variables are held constant in order to learn how much each variable contributes to the overall site value.

Identify Similar Features of Sales

The objective at this step is to carefully locate land sales that are similar to the appraised property in as many aspects as is practicable. For the sake of simplicity, suppose that after culling through a number of land sales, the appraiser has found two sales that are reasonably similar in most respects. Both have approximately the same size, zoning, terrain, and road frontage. They are in the same neighborhood and sold with similar financing terms.

Isolate a Value-Influencing Difference

The only significant difference is that one sale occurred 12 months before the other sale. Generally, in estimating the influence on value of changing market conditions, the first step is for the appraiser to determine if and to what extent mortgage financing has influenced the prices paid for the comparable sale properties. Before the value impact of a particular feature can be isolated, it is necessary to adjust for any other value influences.

Some appraisers seem content to analyze three sales in arriving at an estimate of market value. Such limited analysis is not possible when using the matched pair adjustment method. Imagine, for instance, that six value characteristics are being analyzed. This assignment could necessitate the careful scrutiny of 12 land sale and easily more. Whenever possible, reliance on only two sales to indicate the value contribution of a particular feature should be avoided.

Overreliance on a small pool of sales (data set) can cause a loss of independence among the sales, which in turn may distort the value indicated for the appraised parcel. A more reliable value estimate will be produced with a larger data set of comparable sales. In fact, whenever possible, each adjustment should be supported by more than one pair of comparable sales.

Adjust Price to Reflect a Single Feature

Initially, the information gleaned from the paired sales analysis is used to indicate the value of each feature, such as financing or location. These values then are used to adjust sale prices for each comparable land sale.

Apply Adjustment to Reflect Subject's Value

Once these adjustments have been made, the land sales should provide a reasonably narrow range of indicated unit values for the appraised parcel. The final value estimate is based on the appraiser's judgment as to which sales are considered most similar to the appraised parcel. Care must be taken to avoid the oversimplification of surmising that value attribute adjustments apply uniformly for all classes, locations, and sizes of parcels.

The analytical steps in the paired sales analysis technique are presented in the following example. The appraised site contains 44,500 square feet. It is rectangular, level, and in Dabney Industrial Park, which has public water and sewer. The date of the appraisal is May 2, 2000.

Land Sale 1

Location:	12988 Excelsior Road in Huntington Commerce Park
Zoning:	M-2 Industrial
Grantor:	Package Express Company
Grantee:	Quality Shipping Associates
Deed Book/Page:	1056/768
Date of Sale:	January 16, 1999
Site Size:	43,800 square feet
Sale Price:	$153,500
Price/Sq. Ft.	$3.50
Public Utilities:	Water, sewer, and gas
Comments:	This sale parcel is located in an older office-warehouse district than Dabney Industrial Park and is one mile farther away from the beltway interchange.

Land Sale 2

Location:	11385 Excelsior Road in Huntington Commerce Park
Zoning:	M-2 Industrial
Grantor:	Mayfair Technology Associates
Grantee:	Acme Plumbing Suppliers
Deed Book/Page:	1062/223
Date of Sale:	February 24, 2000
Site Size:	44,260 square feet
Sale Price:	$185,000
Price/Sq. Ft.	$4.18
Public Utilities:	Water, sewer, and gas
Comments:	This sale parcel is located in an older office-warehouse district than Dabney Industrial Park and is one mile farther away from the beltway interchange. It sold subject to the seller agreeing to hold a second mortgage for five years at below-market interest; the broker representing the seller stated that the buyer paid a $5,000 premium for this funding when acquiring the site.

Land Sale 3

Location:	9875 Sanford Road, Dabney Industrial Park
Zoning:	M-2 Industrial
Grantor:	Land Equity Investors
Grantee:	Simco Pallet Company
Deed Book/Page:	1061/878
Date of Sale:	September 2, 1999
Site Size:	41,350 square feet
Sale Price:	$200,000
Price/Sq. Ft.	$4.84
Public Utilities:	Water, sewer, and gas
Comments:	This sale parcel is located in the same industrial park as Sales 4, 5, 6, and the subject parcel and is similar in nearly all respects.

Land Sale 4

Location:	At southwest corner of Hightower and Express Roads in Dabney Industrial Park
Zoning:	M-2 Industrial
Grantor:	Glen Bay Partnership
Grantee:	Matterfact Corp.
Deed Book/Page:	1056/273
Date of Sale:	October 6, 1998
Site Size:	47,000 square feet
Sale Price:	$180,000
Price/Sq. Ft.	$3.83
Public Utilities:	Water, sewer, and gas
Comments:	This parcel is level and readily accessible from a nearby interchange of the Crosstown Expressway. It is in the same industrial park as the subject parcel.

Land Sale 5

Location:	7550 Hightower Road in Dabney Industrial Park
Zoning:	M-2 Industrial
Grantor:	Waldron Electrical Suppliers, Inc.
Grantee:	Capitol Cellular Distributors
Deed Book/Page:	1056/409
Date of Sale:	November 18, 1998
Site Size:	45,800 square feet
Sale Price:	$153,500
Price/Sq. Ft.	$3.35
Public Utilities:	Water, sewer, and gas
Comments:	This sale parcel is located in the same industrial park as Sales 3, 4, 6, and the subject parcel and is similar in nearly all respects. It has a triangular shape, which causes some building design and truck loading-unloading problems.

Land Sale 6

Location:	7229 Hightower Road in Dabney Industrial Park
Zoning:	M-2 Industrial
Grantor:	Bookbinder, Ltd.
Grantee:	Fabricators, Inc.
Deed Book/Page:	1062/339
Date of Sale:	March 11, 2000
Site Size:	45,200 square feet
Sale Price:	$210,000
Price/Sq. Ft.	$4.65
Public Utilities:	Water, sewer, and gas
Comments:	This sale parcel is located in the same industrial park as Sales 3, 4, and 5 and is similar in nearly all respects.

A monthly market conditions (time) adjustment is made as follows:

Land Sale 6	$4.65/sq. ft.	3/11/00
Land Sale 4	$3.83/sq. ft.	10/6/98
Difference	$0.82/sq. ft.	17 months
Total percentage change	$0.82/$3.83 =	21.41%
Monthly rate of change	21.41%/17 months =	+1.26%, say 1.25%

A size adjustment can be derived from a comparative analysis of Sales 3 and 6. First, a time adjustment must be made to bring Sale 3 up to the date of sale for Sale 6. This is a nominal adjustment of plus 7.50% (6 mos. × 1.25%/mo.), indicating an adjusted square foot price for Sale 3 of $5.20. Next, a size adjustment can be computed by dividing the difference in the adjusted price of Sale 3 (1.075 × $200,000) and the price of Sale 6 by the difference in size, which is 3,850 square feet (45,200 – 41,350).

$$\begin{array}{r} \$215,000 \\ -\ \underline{\$210,000} \\ \$5,000 \end{array}$$

This indicates $5,000/3,850 sq. ft., or -$5,000 for every 3,850 square foot increase in area. This amount can then be expressed as a minus $1,300 for every 1,000-square foot increase in size (-$5,000)(1,000/3850).

A shape adjustment can be made by comparing Sales 4 and 5 after making time and size adjustments. A nominal time adjustment of plus $2,250 and a slight minus size adjustment (1.2 × $1,300, or $1,560) are applied to Sale 4. The net adjustment for these two features is plus $690, leaving an adjusted price for Sale 4 of $180,690. Comparing this adjusted price to the $153,500 price for the irregular-shaped Sale 5 indicates a plus adjustment for Sale 5 of $27,190.

A location adjustment is derived from a comparison of Sales 2 and 6. No time adjustment is needed and only a small minus size adjustment is required for Sale 2 (940/1000)($1,300) = $1,220, indicating an adjusted price of $183,780. Comparing this amount to Sale 6 then indicates a $31,220 positive location adjustment for Sales 1 and 2.

A financing adjustment of minus $5,000 is indicated for Sale 2. This adjustment suggests that Sale 2 would have sold for $180,000 subject to typical financing terms. Next, adjustments must be made for time and location.

Table 10.1   *Land Sales Adjustment Grid*

Sale Number	Subject	1	2	3	4	5	6
Sale Price		$153,500	$185,000	$200,000	$180,000	$153,500	$210,000
Financing			−5,000				
Adjusted Price		$153,500	$180,000	$200,000	$180,000	$153,500	$210,000
Date of Sale		1/99	2/00	9/99	10/98	11/98	3/00
		+20.0%	+3.8%	+8.8%	+23.8%	+22.5%	+2.5%
Adjusted Price		$184,200	$186,840	$217,745	$222,840	$188,038	$215,250
Adjusted Price/sq. ft.		$4.21	$4.22	$5.27	$4.74	$4.11	$4.76
Size (sq. ft.)	44,500	43,800	44,260	41,350	47,000	45,800	45,200
Adjustment		−$910	0	−$4,095	+$3,250	+$1,690	+$910
Shape						+$27,190	
Location		+$31,220	+$31,220				
Net Adjustment		+$0.69	+$0.71	−$0.10	+$0.07	+$0.63	+$0.02
Adjusted Price/sq. ft.		$4.90	$4.93	$5.17	$4.81	$4.74	$4.78

In the situation illustrated in Table 10.1, a fairly tight pattern of adjusted sale prices evolved, except for Sales 3 and 5. Excluding these sales, the indicated square foot value for the appraised parcel ranged from $4.78 to $4.93. Often, even after a thorough analysis, one or two sales will fall outside of the cluster of indicated values the other sales suggest.

Summary

The paired sales valuation technique, also known as the *matched pairs method,* requires an appraiser to locate several pairs of sales that are similar in all respects except one. By comparing each pair of land sales on a unit basis, the difference in price explains the value contribution of a particular feature. Rarely will comparable sales provide clear-cut patterns for relevant value attributes such as size, shape, access, public utilities, date of sale, and topography. Nevertheless, this analytical method imposes discipline on the valuation of land.

11

Sale Units of Comparison

It is possible to compare land sales to the appraised property directly, hence the name often associated with this method—*the direct sales comparison method.* While this direct or overall method of comparison is possible, it seldom will be as accurate or as easy to follow as an overall sale price that has been broken down into units of comparison. There are two basic units of sales comparison: density units and physical units. Zoning ordinances specify the first and the latter relates to physical measures, either linear or square units. Invariably, one value unit produces a tighter adjusted price range than other units. Several units of value, when applied to an appraised parcel, may be expected to produce corroborating indications of value.

Density Units

Units Allowed by Zoning

The number of units allowed by zoning for a particular land use greatly influences property value. One measure of zoning density is the number of square feet of building space that can be constructed on the site. This measure of allowable floor area generally relates to land zoned for office use, while a second density measure governs the number of apartment units that the zoning will allow on a parcel.

Floor Area Ratio

The floor area ratio expression of value is most frequently used in appraising office-zoned land. Sale prices for comparable land sales automatically will be divided by either the number of acres or square feet in each particular sale parcel. Next, each sale price is expressed on the basis of square feet of floor area ratio (SF-FAR). The floor area ratio (FAR) set by the zoning ordinance governs the quantity of building area that may be built on a site. It is computed by dividing the area of the building by the site area. This ratio is even more important than the size of the site because the amount of allowable building area is essentially what is being transferred to a purchaser. For example, in a city's downtown business district, the FAR could be as high as 50 or more. In suburban areas, FARs often will be in the 0.50 to 2.00 range. The following examples are presented to demonstrate how this value unit can be used to provide a reliable measure of value and sometimes a narrower range than provided by price per acre or square foot.

Sale No.	Sale Price	Size		Price Per	
		Sq. Ft.	FAR	Sq. Ft.	FAR
1	$450,000	15,943	6.0	$28.23	$4.70
2	929,000	31,406	6.0	29.58	4.93
3	735,000	21,505	6.0	34.18	5.70
4	1,050,000	18,630	6.0	56.36	9.39
5	1,800,000	86,249	4.5	20.87	4.64

In the above example, by using the FAR unit of value, the appraiser was able to use a land sale (Sale 5) that was of a different zoning classification. When reduced to price per allowable building area (FAR), this sale proved to be a reliable index of the appraised site's market value. Sale 4, with the highest unit price among the comparables, would be adjusted downward to reflect its superior location and a highly motivated purchaser.

Price per Apartment Unit

Application of the allowable number of apartment units per acre, or the number of apartments the entire parcel will support (either gross or net acres), generally provides a more consistent indication of value than price per acre. After all, an investor buys land based on how many apartments he or she can build rather than the number of acres a parcel may contain. For example, a 30-acre parcel zoned for garden apartments at a density of 8 units per acre sold for $1,800,000. This price translates into $60,000 per acre and $7,500 per allowable apartment unit. The unit price will vary depending on the usual physical features, but also on the probable rental rate of the prospective apartments and how far the parcel has progressed in the rezoning and site planning processes.

Productive Units

It may be tempting to break sale prices down into productive units for analytical purposes. For instance, land sales could be expressed as so many dollars per hospital bed or theater seat. Such property uses are not zoned on this basis. Instead, they are zoned according to building setback requirements, height limitations, site coverage ratio, or floor area ratio. Likewise, appraisers rarely use such price units. More conventional and readily understood units such as price per square foot or per acre are typically used. It is important for an appraiser to understand how unit prices are expressed in a particular market and use these expressions of value in his or her report.

Physical Units

Front Foot

Generally the front foot value unit is relied on for the purchase, sale, and valuation of retail sites, water frontage parcels, and industrial parcels. In each instance, a purchaser assigns considerable value to the amount of frontage. Highway or street frontage may be highly desirable for traffic exposure or in providing adequate maneuverability for vehicles entering a site. A prime motivator in the purchase of residential water frontage is view and direct access to the water. From a practical point of view, there needs to be sufficient frontage so that a prospective pier will satisfy the side yard setback zoning requirements. Industrial parcels require sufficient frontage to provide for the building, vehicle parking, and sufficient turning space for trucks loading and unloading. An example of this value unit follows, showing how overall sale prices are converted to sale price per front foot. Sales 1 and 2 are not rectangular.

Sale No.	Price	Size (Ac.)	Depth (Ft.)	Front Feet	Price/Fr. Ft.
1	$209,000	4.68	460	495	$422
2	180,000	1.83	223	440	409
3	210,000	3.89	414	409	513
4	230,000	3.75	355	460	500

In addition to possible price adjustments for factors such as the availability of public utilities, shape, date of sale, terrain, and location, site depth influences the front foot price of these sales. As a general rule, the front foot value of a site increases as its depth increases; the opposite value relationship holds as the depth of a site diminishes. In reviewing the four suburban office land sales, one would expect that the highest front foot value would be for Sale 1 because it has the greatest depth. But it also is the largest site, which pulls down its front foot price. Furthermore, this sale occurred earlier than the other sales in a rising market. The lowest front foot price is exhibited by Sale 2, which clearly has the least depth. Its relatively small size, which makes it more affordable than the other three sales, partially offsets the reduction in its front foot price. Sales 3 and 4 are quite similar in size, but Sale 4 has less depth than Sale 3—resulting is a lower front foot price.

Acre

There is no universal point in property size at which sale prices are better expressed on a per acre or per square foot basis for all classes of property.

Nevertheless, there are some guidelines available. Large tracts usually are traded on the basis of price per acre. This is especially true for lower-priced land such as agricultural, residential, and in some instances industrial land. Smaller sites of one acre or slightly larger and higher-value sites, such as retail and office, tend to trade on a per square foot basis. An inverse size-unit relationship exists for price per acre, as compared to the front foot rule stated in the previous section. That is, in general the per acre price tends to decrease as depth increases and the per acre price increases as the depth decreases. That general price-size pattern is demonstrated by the sales shown in the following table. Note that these are the same land sales presented in the previous table. A detailed discussion on size and square units of value is presented in Chapter 6.

Sale No.	Price	Size (Ac.)	Depth (Ft.)	Front Feet	Price/Acre
1	$209,000	4.68	460	495	$44,658
2	200,000	1.83	223	440	109,290
3	210,000	3.89	414	409	53,985
4	230,000	3.75	355	460	61,333

Square Foot

An essential step in using the square foot unit method is to accurately ascertain the size of both the sale and appraised parcels. Of course, this is true for any unit of comparison. A starting point in determining the size of a parcel is to check with the buyer or the real estate agent handling the transaction to confirm how much land was conveyed. A perusal of the deed and accompanying plat will provide additional assurance as to the site size. Records in the municipal assessor's office will further support the size of a parcel. Sometimes the area may not be specified and the appraiser is obliged to compute the area. Some appraisal offices may have surveying software, a compensating polar planimeter, or other means that may be used to compute a parcel's area.

Another method that may be used is to divide the parcel into geometric figures, such as rectangles, parallelograms, trapezoids, and right triangles. The equations for calculating the area of these figures are shown in Figure 11.1.

Figure 11.1   Calculating Area

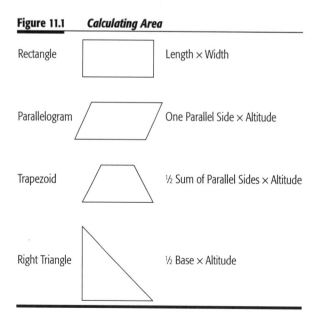

Rectangle — Length × Width

Parallelogram — One Parallel Side × Altitude

Trapezoid — ½ Sum of Parallel Sides × Altitude

Right Triangle — ½ Base × Altitude

| **Figure 11.2** | ***Irregular-Shaped Parcel (145) of Unknown Size*** | **Figure 11.3** | ***Irregular-Shaped Parcel (145) of Unknown Size (Divided into Geometric Units)*** |

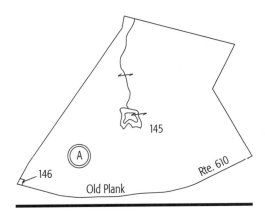

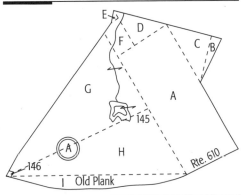

Sometimes the reported area of sale parcels is inaccurate due to unaccounted-for out conveyances, faulty records, inaccurate surveys, etc. For example, Parcel 145 in Figures 11.2 and 11.3 illustrates how a parcel can be subdivided into easily measured areas. The appraiser will need a right triangle drawing instrument to draw and an engineer's scale to measure each division of the parcel. The total area of this parcel has been computed by adding the sum of the nine divisions.

Division	Measurements (in Feet)	Area (in Sq. Ft.)
A	425/335 × 780/730*	286,900
B	$\frac{1}{2}$(60 × 260)	7,800
C	$\frac{1}{2}$(260 × 270)	35,100
D	$\frac{1}{2}$(200 × 200)	20,000
E	$\frac{1}{2}$(40 × 60)	1,200
F	140/120 × 150/125	17,875
G	$\frac{1}{2}$(460 × 780)	179,400
H	$\frac{1}{2}$(395 × 780)	154,050
I	860 × 30 avg.	25,800
Total area		728,125
		or 16.72 acres.

* Area computed by multiplying the average of each side by one another, e.g., 425/335 = 380 and 780/730 = 755. The area then is 380 × 755.

Summary

There are two basic units of sales comparison: density units and physical units. Zoning ordinances specify density units and physical units relate to physical measures, either linear or square units. Several units of value, when applied to an appraised parcel, may be expected to produce corroborating indications of value. Units related to zoning include floor area ratio (FAR), which is most often used in appraising office-zoned land.

Each sale price is expressed on the basis of square feet of floor area ratio. The floor area ratio governs the quantity of building area that may be built on a site. Another unit is price per apartment unit, which involves dividing the sale price of a parcel by the number of allowable apartments.

Physical units include price per front foot. This value unit is relied on for the valuation of retail sites, waterfront parcels, and often industrial parcels, where buyers and sellers assign considerable importance to the amount of frontage. Generally, the front foot value of a site increases as its depth increases; the opposite relationship holds for sites having less depth. Large tracts usually are traded on the basis of price per acre. Smaller sites of one acre or slightly larger and higher-value sites, such as retail and office sites, tend to trade on a per square foot basis. In general, the per acre price tends to decrease as depth increases and the per acre price increases as the depth decreases.

12

Accessibility Adjustments

Corner Versus Interior Sites

It seems that the relative appeal and value of corner and interior sites, like so many decisions in real estate, is appropriately covered by the comment, "It depends." The "it" that largely influences site appeal and value is highest and best use.

For instance, a corner site generally will be preferred and worth more for traffic-dependent businesses such as convenience stores, service stations, fast-food restaurants, and other retail stores. Corner sites offer advantages of better merchandise display, enhanced store visibility, and easier ingress and egress. In contrast, residential land uses and most office buildings do not need the added traffic exposure stemming from a second street at an intersection. Not only do residences not need the additional traffic, their owners typically want to avoid the additional traffic congestion and related noise emanating from the second street.

Appraisers should avoid making the assumption that there is a constant value relationship among all corner locations. This oversimplified notion does not even hold up for sites with the same zoning and highest and best use. Several accessibility factors could cause a difference in value for two parcels with the same zoning and highest and best use. These include locations in different parts of a metropolis or on different sides of a street (going-to-work side versus returning-home side); different parcel shapes and street frontage; differences in public utilities; terrain differences; different traffic controls, including median strips and deceleration lanes; different degrees of visibility via line of sight for approaching vehicular traffic; and different traffic volumes and speed limits.

Each corner must be valued based on the peculiar value influences affecting land value at that particular location. Site value premiums, if any, must therefore be ascertained in each neighborhood and for each site. Sometimes greater accuracy is gained using a sale that requires a relatively large adjustment for a corner location versus an interior location, rather than using several interior lots sales from other neighborhoods that may require numerous minor adjustments.

In the early part of this century when residential row housing was situated on narrow city lots, it was thought that buyers would pay a premium for corner lots to obtain cross ventilation, natural light, enhanced view, and added open space. Later, as larger suburban lots were developed for single-family detached housing, it no longer was necessary to pay more for a corner lot than for an interior lot. In fact, it was argued that there were disadvantages in owning a corner lot due to lack of privacy, increased traffic noise, greater landscaping cost to create a privacy buffer with added maintenance costs, and sometimes increased street or sidewalk special assessment based on the additional street frontage.

In some instances, a smaller building envelope is achievable for a same-sized lot on a corner than an inside lot because the side street setback requirement exceeds that of an interior side yard setback. Gene Dilmore holds "...in most cities, there is no premium assignable to the corner location of residential lots. For example, a study of several thousand lot sales in the Birmingham, Alabama, area discovered no justification for a corner influence in the residential lot market."[1] Unless there is persuasive market evidence to show otherwise, appraisers should not assign a premium value to residential corner lots over similar interior lots.

When comparatively analyzing a comparable site sale and an appraised site, it is important to consider the value contribution of the two street frontages. That is, how much value comes from the main street versus the side street? Corner site appraising becomes more complex if either the comparable site sale or appraised site has two street frontages and the other has three street frontages.

There are instances in which an interior site will be more valuable than a corner site. For example, vehicles can more easily access an interior site from both sides of the street. Such sites may offer superior access over corner sites with restricted access due to median strips and traffic congestion. Because entering and exiting these interior sites by motor vehicles may be easier, they may be superior to corner sites.

Median Strips

As a rule, all types of sites are worth more if there is no raised median strip in front of them. If it is a retail site, approximately one-half of the traffic (and prospective customers) will be lost because drivers are prohibited from making left turns from the far lane (see Site B in Figure 12.1). Site A has unrestricted access and would be more attractive to prospective

---

1. Gene Dilmore, *The New Approach to Real Estate Appraising* (Prentice-Hall, Inc.: Englewood Cliffs, New Jersey, 1971), pp. 78–79.

purchasers. They would be expected to pay a higher price for this site than for Site B. Residential lots in such locations may be worth less than lots with unencumbered access because drivers will have to drive beyond the property and make a U-turn. Industrial parcels may suffer a value loss because truck traffic not only is restricted by the median strip, but U-turns may be impossible for tractor-trailers.

When appraising parcels in the vicinity of proposed highway construction, it is always prudent to check the construction plans. Initially, a site near a future interchange may appear to have substantial value. An examination of the road plans, however, may reveal a proposed median strip in front of the appraised parcel or even a limited access fence.

Speed Limit

High speed limits can sharply reduce the appeal of both residential and commercial sites. In judging the value of an appraised site, the speed limit, braking distance for prospective customers, and visibility must be taken into account. The value of a retail site will be greatly impaired if the speed limit, in combination with limited visibility, prevents oncoming drivers from seeing the site until it is too late. A related value factor is line-of-sight for oncoming traffic. The site may not be readily visible if it is on the inside radius of a turn, especially if there are woods or buildings blocking a clear view of it. The appraiser should put himself or herself in the position of a prospective customer. Will the customer have a clear view of the site and a safe braking distance to enter the premises comfortably?

Traffic Volume

Traffic-dependent land uses, such as service stations and shopping centers, must be along high-volume traffic arteries. Apartment developments

Figure 12.1 *Effect of Median Strip on Customer Access to a Site*

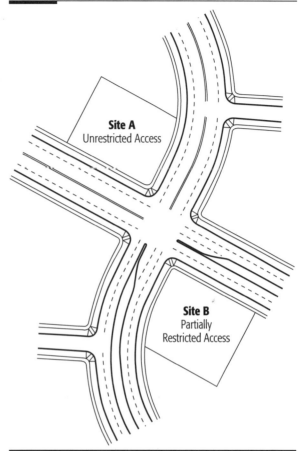

Site A
Unrestricted Access

Site B
Partially
Restricted Access

Source: Wilbur Smith Associates, Richmond, Virginia

generally need to locate adjacent to main traffic thoroughfares. However, well-designed, single-family neighborhoods prohibit primary streets bisecting the immediate area. If the differences are not too significant, appraisers can use average daily traffic counts as a basis for making adjustments for traffic volume. Vehicular traffic surveys are available from local and state transportation departments. Some experimentation and analysis of traffic volume value effects will improve the reliability of the adjustment derived.

At first glance, two physically comparable parcels with the same zoning may appear to have similar values. Yet different traffic volumes for these otherwise similar parcels may cause one of the parcels to have a higher and better use than the other. One parcel may be in a neighborhood that is in transition from residential to commercial land use activities and have substantially higher traffic flows than the other parcel. Municipal and state highway department traffic count reports provide a basis for making this type of location adjustment. A parcel fronting on a primary road invariably will have a higher value than one on a secondary road—due to both road conditions and traffic volume. Progressively higher traffic volume can initially increase business revenue and underlying site values, but as traffic continues to expand, it may reach a point where congestion works against rising land values. In fact, at some point traffic congestion will begin to erode land prices. This is true especially for heavy truck traffic on streets with retail concentrations.

Two identical residential neighborhoods in Grand Rapids, Michigan, were studied during the early 1950s to determine the effects of traffic flow on residential property values. In the neighborhood where traffic was diverted, traffic was reduced sharply and the neighborhood was transformed from one of the city's most dangerous to one of its safest. Over a 10-year period after the traffic diversion, real estate values, as five separate indices measured, showed an increase greater in this area than in the neighborhood with the higher traffic volume. The five methods used were:

1. Changes in assessed value

2. Sales data on homes sold before and after traffic control

3. Changes in sample sales data

4. Census home interviews

5. Econometric analysis[2]

---

2.   D. Gordon Bagby, "The Effects of Traffic Flow on Residential Property Values," *APA Journal* (January 1980), pp. 88, 91–92.

Proximity of Site to Expressways

Ample market transactions underscore the fact that nonresidential land adjacent to either interstate or metropolitan beltway interchanges benefit greatly. Close proximity to interchanges facilitates customers reaching businesses in these locations and assists industrial and distribution establishments in promptly transporting their products to their customers. Generally, the opposite effect on land values occurs when residential properties are located near expressways. For example, a 1970 study of residential properties within 200 to 400 feet from I-495 in northern Virginia (a Washington, D. C. suburban area) versus similar properties located in excess of 4,000 feet from the same beltway found that, "...residential properties located in proximity to I-495 show a tendency to increase in value at a rate significantly less than those more distant from the highway."[3]

Summary

The relative appeal and value of corner and interior sites depends on their highest and best use. A corner site generally will be preferred and worth more for traffic-dependent businesses such as convenience stores, service stations, fast-food restaurants, and other retail stores. Corner sites offer the advantages of better merchandise display, enhanced store visibility, and easier ingress and egress. In contrast, residential land uses and perhaps office buildings do not need the added traffic exposure stemming from a second street at an intersection.

Several accessibility factors could cause a difference in value for two parcels with the same zoning and highest and best use. These include locations in different parts of a metropolis or on different sides of a street (going-to-work side versus returning-home side); different parcel shapes and street frontage; differences in public utilities; terrain differences; different traffic controls, including median strips and deceleration lanes; different degrees of visibility via line-of-sight for approaching vehicular traffic; and different traffic volumes and speed limits.

As a rule, all types of sites are worth more if there is not a median strip in front of them. High speed limits can sharply reduce the appeal of both residential and commercial sites. In judging the value of an appraised site, the speed limit, braking distance for prospective customers, and visibility must be taken into account. Two physically similar parcels with the same zoning may appear to have similar values. Yet different traffic volumes may cause one of the parcels to have a higher and better use than

---

3.   C. John Langley, Jr., "Adverse Impacts of the Washington Beltway on Residential Property Values," *Land Economics* (February 1976), pp. 55, 63.

the other. Industrial and commercial land adjacent to either interstate or metropolitan beltway interchanges benefit greatly. Generally, the opposite effect on land values occurs when residential properties are located near expressways.

CHAPTER

13

Adjusting for Public Utilities

Being able to detect value patterns for parcels with and without public utilities is of tremendous importance to appraisers. Yet a large part of the price difference between land sales with and without public utilities may be caused by their different locations. That is, sale parcels without utilities may be remote from customers, major traffic arteries, and intersections, and even have a lower zoning classification than land sales or appraised parcels with utilities. Small parcels of industrial land may be discounted sharply if they lack public utilities. Their small size may disqualify them for serious consideration for business activities that call for extensive outside storage and ample separation between septic system drain fields and private wells. In addition, these small sites may not satisfy the health department's reserve drain field requirements.

There will be instances when a comparable sale is similar to a subject parcel except it lacks a source of public water. For example, a sale site may have a shallow or drilled private well while the subject site has public water. Generally, the value consequences of this deficiency are relative minor in contrast to a parcel lacking public sewers. The availability of public sewer service is of greater concern than water service in making utility value adjustments.

Influences on Site Size

A preliminary sense of the value differential between sites with and without public water and sewer service can be gained from a review of comparative development intensities. For example, zoning for a residential site with a public source of water and sewer service may specify a minimum lot size of 25,000 square feet, whereas a site without these public services may require a minimum site of 43,560 square feet (1 acre). This is an increase of more than 74% in site size. In some areas, the size differential for residential lots with and without public water and sewer may vary from 20,000 square feet up to 10 acres. However, whether a site has a public supply of water generally has little impact on its minimum allowable size. The key to the size difference is the presence or absence of sewer service.

In some jurisdictions the zoning ordinance does not address minimum site size for industrial or commercial classifications. High water consumption land uses such as apartments require public water and sewer service. Hence, there probably will not be comparable land sales of properties without water and sewer unless the distance to extend these lines to a parcel is fairly short. The size for industrial and commercial parcels with public water and sewer generally will be determined after a municipal review of development plans, which includes a consideration of parking and setback requirements. The size of sites lacking public water and sewer initially is the same as those with public utilities. There is also an allowance for additional land based on the number of employees, daily visitors, and soil texture. (Sandy clay loam generally is a satisfactory subsoil for septic system installations.) In many locales, a reserve field equal in size to the primary drainage field is required, considerably increasing the site size.

Generally, a particular land use does not determine the diameter of water mains or sewer lines and the resulting installation cost. These sizes are set for large utility service districts and influenced by fire protection policies, among other factors. Anticipated land use activities will govern the price differential for sale parcels with and without public utilities. Parcels zoned for high water consumption activities may experience considerably higher unit prices than those uses not having high water demands. The latter category may be able to use septic systems and private wells. Examples of these contrasting uses are restaurants, motor hotels, laundries, apartment complexes (see Figure 13.1), and manufacturing establishments versus self-storage warehouses, churches, small office and retail properties, and detached, single-family houses.

Soil quality can also affect the premium paid for sites not serviced by public sewer. This is true especially for sites with comparatively impervious subsoil that cannot be developed easily for water-intensive activities. Users will pay a premium for fully serviced parcels. Such a site will, of course, have a higher and better use than an impaired site.

Compare Sales With and Without Utilities

Unquestionably, it is preferable to compare land sales with public utilities to an appraised parcel with utilities and likewise comparable

Figure 13.1   *Garden Apartment Complex*

Courtesy of United Dominion Realty Trust (photograph by Chip Mitchell Photography).

sales without utilities to appraised parcels that also lack public utilities. This perfect similarity in comparable sales properties is not always possible, at least for every sale considered. Still, an effort should be made to obtain as many comparable sales as possible. The following sections show some ways in which land sales with different utilities can be analyzed to derive a value estimate for an appraised parcel.

Discounted Sale Prices. If a land sale is sufficiently similar to an appraised parcel, except it lacks public utilities, then it probably should at least be considered as an indicator of the subject parcel's present value. If there is some certainty as to when public utilities will be extended to either the subject or the sale parcel, then the price of the comparable sale either may be discounted or inflated to account for this time lag. Suppose, for example, two parcels are essentially similar except the sale parcel has public water and sewer service available, and the subject property lacks these services. A water and sewer project has been approved and budgeted for the subject's neighborhood. The construction project has been awarded to a contractor by the municipality. Work will begin within 60 days and is scheduled to be completed, tested, and operational in one year. At that time, public water and sewer will be available to the subject property. The sale parcel recently sold for a price of $60,000 per acre. Research indicates that in this market land investors expect a return of 15% on their investments. Thus, the indicated per acre value of the subject parcel is shown to be:

$$\$60,000 \times 0.8696 = \$52,174, \text{ rounded to } \$52,200$$

This lower value recognizes that the subject parcel will not have public water and sewer for another year.

A variation of this utility adjustment can be made when the subject parcel has public utilities and a particular comparable sale lacks these services. As stated in the previous illustration, these utilities will be available to the sale parcel in one year (rather than to the appraised parcel). Now, let's assume that the sale price for the comparable parcel is $52,200 an acre and land investors expect a 15% yield. Hence, the indicated value of the appraised parcel is $52,200 \times 1.15 = \$60,000$ (rounded). In these two examples, the present worth of one factor was first applied to the situation in which the subject parcel would not be fully equivalent to the comparable sale parcel for one year. In the second example, where the subject parcel was superior, a one-year future worth of one factor was applied to the inferior sale parcel to reveal the adjusted value of the subject property.

Outright Comparison. As mentioned at the beginning of this chapter, it is important to discern each influence on the price paid for comparable sales. Location, size, date of sale, topography, or other influences may have caused the differences for which appraisers customarily identify and make adjustments. The paired sales analysis method discussed in Chapter 10 can provide the structure for analyzing each comparable land sale. Once all of the other price influences have been measured, the remaining influence requiring analysis is public utilities.

The presence or absence of public utilities will vary from place to place and among different property classes. Two surveys produced widely different indications of the value of public utilities. A case study of a small New England municipality revealed "...a value premium of 15% to 40% for industrial land serviced with sewers versus similar land only with septic systems."[1] A Virginia survey showed that in the 0–1 acre size category, there was such a huge price premium paid for residential, industrial, commercial, and agricultural parcels with utilities that parcels lacking these amenities could not be viewed as being comparable sales. For example, the average per acre price paid for industrially zoned land sales without public water and sewer was $28,986 versus $262,991 for industrial sales having water and sewer.[2] As always, location played a major role in these price variations.

Compute Cost of Extending Utilities to Subject or Sale Parcel

Sometimes water and sewer service is not immediately adjacent to the comparable land sales or appraised parcel. A utility adjustment can be made when utilities are close to a parcel and the cost of bringing them to the site is not prohibitively expensive. For instance, suppose that the subject parcel has water and sewer service and a comparable sale has water and sewer service 700 feet away. Assume that a local utilities contracting firm has quoted the lineal foot cost of installing utilities for properties similar to the comparable sale parcel at $15 for 6- to 8-in. PVC water mains and $35 for the same diameter sewer lines. Included in these costs are the necessary fire hydrants, manholes, and flushing mains. The reason that the sewer lines are more costly is due to their greater depth (perhaps a minimum of 6 feet versus 3 feet) and the necessity for manholes. In this case, the $200,000 sale price would be adjusted downward by $35,000 (700 l.f. × $50), or 18%. Caution must be employed when using this cost-of-installation adjustment method. The percentage adjustment may be disproportionately large, especially if either a lift station or a major pumping station is required and one landowner has to pay this total cost. Such sales may be ruled out as comparable sales because it is unlikely that a purchaser would pay this high cost to extend utilities to a site.

1. Walter H. Chudleigh, III, "The Impact of the Installation of Public Sewers on Commercial Property Values," *The Appraisal Journal* (April 1991), p. 224.

2. James H. Boykin, "Impropriety of Using Dissimilar-Size Comparable Land Sales," *The Appraisal Journal* (July 1996), p. 316.

In using this method, several other factors must be kept in mind. The municipality may not allow the closest utility source or it may not be the least expensive alternative. The routing of the utilities may require two different easements across other property owners' lands. Lacking the power of eminent domain, the developer may be unable to secure an easement or be required to pay a considerable sum for such access. Depending on the terrain, a sewer line may require costly pump stations and force mains. If any of these potentially expensive problems exists, this adjustment method may be inappropriate because the land sales are not truly comparable or indicative of the appraised parcel's market value.

Summary

Location may be responsible for a large part of the price difference between land sales with and without public utilities. Soil quality can affect the premium paid for sites not serviced by public sewer. This is true especially for sites with comparatively impervious subsoil that cannot easily be developed for water-intensive activities. Certainly it is preferable to compare land sales with public utilities to an appraised parcel with utilities and likewise compare sales without utilities to appraised parcels that also lack public utilities. However, this optimum form of comparative analysis in not always possible. Some ways that land sales with different utilities can be analyzed to derive a value estimate include discounted sales prices, outright comparison, and computing the cost of extending utilities to the subject or sale parcel.

14

Location Adjustments for Resort Lots

Resort lots are specialty assignments for real estate appraisers. In this chapter some key current trends are identified as well as value-influencing factors that should be considered when undertaking such appraisal assignments. It is expected that demand will be strong for resort properties for another 15 to 20 years. Aging baby boomers, with their high disposable incomes and a strong economy will drive this trend. Yet, lessons from the past should sound a note of caution when future demand and values are considered. Properties that are well situated with regard to population centers, airlines, and interstate highway routes and have appealing amenities offer the best chance of secure resort investments. Still, resort property investments can be fickle. Simply being in a resort will not guarantee value enhancement. A lot with frontage on the ocean can be expected to be worth more than an ocean view lot and certainly more than one a short drive from the beach—even if parking is conveniently located. However, there are numerous instances where overbuilding, especially of condominiums, has blighted not only condominium values, but the values of detached homes and lots as well.

Golf-oriented communities have grown significantly in recent years. In 1997 there were 26.5 million golfers in the United States playing on 16,010 golf courses according to the National Golf Foundation. During the past decade, this foundation reports that the number of golf courses has risen by 2,574, or over 19%. Of the more than 400 new courses being built each year, 80% are public facilities.[1]

Ski resort locations are influenced by skier accessibility. Reportedly "...67% of resort areas are within 74 miles or easy commuting distance to major metropolitan population centers. A high proportion of 'weekend areas' require two or more hours of driving time, while vacation destinations are typically in more remote locations where snow conditions are more

---

1. For more detail, see *Trends in the Golf Industry: 1986–1997* (Jupiter, FL: National Golf Foundation, 1998).

consistent."[2] Because ski resorts require snow, appropriate terrain, and climate, they generally are clustered. Hence, skiers have several choices within a limited distance. The average resort has just over 1,900 acres.[3] Consolidation characterizes the ski resort industry with the number of resorts declining from 709 in 1985–86 to 507 in 1995–96.[4] The ski season generally varies from three to four months, with the longest season being in the Rocky Mountains and the Pacific Northwest, and the shortest season being in the southeast and midwest. The level of skier participation has not changed much over the past two decades. In 1978–79, estimated U.S. skier/snowboarder visits were 50.2 million, growing to 54.1 million by 1997–98. The strongest growth was among snowboarders, rising to over 20% of total area visits.[5]

Interview Brokers, Buyers, and Sellers

It probably is more important to interview persons involved in the transfer of resort lots and parcels than other types of real estate. In some instances resort-marketing offices may be willing to provide a chronology of lot sales. Such information can be helpful in discerning price trends. Additionally, these sources can explain aberrations in price trends that have resulted from periodic overbuilding, hurricanes, unseasonably warm winters, or lack of snowfall. Another related source of information is resort rental office staff, who can clarify rental rates, operating expenses, occupancy rates, and popular periods, as well as point out which type of properties and locations are most popular. As always, buyers and sellers can provide useful explanations of price trends.

In some markets, there is a clearly defined two-tier lot sales market. Lots bought in haste frequently will resell for a lower price later. One reason for the reduced resale prices is that resort brokers typically are not enthusiastic about selling owners' lots when they have their own inventory. Further, "for sale" signs by owners may be prohibited, placing the seller at a disadvantage in selling the lot, especially because many lot owners live far from the resort and therefore cannot actively market their lots. In one instance, a purchaser had bought a lot for $109,000 12 years earlier. The owner tried several times to sell the lot after a change in family plans. The latest effort was to try to sell the lot on a best-offer basis. A price of less than $60,000 would have been acceptable to the seller.

---

2. John Packer and Andrea Dixon, *1996–97 Facts & Figures on the On-Snow Industry*, SnowSports Industries of America, McLean, Virginia and National Ski Areas Association, Lakewood, Colorado, January 1998, p. 59.

3. Ibid., p. 59.

4. Ibid., p. 58.

5. National Ski Areas Association, "National Ski Areas Association Releases Final 1997–98 Skier/Snowboarder Visits," Lakewood, Colorado, September 23, 1998, p. 3.

Array Lot Sales by Proximity to Amenities

The value of resort and recreational lots varies considerably depending on their location. There are two levels of location influences on site values. First, there is the macro location influence applicable to lots in different parts of a region or even in different regions. Generally sites subject to great location differences are not comparable sites and should not be used to estimate the value of an appraised site. The other location influence focuses on sites within the same locale and even the same development. For example, in one RV campground there were four categories of lots: privacy, second-tier, first-tier, and waterfront sites. The price of the most remote (privacy) sites was just one-third of the price of waterfront sites. The privacy lots were barely accessible. This is a vivid example of why it may be misleading to rely on lot descriptions of comparable sales instead of actually inspecting them.

Another example involves a tidal riverfront resort in which a first-tier lot is the most valuable category of home site and thus would set the benchmark value of 100% value. A second-tier lot may be worth 25% of the first-tier value. However, if it possesses a scenic view or is near a community swimming pool or boat/swimming pier, then it is worth more—perhaps 50% to 75% of the first-tier lot.

A study of 297 residential lot sales on an Atlantic barrier island south of Charleston, South Carolina between January 1989 and July 1994 revealed distinctive price patterns for different categories of views. It was found that on Seabrook Island "...ocean views add 147% to lot values, location on a creek or marsh adds 115% to lot prices, and golf course location adds 39% to lot values."[6] Little value enhancement was detected for lake views "...because the lakes on Seabrook are small and generally not suitable for swimming and other water sports."[7]

A survey of 18 coastal golf communities in early 1999 by Permar & Ravenel, Inc. of Kiawah Island, South Carolina showed that deep water and oceanfront lots were scarce and brought premium prices. Using interior lots as the basis of comparison (assigned a value of 100%), the value of lots progressed upwardly through lagoon, fairway, fairway/lagoon, marsh, deep water, and ultimately oceanfront lots. Different lot value relationships occurred in each community depending on the lot layout, orientation to amenities, etc., but the general value increases for these developer-priced lots over interior lots were: lagoon (155%), fairway (160%), fairway/lagoon (240%), marsh (260%), deep water (715%), and ultimately oceanfront lots. In the few instances where there were both

---

6. James R. Rinehart and Jeffrey J. Pompe, "Estimating the Effect of a View on Undeveloped Property Values," *The Appraisal Journal* (January 1999), p. 60.

7. Ibid.

deep water lots and oceanfront lots, the latter sold for about 175% over the price of the deep water sites. (A deep water lot provides water of sufficient depth to accommodate a pier for deep draft boats such as sail and shrimp boats.) In one case, a one-acre oceanfront lot was available for $2 million.

Plot Unit Price Pattern

Some developers will create interior lakes or golf courses to stimulate higher prices for lots that otherwise would be worth relatively little. The reason for this price decline from waterfront first-tier lots to interior lots is that prospective buyers tend to be attracted to water amenities and have virtually no interest in a commonplace, off-water lot. Without such value-enhancing amenities, the lot price pattern may look similar to the following example. Prices and ratios will vary from locale to locale, but in most resorts an appraiser should avoid using dissimilar categories of lots as a basis for justifying the value of an appraised lot.

High lot on point	Good water depth & view	Waterfront, with limited view	Off-water lots
$100,000+	$75,000	$40,000–$55,000	$12,000

In appraising resort lots, the term "view lot" requires clarification. For example, in mountain resort areas there are a variety of views. These views may be ranked from least to most desirable as follows:

- *Interior.* These lots are the least desirable of all lots, but they may offer some attractions, such as trees and terrain as well as proximity to resort amenities such as tennis courts, ski slopes, and exercise facilities.

- *Streams.* These views may be seasonal depending on tree foliage and the size of steams, some of which may dry up in the summer. The amount of frontage on a "gold medal" fishing stream usually is an important factor in the price paid for the site. In the Rocky Mountains, there is a reasonably consistent relationship in the price per lineal foot of stream frontage for larger acreage parcels. In analyzing such sales, it is important to determine the width from the centerline of the stream and whether the potential buyer's access is limited to only one side of the stream. Figure 14.1 shows a picturesque view along the Bow River near Banff in Alberta, Canada.

- *Golf fairway or greens view.* These views are appealing because they visually extend the expanse and depth of a lot through additional green space that the lot owner does not have to maintain. Golfers especially enjoy seeing golfing activity. Some lot purchasers will pay

Figure 14.1 *Bow River, Alberta, Canada*

more to be on the left (hook) side than the right (slice) side of a fairway. Because more golfers slice than hook, this purchase strategy is intended to minimize window replacements from errant golf balls.

- *Lake.* Lot prices tend to increase with lake size. Lake views may be attractive and are appealing, especially when there is the prospect of canoeing and sailboat activity. The scenic appeal may diminish when the lake becomes polluted and congested with noisy motorboats and jet skis.

- *Narrow or short distance views.* Sometimes called *keyhole views,* a view is created where a few trees have been cleared between the dwelling and the vista.

- *Sunset views.* These tranquil views can be relaxing at the end of a day and many purchasers prefer this view.

- *Distant view.* These lots are at the edge of a cliff or along a mountain ridge, with no trees interrupting a view of perhaps several mountains and a valley for a distance of 20 to 50 miles. Alternatively, an appealing view for some people is from a valley lot looking up at the mountains. However, these lots generally are worth less than the distant view lots atop mountains.

Lot values at different resorts, and even lots within a particular category at the same resort, can vary substantially. For instance, a distant view lot may be worth more than twice as much as a keyhole view lot. A lake lot may bring a premium over a golf course lot, depending on the circumstances. Either category may enjoy multiple views and added value, such as fairway plus a sunset view (see Figure 14.2). Interior lots may be expected to be worth the least among all categories. Hughes and Nunnick have observed that, "Residential lots adjacent to a quality golf course typically sell for 20% to 60% more than similar lots not on the golf course."[8] Jensen points out the value of hot spots on a golf course, "Typically thought of as the tees, greens, and landing areas, lots located around these areas usually fetch higher premiums than lots on fairways or most any other part of a development." Further, he observes that, "Elements that can create additional hot spots include ponds, natural streams or wetland conservation areas, wooded areas, sculptured bunkers, contoured fairway edges, dramatic sand traps, and the utilization of high points for views overlooking the golf course."[9]

In mountain recreation areas, the appraiser will find it helpful to test the following units of comparison in narrowing the range of indicated values:

- Price paid per square foot of site area

- Price paid per linear foot of river or lake frontage

- Price paid per square foot of buildable area

- Price paid per lot (building site)

Apply Price Pattern to Appraised Lot

Sound advice in making location adjustments for resort lots, as well as for all classes of real estate, is— don't. That is, whenever possible conduct exhaustive research to discover recent sales of similar lots

Figure 14.2   *Multiple View Lot—Golf Course Fairway and Mountains*

Source: Wintergreen Resort, Wintergreen, Virginia

8.   Stephen R. Hughes and Kevin K. Nunnink, "Appraising Golf Courses for Ad Valorem Tax Purposes," *The Appraisal Journal* (October 1993), p. 612.

9.   David Jensen, "'Windows' and 'focals' maximize golf community real estate values," *Resort Development* (April 1990), p. 10.

or parcels having equivalent location attributes. As shown in this chapter, lots that are dissimilar in their orientation to amenities and views command quite different prices. If, however, it is not possible to obtain recent sales of nearby lots in the same location or class, then the appraiser is obliged to fully investigate the location factors that produce different value discounts and premiums.

Summary

Properties that are well situated with regard to population centers, airlines, and interstate highway routes and have appealing amenities will offer the best chance of protecting investors' investments. But, simply being in a resort does not guarantee value enhancement. Skier accessibility influences ski resort locations. Because ski resorts require snow, appropriate terrain, and climate, they generally are clustered.

In some markets there is clearly a two-tier lot sales market. Lots bought in haste frequently will resell for a lower price later. The value of resort and recreational lots vary considerably depending on their location. There are two levels of location influences on site values. First, there is the macro location influence, affecting lots in different parts of a region or even in different regions. Generally land subject to large location differences are not comparable sites and should not be used to estimate the value of an appraised site. If it is not possible to obtain recent sales of nearby lots in the same location or class, then the appraiser must fully comprehend the location factors that produce different value discounts and premiums. Other location influences affect sites within the same locale and even the same development.

There are a variety of view lots. For example, in mountain resorts the following views may be available, ranked from most to least desirable: distant view, sunset view, narrow or short distance view, lake view, golf fairway or greens view, stream view, and interior.

15

Depth Adjustments

Adjustments are required to account for the differences between the depth of comparable land sales and an appraised parcel if the difference affects value. An adjustment is justified if the difference in depth measurably affects the values of the comparables and the subject parcel. Depth value analysis is one of the most obvious illustrations of the principle of contribution, which states that "...the value of a particular component is measured in terms of its contribution to the value of the whole property, or as the amount that its absence would detract from the value of the whole."[1]

This principle as applied to site depth is illustrated in Figure 15.1. The appraised site has a depth of 250 feet whereas the sale site has additional depth of 50 feet, for a total depth of 300 feet. The question to be answered by the principle of contribution is how much, if any, value did the additional 50 feet contribute to the price paid for the sale site? Suppose that all other features of the two sites are similar. Through market analysis it is found that $5,000 of the total sale price of $80,000 for the comparable site can be attributed to the additional depth. Therefore, the indicated value of the appraised site is $75,000 ($80,000 − $5,000).

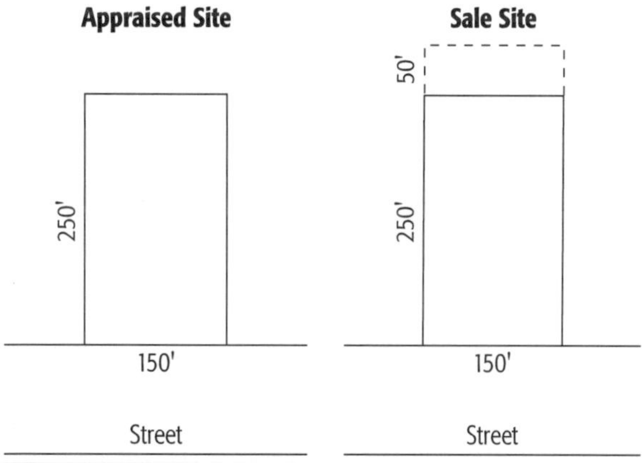

This paired sales valuation technique was covered in detail in Chapter 10. It involves isolating a value-influencing feature that can be explained by comparing two or more sale properties. The sale and subject sites analyzed in this illustration reveal that the contributory value of the rear 50 feet of depth is $5,000.

Figure 15.1   *Principle of Contribution Illustrated*

1.   Appraisal Institute, *The Appraisal of Real Estate,* 11th ed. (Chicago: Appraisal Institute, 1996), p. 45.

As will be illustrated later, the goal in making a depth adjustment is to arrive at a dollar adjustment for the difference in depth between comparable land sales and the appraised parcel. Two depth-value relationships generally hold true for parcels of varying depths.

- The front foot value of a parcel increases as its depth increases.
- The square foot (or acre) value decreases as a parcel's depth increases.

Of course, there are exceptions to this rule as well as different unit value patterns. The highest square unit of value is to be expected in the front portion a site's depth. Yet, if a site is so shallow as to not allow a building to be constructed, then it will have diminished square foot and front foot value.

Earlier Depth-Value Estimation Method

Early in this century, appraisers searched for scientific means to improve the uniformity of appraisals, especially those made for municipal assessment purposes. In his 1924 book, John A. Zangerle observed that the first depth curve was the 4-3-2-1 rule. Under this rule, a parcel was divided into quarters, with the first quarter of depth from the street being worth 40% of the total value; the second quarter contributed 30% of total value; the third quarter was worth 20%; and the rear quarter was worth 10%.[2] He credited Judge Murray Hoffman of New York City as having established the first recognized rule for appraising lots of varying depths.[3] Hoffman estimated that "...the first fifty feet of a lot one hundred feet in depth was worth two thirds of the value of the entire lot. On this basis the first twenty-five feet of a lot one hundred feet in depth equaled $37^1/_2$ percent; the first half equaled 67 percent; three quarters, $87^1/_2$ percent and one hundred feet equaled 100 percent."[4]

During this period several large cities prepared their own variations of depth tables. They were of great assistance to assessors as a way to establish equality and uniformity in assessing since it was impossible to individually appraise each lot in a city.[5] Babcock suggested that different types of land would reveal different depth-value patterns. "The rate of [lot] value increase will be very low in retail districts, will be relatively higher in wholesale districts and in apartment districts, and will very nearly

---

2. John A. Zangerle, *Principles of Real Estate Appraising* (Cleveland: The Stanley McMichael Publishing Organization, 1924), p. 91.

3. Zangerle, p. 91.

4. Zangerle, pp. 91–92.

5. Stanley L. McMichael, *McMichael's Appraising Manual,* 3rd ed. (New York: Prentice-Hall, Inc., 1945), p. 484.

approach direct proportion in industrial property."[6] He cautioned that a variety of rates of value change would occur between the front and rear portions of various kinds of properties. A difficulty in attempting to use depth tables is their limited applicability to a variety of properties in different locations and for differently zoned parcels with various highest and best uses. This misapplication is illustrated with the following story.

A young appraiser had just finished answering questions under direct examination in an eminent domain case. In his presentation, the appraiser discussed at some length how he accounted for the difference in depth among the several comparable residential lot sales and the appraised lot. At this point, the opposing attorney began his cross-examination by complimenting the appraiser on the thorough description of his depth adjustment methodology. The veteran attorney's reassuring comments increased the confidence of the already smug appraiser. Then, the lawyer almost meekly asked the appraiser if he would please explain the basis for his rather precise depth adjustments. The appraiser was quite willing to accommodate the attorney and brought forth from his briefcase a well-worn set of depth tables. At this point, the attorney requested that the overly confident appraiser state for the jury the publication date of the book and where it was published. He then destroyed the appraiser's testimony by stating, in an incredulous and mocking tone, "You mean to tell us that you arrived at the value of this home site just down the street from this courthouse by relying on a so-called depth table that was published over a half century ago halfway across the United States by someone you don't even know! Your honor, I have no further questions for this witness." Based on the award recommended by the jury, the appraiser's testimony was virtually ignored.

A general rule of thumb for appraisers is to avoid use of published depth tables and curves for the valuation of individual parcels. However, convincing and accurate reports **can** result from preparing such benchmarks from local market data.

Comparative Depth of Sales and Subject Parcel

Before any adjustment can be made for variations in depth between comparable land sales and a subject parcel, either a common unit of measurement or value pattern must be established. For example, land sales may either be expressed on the basis of price per acre or per front foot. A lower per acre (or square foot) price and a higher front foot price may be expected as the depth of a parcel increases beyond the local norm. One way to gauge the value of the appraised parcel is to compile a number of

---

6. Frederick M. Babcock, *The Appraisal of Real Estate* (New York: The MacMillan Company, 1927), p. 287.

similar land sales and plot the value pattern. The value unit-depth patterns may appear as shown below, keeping in mind that the rate of unit value change can vary considerably from site to site. In Figure 15.2, several recent land sales of varying depths have been plotted to show the pattern of their prices per front foot. It can be seen that each foot of additional depth for shallow lots contributes more value than the incremental depth some distance from the street. For instance, an increase of 25 feet from 125 feet to 150 feet adds $50 per front foot, from $1,050 to $1,100 in value (+4.8%). A much lower value increase occurs between 250 and 275 feet, increasing from approximately $1,240 to $1,265. This is a value increase of only $25 (+2.0%).

A different and inverse unit-value progression can be seen when using sale price per acre as shown in Figure 15.3. As the depth increases, the price per acre decreases. An increase in depth from 100 to 125 feet results in a per acre price decline of about $35,500 from $345,000 to $309,500 (-10.3%). By contrast, when the depth increases from 250 to 275 feet, the per acre price falls off by approximately $14,000, from $229,000 to $215,000 (-6.1%). Either of these graphs would be useful in making depth adjustments for comparable sales of the same type parcels (i.e., same zoning, utilities, terrain, etc.).

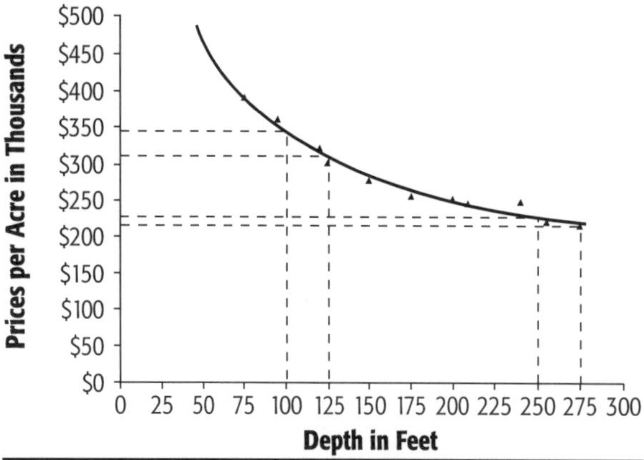

Using Figure 15.2, suppose that the subject parcel had 170 feet of road frontage and was 150 feet deep. By drawing perpendicular lines from 150 feet up to the curve and then horizontally from the point of intersection to the vertical axis, a value of approximately $187,000 (170 × $1,100) is indicated. A similar value estimate of another parcel could be made by using Figure 15.3. This illustrative parcel contains four acres and is 250 feet deep. This graph indicates an approximate value of $904,000 (4 ac. × $226,000).

Figure 15.2   Land Sale Prices per Front Foot

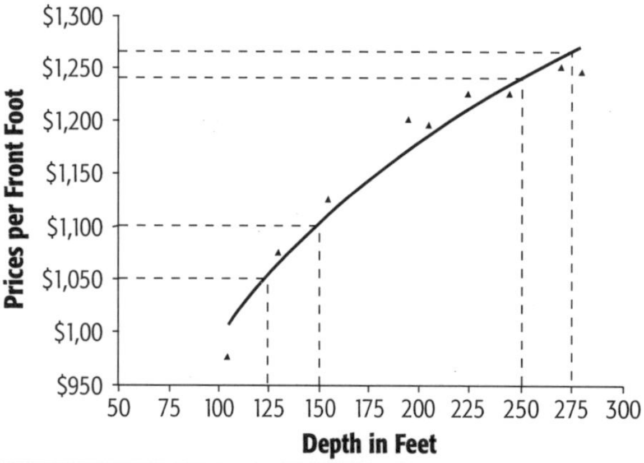

Figure 15.3   Land Sale Prices per Acre

Summary

Adjustments are required for the difference between the depths of comparable land sales and an appraised parcel. An adjustment is justified if the difference in depth measurably affects the value of the comparables and the subject parcel. The two depth-value relationships that generally hold true for parcels of varying depths are: the front foot value of a parcel increases as its depth increases and the square foot (or acre) value decreases as a parcel's depth increases. One difficulty in using depth tables is their limited applicability to a variety of properties in different location and for differently zoned parcels with various highest and best uses. Before any adjustment can be made for variations in depth between comparable land sales and a subject parcel, either a common unit of measurement or value pattern must be established.

16

Sites in Mature Neighborhoods

One method that may be applied in appraising vacant sites in mature (built-up) neighborhoods is the site value-to-total property value ratio method. This method is also known as the *allocation method.* It can be used to corroborate the value of an improved site for real estate assessment purposes, in federal income tax matters, in the depreciated cost approach, and when a separate estimate of the site value is needed.

Insufficiency of Lot Sales

In certain appraisal assignments, the nature of the property, the age of the neighborhood, supply and demand conditions, or the stage of the real estate cycle will require departure from the usual valuation methodology. As a rule, an appraiser will initially rely on an analysis of land sales to derive an estimate of a parcel's market value. Lacking reliable and current information of this nature, alternative methods such as the subdivision development, land residual, or extraction methods may be applied. At other times, an appraiser may either want to make a preliminary estimate of a site's value or use a more common method to corroborate the reasonableness of an estimate. An appraiser should be cautious about relying too greatly on the site value-to-total property value method because it only provides a general benchmark of value. A more precise indicator may be produced by a rigorous analysis of recent comparable land sales.

Establish Neighborhood Lot Value-to-Property Value Ratio

This valuation technique is most successfully used for standard-size lots in a new residential subdivision where there is a combination of lot sales and home sales. It is easy to apply in a newly developed subdivision because a fairly uniform lot value-to-total property value pattern can be established. Paradoxically, because there are ample recent lot sales, it is redundant. In any situation, it is an indirect measure of market value. The method probably is most difficult to apply to industrial parcels with wide-ranging sizes and varying intensities of development. Similarly, it is difficult to apply to properties that have excess land. More intensive land uses, such as central business district multistory office buildings, generally result in a lower land value-to-total property value ratio than less intensive land uses such as suburban warehouse development.

By analyzing similar neighborhoods or districts where occasional site sales can be located, the appraiser can create a fairly accurate land value ratio for the subject neighborhood. In time, he or she may be able to construct a table similar to Table 16.1 to use as a general guideline for appraising sites with different land uses.[1]

Table 16.1   *Site Value-to-Property Value Ratios for Different Classes of Real Property*

Land Use	Site-to-Property Value Ratio (%)
Commercial	20–50
Office	10–30
Residential	15–25
Apartment house	10–15
Industrial	5–10

Apply Neighborhood Ratio to Appraised Property

For example, suppose that an assignment involves the appraisal of a residential home site in a neighborhood where the homes typically are 30 to 35 years old. The subject lot is improved with a 3,000-sq. ft., two-story dwelling; the lot is typical for the area and there have been no lot sales during the past 10 years. A few lot and improved sales in other neighborhoods suggest a lot value ratio of 20% to 23%. Also, the following improved sales were located in the subject neighborhood. Applying this value ratio to these home sales indicates the following lot values.

Sale No.	Sale Price	Lot Value Ratio	Lot Value
1	$265,000	20–23%	$53,000–$60,950
2	$250,000	20–23%	$50,000–$57,500
3	$253,500	20–23%	$50,750–$58,305
4	$264,000	20–23%	$52,800–$60,720
5	$248,900	20–23%	$49,780–$57,247
6	$251,500	20–23%	$50,300–$57,845

These improved sales indicate a fairly wide lot value range of $49,780 to $60,950. While appraisers may dislike using averages, it may be appropriate to rely on this measure of value because a direct comparative analysis is not possible in this case. Thus, based on average values derived from these sale ratios, the probable value for the subject lot is in the range of $51,105 to $58,761.

---

1.   James H. Boykin and Alfred A. Ring, *The Valuation of Real Estate* (Englewood Cliffs, NJ: Regents/Prentice Hall, 1993), p. 161.

As demonstrated in the example, this method is not precise. For instance, even if a narrower range of lot values had been indicated, the subject lot may have been atypical in size, corner orientation, depth, or any of several other value-influencing factors. The best that can be expected from this method is to obtain a reasonably close approximation of a lot's value.

The site value extraction method is discussed in Chapter 9. This method is well adapted to sites with nominal or dilapidated improvements that contribute relatively little to the property's overall value. For most valuation assignments, it is not applicable because considerable effort must be made to estimate the building value of each comparable sale. This time-consuming effort generally does not yield a reliable estimate of site value. Imagine the degree of inaccuracy involved in estimating the amount of accrued depreciation in a 40-year-old office building with a current replacement cost new of $5 million. First, the replacement cost and then the accrued depreciation estimate must be made to estimate the value that the building contributes to the sale price. This value then is deducted from the sale price—supposedly producing an indication of the value of the underlying site. However, it is extremely difficult to accurately gauge the depreciated cost of substantial buildings on comparable improved sale properties.

Summary

Lot appraisals in mature neighborhoods may require a departure from the customary valuation methodology and use of the site value-to-total property value method. Appraisers should be cautious about relying on this method too much because it only provides a general benchmark of value rather than the more precise indicator derived from a rigorous analysis of recent comparable land sales. Through an analysis of similar neighborhoods, where occasional sites sales can be located, the appraiser may create a fairly accurate land value ratio for the subject neighborhood. Applying this value ratio to home sales in the subject neighborhood will indicate a range of lot values from which an estimate of the appraised lot can be made.

17

Prospective Subdivisions

The underlying rationale for the subdivision development approach is to estimate the price that an investor would be justified in paying for land that has subdivision potential. It is best applied to estimate the bulk sale value of improved subdivision lots rather than undeveloped land. Frequently, this technique is used in valuing residential land, but it may be used when a tract's highest and best use is for development and marketing as multiple nonresidential sites.

The approach is not a shortcut or an easy means for deriving a value estimate. In fact, to apply this valuation method properly, the appraiser must be familiar with the land development process and thoroughly understand all aspects of the market in which the property is situated. Every input into this discounted cash flow method must be market-derived because this method simulates reality. Thus, the validity of this method varies directly with the level of research the appraiser performs. It is prudent to always back up this method with the direct sales method, even if the market is not robust and some land listings must be used.

The subdivision development method can produce unrealistic indications of market value when applied improperly. In fact, it probably is the least accurate raw land valuation technique. Some reasons for value distortions are:

- Inaccurate highest and best use analysis
- Inaccurate estimates of expenditures required to generate forecast sales revenue
- Overstated project income or failure to accurately graduate lot prices as development matures
- Inaccurate derivation and application of discount rate

The nine steps to be followed in preparing a value estimate using the development technique are:

1. Create a sound development plan.

2. Forecast a realistic pricing schedule.

3. Forecast the lot absorption rate and price mix.

4. Estimate the staging of land development and related expenses.

5. Forecast marketing and related expenses.

6. Estimate annual real estate taxes.

7. Estimate overhead and profit allowance.

8. Determine the expected discount rate.

9. Select a discount rate that reflects the timing of lot sales.

Create a Sound Development Plan

An appraiser must be familiar with proper development design and practices and with local governmental subdivision approval delays and developer monetary extractions to estimate the appropriate development density, lot prices, site preparation costs, and absorption of lot sales. In some municipalities, the sizeable carrying costs and cash proffers incurred during the planning and development process not only reduce the present value of the tract, but can render its development financially infeasible. If the appraiser lacks knowledge of the development process or is unwilling to acquire it, this valuation technique definitely should be avoided.

A development plan does not have to be a detailed engineering drawing. However, value-influencing factors such as lot size; street layout; engineering and utility costs; the prospect of installing surface water infiltration devices, offsite storm-water drainage systems, and required easements; lot pricing; and competition should be understood. A simple mistake such as relying solely on the lot density permitted by the zoning ordinance can cause an appraiser to overstate a parcel's present value. Other factors such as topographical and drainage problems can reduce development density or limit design options.

Forecast a Realistic Pricing Schedule

The key to establishing a realistic site pricing schedule is to study the competition. Although it may be grueling work, there is no substitute for surveying competitive projects to determine the prices being charged for similar sites. It is wise to profile each project over its marketing phase to see the pattern of price changes—that is, by what percentage have the prices changed each year? Additional information usually can be acquired from knowledgeable brokers and trade association publications. A study of neighborhood home prices can provide a starting point for estimating the expected price range of completed homes in the proposed subdivision. By analyzing competitive lot prices and applying a lot value ratio to the improved home sales in the area, an indication of lot pricing can be obtained.

Forecast the Lot Absorption Rate and Price Mix

This phase of analysis is based on common sense, but requires some effort to execute properly. The appraiser simply is estimating how much time will be required to sell off the prospective site inventory and how the inventory should be priced to be competitive. Both answers are derived from a close analysis of similar developments and an awareness of the competitive environment in which the subject development's sites will be delivered. Proximity to shopping facilities, a location in a popular public school district, and access to employment centers and recreational amenities affect lot demand and pricing. The appraiser will want to be familiar with the state of the economy, mortgage interest rate levels, and supply-demand conditions, including future lots in the pipeline. The appraiser needs to have a clear idea of the extent of competition and probable market conditions when the subdivision marketing effort gets underway.

Municipal planning department personnel can provide information on the number of zoned lots, those that are undergoing rezoning approval, and those that are currently under construction. Care must be taken to avoid forecasting lot absorption based on a developer's marketing schedule. There may or may not be a close relationship between the two timelines. Also, there will be a lag between the purchase date and commencement of the lot sales program. There is the initial delay until the subdivision has received the requisite municipal approvals and sufficient infrastructure has been completed to allow builders to buy lots for construction. This phase may take one year or more. Then the individual builders must receive plan approval and generally will delay settlement until the first construction draw, which may take two or three months.

It is rare that all lots in a development will be marketed at the same price. Developers generally will grade their lots from A to C from the most choice to the least desirable lots. Then competitive individual lot prices are set. These prices are based in part on the ultimate prices of the properties to be sold. Typically, view lots, moderately flat lots, wooded lots, and larger lots will be priced at the highest level. Hillside lots, poorly drained lots, lots requiring additional site preparation costs, or inferior location lots will receive lower prices. In one development of second homes, there were the usual lot categories, but the appraiser was unfamiliar with the term "privacy sites." The developer, with a mild sense of exaggeration, explained, "You can't get to those sites, that's why they're called 'privacy lots.'"

Estimate the Staging of Land Development and Related Expenses

It is possible to obtain generalized land development cost estimates from developers and civil engineering firms. An effort should be made, however, to relate these expenses and their scheduling to the particular parcel being appraised. An illustration of these expenses and their scheduling is shown in Table 17.2 at the end of this chapter. Sometimes the developer will handle much of the interaction with the municipal planning, environmental engineering, and highway departments. In other situations, an engineering company manages these efforts. Some expenses must be borne before any sales begin. In fact, it can be self-defeating for the developer to attempt to market lots to either prospective home buyers or builders before the streets are paved. It is hard to get prospective buyers to return for a second look if they did not like what they saw initially.

Expenses that typically are incurred before the first lot is sold include the land purchase price and closing costs. These costs are excluded from this valuation technique because the goal is to estimate the price that should be paid for the undeveloped tract. Typical expenses include the costs of title search, boundary survey and environmental investigation, soil analysis for bearing walls and/or septic drain fields, engineering fees, real estate taxes, utility easement acquisition, mortgage interest carrying costs, subdivision plan preparation, advertising, parcel clearing and stump hauling, silt fences, road grading, storm sewers, utility installation, subdivision bond, and plat recording. The cost to seed and straw roadside slopes may also be included. Once the sales stage commences, payments are due for preparation and recording of restrictive covenants, marketing expenses, ongoing mortgage debt service, legal fees and any bond renewals, and "punch list" road work such as reshaping roadside ditches and replacing damaged concrete culverts, curbs, and gutters.

Forecast Marketing and Related Expenses

These expenses vary with local customs and the magnitude of a development. Marketing may be limited to newspaper advertisements or local real estate home sales magazines. Larger-scale projects may include a model home, which becomes the on-site sales office, possibly limited to weekend use. Lot commissions may range from 5% to 10% or, in some cases, commissions may be prohibited. Some developers will not allow "double dipping," in which an agent collects one commission for the sale of a lot and then another for the sale of the lot and completed house. Marketing expenses will normally diminish toward the end of the marketing phase, when the project amenities and character are established and word-of-mouth advertising replaces print advertising.

Estimate Annual Real Estate Taxes

Estimation of the annual real estate taxes is not complicated if the proposed development is expected to be developed and completely sell out within a single tax year. More likely, however, is the prospect of a multi-year development and marketing program. The real estate taxes for the first year and before actual subdivision has occurred is based on the raw acreage value. Once subdivision has occurred, the recorded lot part of the land will be assessed, likely as finished lots, and the undeveloped part will be assessed as raw land, possibly reflecting some increase in value due to its proximity to the finished lots. The appraiser would be wise to check with the local assessor's office to determine when it converts land to lot value for developing subdivisions. An accounting of real estate taxes then should be made based on the proposed development schedule.

Estimate Overhead and Profit Allowance

The normal profit expectancy for developers may be handled several ways. Certainly an allowance should be made for overhead or contingencies as well as profit. Failing to do so will overstate a proposed project's revenue and inflate the present value estimate. An insufficient yield would not encourage a developer to take the risk of developing the raw land or motivate a lender to provide acquisition and development financing. When discounting the net sales revenue of a prospective development, it is preferable to omit a profit line and include that rate as part of the discount rate. Because profit already is built into the sale prices of the finished lots, there is no need to add it in again. However, some clients may require the appraiser to split the discount rate into a separate line-item profit percentage and a complementary discount rate.

Determine the Expected Discount Rate

The discount rate usually will be market-derived rather than imputed from a single investor because most valuation assignments require estimates of market value and not investment value. When a given investment is low in the real estate food chain, investors expect a higher yield rate. Hence, land investors and developers may expect a return two or three times greater than that anticipated for a well-leased, stable, multitenant office building. Discount rates rarely can be computed directly from market data because an appraiser would need to determine the initial acquisition price of the comparable property, the amount and dates of all of its income and expenses, and its eventual resale price. Sources of discount rates include personal interviews with informed investors to ascertain their yield requirements for similar ventures and published surveys. Alternatively, the appraiser can find the sum of the weighted average of the respective lender and equity investor internal rates of return or adjust for the illiquidity, risk, and management burden of real estate developments over bonds of similar duration or equity real estate investment trusts.[1] The discounting process takes into account delays that municipal approvals, utilities and road construction, and marketing time cause. That is, the land does not have to be immediately ripe for development, but the starting time should not be so remote that an appraiser cannot accurately compile and analyze pertinent information.

Some published sources of land yields include the "Pricewaterhouse-Coopers LLP National Land Market Report" in the *Korpacz Real Estate Investor Survey*. In studying these surveys, it is important to determine whether the yield is for holding land for speculation, leasing, or development; whether it is leveraged or unleveraged; and if it has municipal approvals or not. Land held for development without municipal approvals and using leverage that involves considerable risk will necessitate the highest return. An illustration of the PricewaterhouseCoopers Survey is shown in Table 17.1.

Table 17.1	Land Yield Survey, Mid-Year 1999	
	Range	**Median**
DCF analysis		
Property discount rate *(IRR)*[a]	9.00%–30.00%	14.00%
Equity discount rate *(IRR)*[b]	20.00%–35.00%	24.00%

a. Rate on unleveraged, all-cash transactions.
b. Rate on leveraged transactions.
Source: *Korpacz Real Estate Investor Survey*, second quarter, 1999, p. 34.

Select a Discount Rate That Reflects the Timing of Lot Sales

As a rule, an end-of-period (EOP) discount rate will be used in determining the present value of the underlying land for a prospective development. (Financial tables are set up on this basis.) There are situations in which the EOP discount premise does not reflect accurately the timing of the revenue stream. For example, for seasonal lot sales in resort areas, sales activity tends to be heavily concentrated during the spring, summer, and fall seasons and especially during summer. If this kind of sales clustering occurs, then a mid-year discount factor would most accurately gauge the present value of the income stream. Of course, the same methodology should be used in extracting yield rates from available market sources. If the selected discount rate were 30% and the appraiser was using the mid-year factor for Year 1, the correct present value factor would be 0.869565 and not 0.769231, which would be the EOP factor.

Table 17.2 relates to a 40-acre tract of land that is zoned to allow for the construction of 100 single-family, detached dwelling units. The development is forecast to take three years and it is expected that the sale

---

1. James H. Boykin, "A Comparative Evaluation of the Direct Capitalization and Discounted Cash Flow Methods in Development-Construction Loan Appraising," Proceedings of International Conference on Financial Management of Property and Construction (Newcastle, Northern Ireland: University of Ulster, May 1995), p. 204.

Table 17.2 _Present Value of Proposed Subdivision_

	Year 1	Year 2	Year 3	Year 4
Lot Sales:				
10 @ $40,000	$400,000			
30 @ $42,000		$1,260,000		
40 @ $44,500			$1,780,000	
20 @ $47,000				940,000
Less:				
Development costs:				
1. Streets & drainage @ $6,000/lot	$180,000	$300,000	$120,000	
2. Sewer lines @ $3,500/lot	105,000	175,000	70,000	
3. Water system @ $2,500/lot	75,000	125,000	50,000	
4. Engineering & surveying @ $1,500/lot	45,000	75,000	30,000	
Miscellaneous expenses*	43,200	72,000	28,800	7,000
Loan interest & points @ 9.0%†	40,338	67,230	26,892	630
Sales commission/management @ 6%	24,000	75,600	106,800	56,400
Marketing & promotion	15,000	25,000	20,000	10,000
Total expenses	$527,538	$914,830	$452,492	$74,030
Net sales revenue	($127,538)	$345,170	$1,327,508	$865,970
Discounted @ 30%	($98,106)	$204,243	$604,237	$303,200
Total present value of 40-acre tract:				$1,013,574
			Rounded to: $1,000,000, or $25,000/acre	

* 12% of items 1, 2, & 3 to allow for rock, hardpan, inspection fees, bonds, real estate taxes, soil studies, closing costs, etc., except in Year 4, in which only real estate taxes and closing costs are incurred.

† Loan funds all development and miscellaneous expenses.

of the lots will require four years. The development expenses are set to reflect 30 lots being prepared in Year 1, 50 in Year 2, and 20 in Year 3. Similarly zoned tracts are currently selling for $22,000 to $26,000 per acre.

Summary

The subdivision development valuation method provides an estimate of the price that an investor is justified in paying for land that has subdivision potential. It is not a shortcut or an easy means for deriving a value estimate. In fact, to apply this valuation method properly, the appraiser must be familiar with the land development process and thoroughly understand all aspects of the market in which the land is located. This method may produce an unrealistic value indication if it is applied improperly. The suggested steps to be followed in preparing a value estimate using the land development technique are: create a sound development plan; forecast a realistic pricing schedule, forecast accurately the lot absorption rate and price mix; accurately estimate the staging of land development and related expenses; forecast marketing and related expenses; estimate the annual real estate taxes; estimate a reasonable overhead and profit allowance; determine the expected discount rate; and select a discount rate that reflects the timing of lot sales.

Residential Waterfront Property

Water frontage as a residential lot amenity may vary considerably in appeal and value within the same geographic area and certainly in different regions or states. That is, what is an important value consideration for a Maine coastal cottage may not be important on a California beachfront. Although the elements of value covered in this chapter have general applicability to all of the coastal and inland states, the appraiser must continually exercise sound judgment in identifying and analyzing local value factors.

The following five elements of value generally are important for waterfront property. Some of these also are relevant to appraising off-water land as well.

1. *Boating.* This is probably the most important value factor. Boating includes sailing and power boating. Sailboats generally require water deep near the shoreline. Unless a power boat is large, only moderate water depth is needed at the water boundary. In recent years, the growing popularity of personal watercraft, such as jet skis, has increased the appeal of previously unusable water frontage.

2. *Swimming and water sports use.* Most waterfront properties are used part of the year for swimming or water sports. In northern climates, wetsuits or other protective clothing is often required to enjoy the water.

3. *View amenity.* A water view almost always is pleasant and often prospective lot purchasers seek it out.

4. *Light and air.* Property owners typically favor waterfront lots for the open feeling and the breeze off the adjacent body of water.

5. *Privacy.* Depending on the nature and volume of boating activity and the width of the body of water, a greater sense of privacy may be achieved by owning a waterfront lot than an off-water lot of similar size.

Before considering waterfront lot valuation methods, factors that influence the value of these lots must be understood. One multiple regression study involving 115 residential ocean beach lots at Emerald Isle, North Carolina, revealed that the following factors significantly influence the value of such lots: distance of lots to the beach, view of the ocean, average value of surrounding lots, shape of the lot, and amount of beach frontage as measured in feet.[1] Although this study was limited to ocean-oriented lots, these same value influences apply to other water-oriented lots such as those on rivers, creeks, and lakes. These and other factors are explained in this chapter.

Driving Time From Population Centers

Land prices often vary directly with proximity to metropolitan areas. As a rule, most second home owners and tenants prefer limiting their driving time to two or three hours. Properties located within this driving range are able to draw from a larger population pool and, in turn, realize higher demand and prices. Within a water-oriented area, higher prices are paid when open sailing water can be reached in two hours or less under sail. People will pay airfare or drive eight or more hours to reach an area that offers distinctive amenities, such as Myrtle Beach, South Carolina, with its extensive entertainment, golfing, and mild weather; coastal Florida with its subtropical weather; or Lake Tahoe, California-Nevada, with its scenic vistas.

Elevation and Slope of Lot

An elevated lot generally is preferable to a low-lying lot. It offers a superior view as well as protection from flooding and storm damage. On lakes and rivers, a gently sloping lot is desirable because generally it provides a superior view and an easy walk from the house to the water. Along oceanfronts, it may not be possible to find any appreciable elevation, but here it is highly desirable to be behind the first row of sand dunes. In some places, it is not possible to get a building permit or insurance to build a home between the ocean and the first dune line. Coastal construction control lines mandate building setbacks in many areas. Adequate site elevation also gives greater assurance of septic drain fields operating satisfactorily during periods when the seasonal water table rises. Although a lot should have a reasonably high elevation, it should not be so high that a large expense will be incurred in building a bulkhead to retard shoreline erosion.

---

1. Paul Wertheim, Margaret Capen, Jon Jividen, and Dave Chatterjee, "Characteristics that Affect Market Value of Beach Lot Property," *The Real Estate Appraiser* (August 1992), p. 63.

Land Valuation: Adjustment Procedures and Assignments

Beach Versus Marsh Frontage

Certainly individual preferences may lead one person to choose marsh frontage over beach frontage as a home site. They may enjoy the privacy offered by a marsh because no one will be walking or even riding in a four-wheel drive vehicle in front of their house and no noisy boats will tow water skiers close to their cottage. In some areas there is a distinction between soft and hard marsh, with the latter being sufficiently firm that one can generally walk without miring down in mud. Some salt marshes are interlaced by guts (gullies) that allow shallow-draft boat traffic. Marshes are appealing to naturalists and duck hunters. See Chapter 23 for a detailed discussion on the related topics of floodplains and wetlands.

Within the same area, it can be expected that ocean frontage will bring peak prices and that land values will decline from bay frontage to marsh frontage. For example, in rural areas marsh frontage may bring 20% to 30% of the price of bay or river frontage; creek frontage may command 30% to 60% of bay and river frontage lots. In such areas, buyers may pay approximately the same for bay and river frontage, as shown in Table 18.1.

Each market is different. The above value relationship may be altered in favor of fishing rather than water skiing and swimming if the waters become infested with sea nettles. Their painful presence may place a value premium on lots that allow moderately-priced pier construction and a discount from the expected higher prices for lots with sandy beaches. Fishing and boating become more important than swimming and water skiing when an area is overrun by sea nettles.

Table 18.1	*Illustrative Waterfront Value Scale*		
Bay	**River**	**Creek**	**Marsh**
View	Lesser view	Short view	Privacy
No dockage	No dockage	Protected dockage	Limited dockage
100% value	100% value depending on river width and view	30%–60% value of bay/river lots	Insects when no breeze
			20%–30% value of bay/river lots

Beach Width

It has been found that increased beach width positively affects oceanfront home values. For instance, a multiple regression study of sales in the Myrtle Beach area focused on improved residential sales, but the results are indicative of vacant lot value patterns. Safety from storm water surges and erosion is foremost in the minds of buyers considering beachfront property. Rinehart and Pompe found, "Any increase in beach width provides greater land protection and consequently increases property values. In addition, the wider the beach the greater the recreational benefits."[2] The study further concluded that "...for an increase in beach

---

2.   James R. Rinehart and Jeffrey J. Pompe, "Adjusting the Market Value of Coastal Property for Beach Quality," *The Appraisal Journal* (October 1994), p. 605.

width of 10%, the house value will increase by 2.6%." It also found, "The value of a wider beach is greater for property near the ocean than for property located farther back."[3] Figure 18.1 depicts a beach along the Atlantic Ocean.

Figure 18.1 *Undeveloped Ocean Beach Frontage*

Source: Virginia Institute of Marine Science, Gloucester Point, Virginia.

Direction of Prevailing Winds/Shoreline Erosion

The direction of prevailing winds can impact the desirability, maintenance costs, and value of a waterfront site. For example, along the Eastern Seaboard land with northeastern exposure tends to experience the worst shoreline erosion from winds, especially by winter storms called "nor'easters." As the expanse of open water increases, the prospect of water energy rises.

Oceanfront lots are especially susceptible to erosion during late summer and early fall hurricanes and from winter storms. In some areas, more than 200 feet of beachfront depth may be lost in a couple of storms and homes may be lost to the sea. Figure 18.2 illustrates the migration and even disappearance of shoreline. In 1852 the lighthouse at New Point Comfort in Virginia was approximately 750 feet north of the southern shoreline. By 1985 the lighthouse was about 3400 feet south of the nearest land mass. The annual rate of erosion during this period amounts to more than 31 feet, or almost one mile of shoreline lost. In the summer of 1999, Cape Hatteras Light Station in North Carolina was moved 1,900 feet from the Atlantic shore. This lighthouse was about 1,600 feet from the ocean when it was built in 1870, but by 1987 it was just 160 feet away. Historically, ocean water levels have been rising at the rate of one foot every one hundred years. Using a somewhat typical seashore area, where the topography rises five feet vertically for every 2,500 feet horizontally, this 1:500 gradient indicates that the ocean will move inward 500 feet every 100 years. As shown in Figure 18.3, land is accreting in some coastal areas while it is eroding elsewhere.

In Florida, accretion occurs on the upstream side of current flow, wherever there is a man-made inlet. That is, where an inlet impedes the normal current flow (such as the Gulf Stream), the beach on the upstream side (north) of the inlet will accrete and grow larger while the beach on the

---

3. Ibid., p. 608.

downstream side (south) will erode and shrink in size. It is helpful for an appraiser to have knowledge of shoreline trends.

Dolan points out that, over the last 100 years, the sea level has risen about 15 centimeters (nearly 6 inches). He notes:

> The Virginia barrier island, Maryland, and New Jersey have the most pronounced erosions rates, up to 4.2 m/yr. [i.e., 13.8 ft./yr.]. Georgia, New York, and Delaware have, in the aggregate, only slightly eroding, stable, or accreting coasts. Overall, the Atlantic Coast is receding. States bordering the Gulf of Mexico have the most rapid average erosion rates, [especially] the coast of Louisiana (4.2 m/yr.). The Great Lakes shorelines are eroding at an average rate of 0.7 m/yr. [i.e., 2.3 ft./yr.] The Pacific Coast, including Alaska, has the lowest erosion rates (0.005 m/yr.) [i.e., 0.20 in./yr.], as well as the lowest overall percentage of eroding areas.[4]

Figure 18.2   *Shoreline Migration*

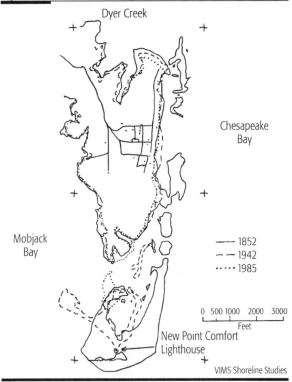

Source: "VIMS Shoreline Studies," Virginia Institute of Marine Science, Gloucester Point, Virginia.

Millions of dollars may be necessary to stabilize and replenish beaches periodically. In one area, a gap breakwater system built of stacked 200- to 300-pound rocks was proposed to retard beach erosion. The per household cost of this preventative measure was expected to be $25,000 to $35,000 for waterfront lots and $5,000 for each interior lot. In some resort communities, special sand taxes are levied. The appraiser should determine whether a dwelling can be rebuilt on a lot if a storm such as a hurricane demolishes an existing cottage. If it cannot, the highest and best use of the underlying lot is impaired severely.

Appraisers should be careful to note whether any comparable sales selected occurred shortly after hurricanes. Sellers may be more inclined to unload lots cheaply after severe storm damage and buyers, being aware of recent damage from personal inspection and sensationalized media reports, may be willing to purchase only at discounted prices. Use of these below-market sales without adjustment for special seller motivation will, of course, understate the appraised value of a subject lot.

---

4.   Robert Dolan, Fred Anders, and Suzette Kimball, *Coastal Erosion and Accretion* (Reston, VA: U. S. Geological Survey, 1985; 38077-AU-NA-07M-00).

Figure 18.3   *Shoreline Reshaping Process, Chesapeake Bay and Vicinity*

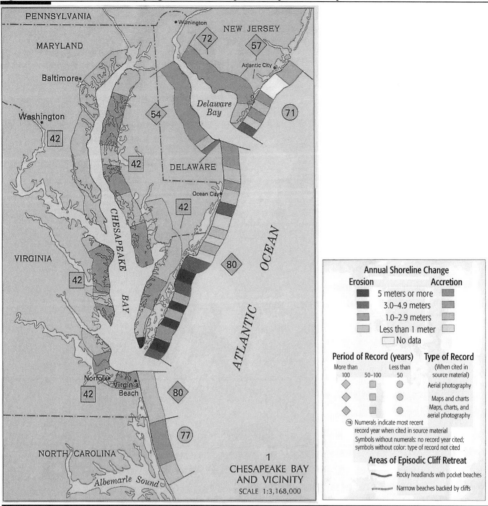

Source: Robert Dolan, Fred Anders, and Suzette Kimball, *Coastal Erosion and Accretion* map (Reston, VA: U. S. Geological Survey, 1985; 38077-AU-NA-07M-00).

Added Cost of Riprap or Bulkhead

A site with a high bank subject to strong prevailing winds may require the installation of expensive bulkheads and/or stone riprap. This added expense might reduce the value of affected lots in comparison to lots not requiring these added erosion-protection costs. The erosive effect of continuing wave action on high waterfront banks can add significantly to the total cost of a lot. As a consequence, a prospective purchaser may discount the price he or she is willing to pay for a lot if additional construction expenses will be incurred to protect the shoreline.

For example, it may cost $85 to $90 a lineal foot to install a 4-ft. high, tongue-and-groove, salt-treated bulkhead in fresh water. Due to extra preservation treatment, this cost may increase 10% for lots on bodies of salt water. Suppose a person is considering buying a 100-ft. lot for $100,000. The added cost of a bulkhead may increase the real purchase cost by $9,000 to $10,000 in this case. Oceanfront steel or reinforced concrete bulkheads, used to contain sand in front of a cottage, may cost $400 a lineal foot, but these structures may be breached by wave action. Better-constructed sea walls may cost three times as much as bulkheads, but will last much longer. Often by the time that either of these structures are built, the beach is virtually nonexistent and owners are attempting to save their cottages.

Installation of riprap (stones or rocks) along the shoreline may cost less than bulkheads. If the stone must be offloaded and then moved some distance to the water bank, it can cost more than a bulkhead. It offers the advantage of permanence over bulkheads, which ordinarily may have a 20-year life, but less if breached by severe storms. Note the loss of beach and damage to stairs shown in Figure 18.4. In some cases, an owner will want to place riprap at the base of a bulkhead to prevent scouring and the eventual undermining of the bulkhead. Armor stone (large stones) also may be used to preserve beach frontage. However, use of either riprap or armor stone may leave a property owner with no option but walking over stone (a favorite habitat for snakes) to reach the beach.

Variance Between High and Low Water Levels

Tidal

Sharp swings between high and low tides of as much as seven to eight feet can measurably affect the utility and value of a site. A one to two foot variance may not be significant unless there is minimal water depth at high tide. If the low tide depth is shallow, access in and out of creeks may be possible only at high tide, which greatly reduces the appeal of a site. For a stern drive boat, a minimum of three feet of water is needed at average mean tide. A fixed-keel sailboat or even one with a swing keel probably should have four to six feet of bottom clearance. Prices of lots will vary significantly depending on the water depth. The greater the depth, the wider the pool of prospective buyers. Figure 18.5 shows a protected creek site with easy access out into a larger body of water, which is seen at the top of the photograph.

Figure 18.4 *Oceanfront Cottages After a Hurricane*

Source: Virginia Institute of Marine Science, Gloucester Point, Virginia.

Figure 18.5   *Protected Creek Site (in foreground)*

The tide changes twice each day. During its rise, it is known as *flood tide* and during its fall, *ebb tide*. The highest tides occur when the moon is new or full. During the moon's first or third quarter, the tide is unusually low. The world's highest tides occur in the Bay of Fundy (an inlet of the Atlantic Ocean between the Canadian provinces of Nova Scotia and New Brunswick) where 70-ft. tides have been reported. By contrast, inland seas such as the Great Lakes have only slight tides. The timing of low and high tides changes in a cyclical manner. Weather pressure systems can influence the level of tides also. For example, a low pressure system can force coastal water into rivers and creeks. Another tidal action that can negatively influence the appeal of waterfront property is a rip tide. This current runs perpendicular to the shore at some inlets during tidal changes and is sometimes dangerous.

Water Impoundment Lakes

Lakes that are used for hydroelectric power and flood control have water levels that may vary from one foot to six feet. Lakes in the Tennessee Valley Authority control vary as much as thirty feet in depth. Wide swings in water level can greatly impair lake usage and cause damage to boats that are not moored properly. Moreover, special and expensive pier construction may be required. At times, there may be insufficient water depth adjacent to the shoreline for recreational purposes. Boats may become grounded.

Water impoundment lakes sometimes are created by electric power generating companies. The primary purpose of such lakes is to produce electricity at a competitive rate. One way these impoundments are designed is to create a pair of lakes. The upper (main) lake may be designed to recirculate its water through immense penstocks to a lower lake. During periods of low power demand, such as at night, the turbines are reversed and water in the lower lake is drawn up through large pipe(s) behind the upper dam.

The crucial value influence is the variation in the water height of each lake. For example, the daily variation in the upper lake's water level may range from six inches to two feet, while the water level of the lower lake may vary between six and 10 feet. During limited periods each year, both types of lakes will vary even more to allow residents to repair piers or to treat invasive aquatic plant life such as hydrilla and elodea. (These plants tend to proliferate in shallow water at the head of creeks or coves.)

The value implications of these vastly different water heights are significant. Typical lot prices on the upper lake may be from 10 to 20 times those on the lower lake. The sharp variance in water levels on the lower lake requires owners to construct floating docks that either have steep steps from the top of the home site or a gradual, long set of steps to the dock. People do not like steep steps and the longer series of steps frequently will twist in the wind and need repairs. Thus there will be a lack of residential development on the lower impoundments; there generally will be only minimal commercial development such as stores and marinas.

Access From Water and Land

The value of residential waterfront land often falls into two categories: the lower-value land, which can be reached by water only in skiffs and other shallow-draft boats requiring two feet of water, and the more valuable sites that appeal to a broad segment of prospective home owners. Sites in this latter category have water depth of four to six feet or more at low tide. The greater appeal of deeper-water lots often is seen in advertisements for sailboat depth lots. These boat owners cannot use shallow-water lots for fixed keel sailboats or cabin cruisers unless long, expensive piers are built or their larger boats are moored some distance offshore or at a boat club. Also, the prospective owners are confronted with mud flats during low tide twice daily for approximately four hours per tide change. There is the added inconvenience of only being able to use their boats during high tide periods.

An initial perspective on probable access can be obtained from viewing a quadrangle map published by the United States Department of the Interior Geological Survey. (Order information is provided in Appendix C, "Maps.") As shown in Figure 18.6, the depth of water is depicted in these charts with areas exposed at low tide denoted by the color gray. (All depths are given at low tide.) The mooring of sailboats on a creek is a reliable indication of deeper water. Identification of such areas is especially important at the mouths of creeks because access to and from a home site may be limited by tidal changes. This differential in water depth is expressed in lot pricing. For example, in one development on a small peninsula, the water depth on one side averaged three feet at mean low tide and five feet on the other side. Similar lots on the deeper-water side were priced at more than double that of the shallow-water lots.

Ease of access to waterfront home sites over land has five key dimensions.

Figure 18.6   Water Depth Chart

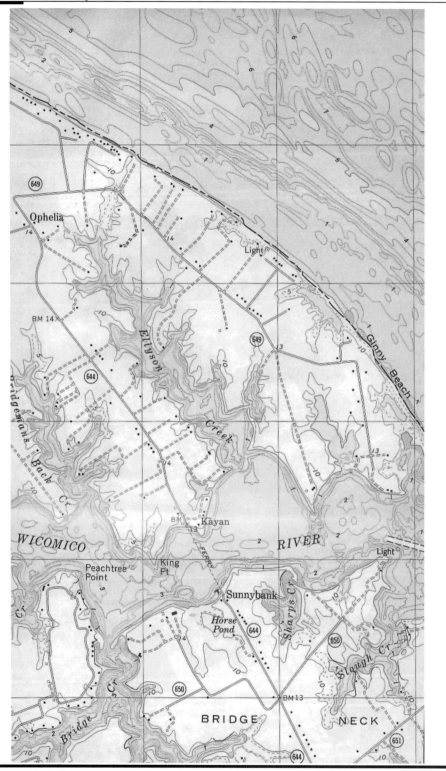

Source: U.S. Department of the Interior and National Oceanic Survey , Burgess Quadrangle Virginia-Maryland, photo inspected 1973.

Land Valuation: Adjustment Procedures and Assignments

1. Legal access
2. Winter access
3. High tide access
4. Rough terrain
5. Length and paving of access route

Legal access relates mainly to easements and rights of way over the lands of others. The conditions pertaining to such access and any shared responsibilities, such as road maintenance, should be spelled out or at least referenced in prior deeds as well as in title insurance policies.

The lack of *winter access* may pose serious problems on the use of a waterfront property. In many northern areas, especially mountainous regions, cottage use is limited to spring through fall.

High tide access can be an issue for low-lying parcels and peninsulas, and if there is a section of road subject to flooding during high tides. Such conditions either restrict access to affected properties or may isolate land owners already on such property. *Rough terrain access* becomes a matter of physically being able to reach a site. The owner may incur substantial road-building expense and the additional cost of buying a four-wheel-drive vehicle. Each of these factors may limit the market and drive down the price that prospective buyers will pay for a site. An appraiser can get a clear idea of terrain conditions by superimposing an acetate topographical map over an aerial photograph of the tract. Of course, both must be set to the same scale.

The length and paving of the access route initially can be identified by perusing aerial photographs, local road maps, or county maps to determine road surface conditions and the distance from a paved road to the comparable sale parcel or subject parcel. The map may indicate that it is a hard surface (stone base and either concrete or bituminous surface) road, all-weather surface (stabilized base of soil and gravel with treatment, often referred to as tar and gravel surface) road, light surface (loose gravel) road, or non-surface (graded dirt) road. Replacing loose gravel every two or three years can be fairly burdensome for an owner.

Low Bridges Between the Site and the Mouth of a River or Creek

The true nature of waterfront comparable sales and the subject lot cannot be appreciated without viewing both from a boat. Whereas a traditional land-bound neighborhood is viewed from a motor vehicle or on foot, part of the neighborhood inspection for waterfront land is ideally made from the water (and sometimes from an airplane). A site that allows unrestricted access to the lot from both ends of a creek or river will realize the highest value. A low bridge, overhead power lines, or a boat tunnel on man-made lakes will reduce the number and size of boats that can access a particular site. Large sailboats and power boats with fishing outriggers and flying bridges may be unable to reach a site because of these obstacles. Limited boat access restricts the user market and, in turn, the price that can be obtained for an affected site. For example, in the Jupiter/Tequesta area of Florida, waterfront lots on the Loxahatchee River that are upriver from a fixed bridge are worth as much as 40% less that sites that are downstream from the bridge.

Location and Depth of Channel

Location and depth of channel are not readily apparent, except perhaps to boaters who are familiar with local waters or those who have access to nautical charts. Being familiar with channel buoy locations and their meaning also will guide one in determining channel locations. An oft-quoted guide to boaters is "red-right-return" which means to keep the red side of a buoy to the right (starboard) of the boat when returning from the sea (open water) and approaching a harbor. When leaving a harbor for open water, such as leaving a creek for a river or bay, keep the green side of the buoy to the right of the boat. Nautical charts and the previously mentioned quadrangle maps reveal water depth. The significance of this information is that open and reasonably straight, non-shifting channels encourage boaters (who buy waterfront property) whereas narrow, twisting channels subject to silting discourage boating activities. If the channel is on the opposite side of a body of water and the depth between it and a parcel is shallow, then the marketability and value of that site will suffer.

Pier Construction Cost

Recreational boating, including fishing and water skiing, are important to people owning waterfront property. Piers are associated with those water activities. Obtaining a construction permit generally is not difficult. The length of a pier may vary considerably, depending of the depth of the water. The permitting agency may be expected to allow a pier to be extended to the near edge of a channel if the pier will not interfere with boaters' use of the channel. Water depth becomes a factor when buying a waterfront lot where a pier needs to be built. For example, a 100-ft. pier on a freshwater lake may cost approximately $7,000 to $10,000, assuming a 6-ft. pier width.

Valuation Techniques

Several contrasting location possibilities are discussed in this chapter, such as beach versus marsh frontage, sheltered lots or those exposed to strong winds, lots with minimal water depth versus navigable water, lots with varying degrees of land and water access, lots affected by low bridges, and lots located near channels. It is important for an appraiser to recognize each of these value-influencing factors. Whenever possible, lots with these contrasts should be avoided in selecting lot sales for comparative analysis. For instance, shallow water lots should not be used to measure the value of a site with deep water a short distance offshore.

Once several, recent, similar lot sales have been located in the same area as the subject parcel, the usual adjustments would be made as discussed in Part II. Customarily, lot prices are analyzed on a lot, square foot, acre, or front foot (of water) basis. An appraiser should not rely on plats to determine the amount of water frontage. The frontage, especially usable frontage, may have changed considerably since the survey was made. Currents and wave action, erosion from boating activity, or the formation of mud or sand bars may have altered the frontage. Also, without actually inspecting a comparable sale, there can be no accounting for views, shorelines, beaches, or water conditions.

Marketing time for waterfront land will vary considerably in different markets. In markets with substantial infrastructure and a favorable supply-demand situation, sales may occur within 90 days. In outlying, overbuilt markets, it may take an average of two to three years to sell a lot. This extended marketing time is especially prevalent for ill-conceived developments with inadequate protective covenants.

Summary

Second home waterfront land prices vary directly with proximity to metropolitan areas. Properties located within two to three hours driving time are able to draw from a larger population pool and, in turn, realize higher demand and prices. Elevated lots generally are preferred over low-lying lots; they offer superior views as well as protection from flooding and storm damage. Within the same area, site values may be expected to decline from ocean frontage, to bay frontage, to marsh frontage.

The value of waterfront land can vary according to the direction of the prevailing wind and whether the shoreline is accreting or eroding. A site with a high bank subject to strong prevailing winds may require the installation of expensive bulkheads and/or stone riprap. This added expense may reduce the value of affected lots in comparison to lots not requiring the added erosion-protection costs. Prices of lots will vary significantly with the water depth. The greater the depth, the wider the pool of prospective buyers. Wide swings in water level can greatly impair lake usage and cause damage to boats that are not properly moored.

Ease of access to waterfront home sites over land has five key dimensions: legal access, winter access, high tide access, rough terrain access, and length and paving of access route. A site that allows unrestricted access to a lot from both ends of a creek or river will realize the highest value. A low bridge, overhead power lines, or a boat tunnel on man-made lakes will reduce the number and size of boats that can access a particular site. Open and reasonably straight, non-shifting channels encourage boaters to buy waterfront property whereas narrow, twisting channels subject to silting discourage boating activities. If the channel is on the opposite side of a body of water and the depth between it and a parcel is shallow, then the marketability and value of that site will suffer.

Office, Retail, and Industrial Land

This chapter focuses on three urban, nonresidential categories of land, exploring factors that influence the value of office, retail, and industrial land. These factors include access, visibility, proximity to a variety of transportation modes, freestanding and business park locations, size and shape of sites, and real estate taxes. Also covered are units of comparison and the reliability of the comparable sales method.

Office Land

There are three principal types of office sites: central business district sites, which typically accommodate large, high-rise structures with parking garages; freestanding outer city or suburban sites; and business park sites. Master-planned business parks are characterized by well-designed streets, attractive landscaping, and strong building design standards, which create an attractive environment.

Convenient day care facilities often are incorporated in these campus-like parks. The site development intensity, site coverage (the building footprint versus site size), and unit value of office sites tend to be lower in suburban areas than in central cities. An example of a business park is shown in Figure 19.1.

Figure 19.1   *Suburban Office Park Building*

Building located in Oakhill Business Park in Charlotte, North Carolina. Courtesy of Highwoods Properties.

Retail Land

Adequate space for customer parking, ease of access, and strong economic trends within the primary trade area are important to successful business operations at retail sites. These factors ensure the sustained purchasing power of prospective customers. Customer access to the site via private vehicles and public transit is important and traffic volume is of concern. A retail business will suffer if there is inadequate traffic flow or if the traffic volume is so heavy that it discourages customers driving to a site. Similarly, traffic moving too fast can intimidate customers trying to reach a particular business.

The path of population growth and its demographic composition are important to the success of retail establishments. Prospective sites should not be too far ahead of residential development. Retail site purchasers understand that the number of rooftops drives retail demand. Average household income, size, median age, age distribution, and type of consumer expenditures such as groceries, apparel, footwear, home furnishings, and electronics affect retail site selection.

Of great concern to retail site purchasers is the size of the trade area for a particular retail use or combination of uses. A trade area seldom has a regular shape. Its shape and size are influenced by demographic characteristics such as age, income, and household size; existing and proposed residential developments; natural or fabricated barriers such as expressways, rivers, and ravines; psychological barriers such as neighborhoods perceived to be dangerous; the number and location of competitive establishments; and transportation services. Commuter patterns influence the location of certain retail activities. (See Chapter 12 for more details on accessibility adjustments.) There are distinctly different highest and best uses for different classes of retail sites. Freestanding parcels, such as pad sites in shopping centers, may front along roads and contain approximately one acre. These pad sites frequently are used for branch banks, fast food restaurants, and video stores. Larger sites may be used for small, neighborhood strip shopping centers or even regional shopping centers. Strip center sites may range in size from three to 10 acres while regional centers may require 75 to 100 acres or more.

Line of Sight

The value of otherwise similar retail sites may vary considerably depending on their relative visibility to prospective customers. An important part of visibility is line of sight. This value-influencing factor takes on particular importance for sites located on road curves. Obstructions that can restrict the visibility of a site to oncoming motorists include vegetation, buildings, moving and stationary vehicles, and elevated and depressed roadways. A site may have reasonably good visibility during the winter, but an impaired view in the spring, summer, and early fall. Greater visibility is required for a retail business to succeed as speed limits increase. Otherwise, prospective customers will pass the business because they will have seen it too late.

Industrial Land

Key considerations in industrial site selection and valuation include ample and reasonably priced public utilities; proximity to customers and raw materials and suppliers; good access for warehouse facilities; access to water transport, air, rail, and highways; level site topography; a sufficient labor supply; reasonable labor costs; and favorable labor-management relations. (Some industries prefer locating in right-to-work states where there is less threat of work stoppages.) Industrial sites should have an adequate supply of reasonably priced water and sufficient water pressure.

Plant location influences most often mentioned by the management of industrial firms are:

1. Proximity to good highways
2. Abundant labor supply
3. Availability of suitable land
4. Proximity to markets
5. Availability of rail service
6. Availability of raw materials
7. Favorable state and local tax structure
8. Favorable leasing or financing
9. Abundant water supply
10. Proximity to related industry
11. Existence of building at site
12. Community cultural/recreational assets
13. Nearby vocational training facilities[1]

A study of warehouses in the Los Angeles area found the following location factors to be most important:

1. Size, shape, and adaptability of site
2. Location of customers
3. Highway system, access, and delivery cost
4. Traffic and congestion
5. Neighborhood environment and land use controls
6. Community protection services (fire and police)
7. Parking and loading facilities
8. Availability of rail service[2]

---

1. James H. Boykin, consulting editor, *Industrial Real Estate* (Washington, D.C.: Society of Industrial Realtors, 1984), p. 62.
2. Ibid., p. 64.

Access to Rail, Airports, Interstate Highways, Expressways, and Ports

Depending on the nature of the raw materials, production process, and finished product, different types of transportation will be important. Heavy, low-value products often travel by rail or water while lightweight and expensive electronic products may require airline freight service. The truck transportation required for many industrial activities includes interstate service and local pickup and delivery of materials and the finished product.

Desired onsite and offsite conditions for industrial land include level to moderately sloping land, generally not in excess of 10% slope; soil that drains well and possesses sufficient load-bearing capability; and reasonable proximity to suppliers and customers. The nature of the production process, raw materials, and the finished product influence the relative importance of the proximity of each of these elements to the industrial property.

Access to deep-water terminals is of great value to some industrial land users. A waterfront parcel may not be suited for water transport unless there is sufficient water depth and, in some instances, a nearby turning basin for cargo barges and freighters. Permission from regulatory bodies for dredging permits to enhance water access may be difficult to obtain. The combined delays of obtaining dredging permits and constructing wharves and docks can influence both the financial feasibility of developing a water-oriented industrial parcel and its market value.

Freestanding Sites Versus Business Park Sites

Freestanding office or industrial sites often suffer from obsolete zoning ordinances that allow wide-ranging and sometimes incompatible activities on adjacent parcels. Also, traffic congestion can be a problem. The capacity of public utilities may be insufficient for modern user requirements and real estate taxes may be high. However, close proximity to customers and specialized outside support services, fast delivery services which allow for small inventories, and reliable public transportation may offset some disadvantages. Suburban sites may lack sufficient public utility capacity, but provide large tracts of comparatively inexpensive land for one-story, modern, industrial-office users. Close proximity to their workforce and convenient expressways for moving employees, materials, and finished products offer important advantages for outlying site users. Outlying locations generally provide room for future expansion of operations as well as flexibility. Users can establish a desired company image via signage and building design and enjoy visibility from a main traffic artery.

Industrial firms located in a master-planned office-industrial park may have the following advantages:

- *Low unit site development costs.* Because costs are distributed over a large area, the cost per unit is often lower than the cost of single-site developments. This reduced cost frequently is passed on to the user in the form of a lower unit price.

- *Operating economies.* Better access to necessary services in a park location usually results in reduced unit operating costs for the tenant.

- *Availability of building space.* An industrial firm is able to obtain better-located space more quickly in a planned district, than outside an industrial park.

- *Site availability.* For a firm that is a frequent purchaser or lessee of new industrial space, the availability of prepared sites, with all facilities ready to accept a new building, is a definite attraction.

- *Flexibility of site choice.* A variety of different sizes and shapes of sites generally are available within the park, as are several different specific locations, all with the same basic access and location amenities.

- *Stability in location.* The environment in an industrial park is essentially controlled. The occupant firm can rely on the stability of the location and the character of its neighbors over a substantial period of time.

- *Protection of investment.* Sites and buildings in planned industrial districts generally have greater marketability, and the environment is usually stable. The industrial firm's investment is therefore protected against premature depreciation.

- *Profit on resale or sublease.* The industrial occupant generally is assured of a ready market for the space he or she purchases or leases should resale or subletting become necessary later. Some developers contend that the customer makes more profit reselling sites in industrial parks than the developer does in initial sales.

- *Compatibility.* An industrial firm in a planned park finds itself within a group of compatible industrial establishments. There is a controlled environment, not only among the occupants of the park itself, but also between the park and the community. Industrial occupants note an absence of hostile residential neighbors, which are often found adjacent to single-site developments or unplanned districts.

- *Proximity of industrial and employee services.* An efficiently planned industrial complex usually provides services to employees nearby, sometimes within the park itself. Increasingly, occupants expect and receive amenities such as on-site banking, restaurants, and even exercise facilities for their employees.

- *Security.* Industrial parks usually offer security provisions so that there is less danger of vandalism, robbery, or fire. Patrols, open space, ease of identity, lighting, off-street parking, and alarm systems all add to the security of the park.

- *Park services.* In addition to utilities, streets, and other necessary site facilities, planned parks often offer landscaping services, snow plowing, street cleaning, and supplementary security protection. In many instances, these services will be available through an occupants' association. Whatever the source, the cost to the occupant generally is less than it would be to acquire the same services individually and independently.[3]

Industrial Land Classification

There are different ways of classifying industrial land. In addition to the obvious use categories zoning ordinances permit, land may be acquired and used by local, regional, or national firms. Typically, firms serving large geographic markets require large sites. Industrial land may also be classified as manufacturing, distribution and warehousing, research and development, and support services. The latter category may include such businesses as suppliers, maintenance and repair services, security services, personnel agencies, and consultants.

Size and Shape of Site

A site will have greater value when it is of regular shape and sufficient size for a particular use or uses. These two site features influence truck maneuvering, such as the ability of trucks to turn and easily back into loading bays. Affected as well are the outside storage of materials and employee, visitor, and customer parking. Outside space often is required for repair shops and truck fleet parking. Thus, the value of a narrow, undersized site will be lower.

Jurisdictional Taxes

All forms of taxes, including real property, equipment, inventory, and income, influence the relative desirability of industrial sites. If the quantity and quality of public services provided are comparatively low with respect to the taxes levied, the value of the underlying land will be impaired. Also, if the real estate or other taxes are higher than for other service districts or competing municipalities, land value likely will decline. Some jurisdictions

---

3.   Ibid., pp. 580-581.

induce industrial companies to locate within their borders by offering partial or full real estate tax abatements. Any of these positive or negative tax practices may affect tax bills and, in turn, the value of industrial land.

Units of Comparison

Comparative analysis of recent, similar land sales is the predominant valuation technique used in appraising industrial land. Great care must be taken to distinguish among different categories of industrial zoning and highest and best use. Wide ranges of prices may be observed among these different groupings. Also, sites in master-planned business parks generally will bring higher unit prices than freestanding sites.

The two, most common units of comparison for office sites are square feet of site area and square feet of floor area ratio (FAR). For example, suppose a site containing 15,943 square feet sold for $450,000. Its square foot price would be $28.23. If the same site's zoning allowed six square feet of building area for every one square foot of land area, then its sale price per allowable square foot of floor area would be $4.70 [$450,000/(15,943 × 6.0)]. The FAR method allows an appraiser to consider similar land sales with different zoning and known FARs. Generally, these sales will produce fairly similar sale prices per square feet of FAR, while prices of different-zoned office categories may indicate widely divergent prices per square foot of land area. This topic is discussed in more depth in Chapter 11.

Retail sites typically are appraised on a square foot or front foot basis. Large parcels, however, may be appraised on a per acre unit basis. Retail sites with road or street frontage derive most of their business from customers visiting their sites via motor vehicles, hence, there is a fairly direct correlation between the quantity of street frontage and sale price. Other strong influences on retail land prices are location, terrain conditions, depth of site, and availability of public utilities, especially for land use activities requiring large quantities of potable water. The usual measure for industrial parcels of 10 to 20 acres and larger is price per acre. Prices for smaller sites may be expressed on a square foot basis.

Reliability of the Comparable Sales Method

There can be a wide variance in the highest and best uses of retail, office, and industrial parcels. Even within the constraints of a particular zoning ordinance, the range of prospective site uses may be substantial. Each potential site user has a different outlook on the potential of a site for a business endeavor or as a real estate investment. Thus, it is important for an appraiser to compile an adequate number of land sales for comparative analysis. Just as "One robin does not make a spring," it is also true that "One sale does not make a reliable appraisal." Generally a minimum of five to seven land sales are recommended to depict accurately the estimated value of a retail, office, or industrial site. More land sales may be needed if a reliable pattern cannot be found. Typically, the most accurate and reliable comparable sale is one that has required the fewest gross number and dollar adjustments.

Suppose that one comparable property sold for $300,000 and required positive adjustments of $60,000 and negative adjustments of $55,000, for a net adjustment of plus $5,000. A second sale brought $325,000, but had positive adjustments of $15,000 and negative adjustments of $25,000, for a net negative adjustment of $10,000. On a net basis, the first sale would appear to be more indicative of the appraised parcel's value. However, a closer examination reveals that the first sale required gross adjustments of $115,000, while the second sale needed gross adjustments of only $40,000. Thus, because of smaller gross adjustments, the latter sale may be the better indicator of the appraised parcel's value.

In confirming sale prices with sellers, buyers, or their representatives, an appraiser will want to determine the motivation for each purchase. Particular scrutiny is called for in considering purchases of land adjoining a purchaser's present operation. A premium may have been paid to satisfy an urgent need for employee parking or plant expansion. Was the land price subsidized by a government agency anxious to attract the company onto its tax rolls? Perhaps the buyer was a land speculator, end user, or a developer. Price variations may be detectable among these different groups of purchasers.

Summary

Factors that affect the value of office, retail, and industrial land include access, visibility, proximity to a variety of transportation modes, freestanding and business park locations, size and shape of sites, and real estate taxes. The three principal types of office sites are central business district, freestanding outer city or suburban, and business park. Important to successful operations at retail sites are adequate space for customer parking, ease of access, and strong economic trends within the primary trade area. The path of population growth and its demographic composition are important to successful retail operations. Of great concern to retail site purchasers is the size of the trade area for a particular retail use or combination of uses. The value of otherwise similar retail sites may vary considerably with their relative visibility to prospective customers. A variety of obstructions can restrict the visibility of a site. Some of these are cut slopes, vegetation, buildings, and moving and stationary vehicles.

Key considerations in industrial site selection and valuation include ample and reasonably priced public utilities; proximity to customers and raw materials and suppliers; good access for warehouse facilities; access to water transport, air, rail, and highways; generally level site topography; a sufficient labor supply; reasonable labor costs; and favorable labor-management relations. Different types of transportation are important depending on the nature of the raw materials, production process, and finished product. Desired onsite and offsite conditions for industrial land include level to moderately sloping land; soil that drains well and has sufficient load-bearing capability; and reasonable proximity to suppliers and customers. Industrial land may be classified as manufacturing, distribution and warehousing, research and development, and support services. A site will have greater value if it is of sufficient size and has a regular shape.

The two most often used units of comparison for office sites are square feet of site area and square feet of floor area ratio (FAR). The FAR method offers the advantage of allowing an appraiser to consider similar land sales with different zoning and known FARs. Retail sites typically are appraised on a square foot or front foot basis. Large parcels may be appraised on a per acre basis. It is important for an appraiser to compile an adequate number of land sales for comparative analysis. The most accurate and reliable comparable sales are those that require the fewest number and dollar amount of adjustments. In confirming sale prices with sellers, buyers, or their representatives, an appraiser will want to determine the motivation for each particular purchase.

20

Agricultural Land

The value of farmland, like most other types of land, vacillates over time. For instance, between the late 1950s and late 1970s, per acre land productivity tripled due to modern farm machinery, hybrid seeds, fertilizers, pesticides, and irrigation equipment. Surging farm income boosted land prices twelvefold. During the early 1980s, annual farm incomes dropped, in part because of increased debt service required on higher land values. Congress took inappropriate action to raise and stabilize farm incomes. The result was to encourage more bidding up of land prices when prices already were overheated.[1] Prolonged periods of drought, declining commodity prices, or shrinking farm exports can have the opposite effect, reducing farmland values.

Definitions

The following definitions are fundamental to rural appraisal:

- *Animal unit (AU)*. A unit of measurement that provides a benchmark against which different sizes of cattle, sheep, or horses can be measured. For instance, a two-year-old beef cow weighing 1,000 pounds, a bull, and a horse each are 1 animal unit, whereas a lamb (from weaning to 1 year) is 0.15 AU.

- *Cash crop*. Crops raised for sale to customers rather than as feed for livestock on the farm.

- *Crop allotment*. The number of acres the federal government allots to a farm—e.g., a tobacco, cotton, or rice allotment.

- *Dry farming*. A type of farming associated with semiarid areas in the southwestern United States. It generally involves water conservation and harvesting crops once every two years.

---

1. Thomas G. Gillentine, "Valuation of an Agricultural Operation," *The Appraisal Journal* (October 1986), p. 554, citing *The Wall Street Journal,* which cited a paper by Lawrence Shepard, an agricultural economist at the University of California at Davis (August 1985).

- *Farm.* The U.S. Department of Agriculture (USDA) defines a farm as any establishment from which $1,000 or more of agricultural products were sold or would normally be sold during the year.

- *Farmland.* Agricultural land associated with a farming operation, which includes all categories of tillable and untillable land as well as wood lots.

- *Farmstead.* The part of a farm where the farm buildings and house are located.

- *Sharecrop rent.* An agreement between a farm owner and a tenant who works the land. A variety of share arrangements may be used, including respective contributions by each party for the purchase of fertilizer, seed, irrigation, and harvesting costs.

- *Subsoil.* Generally thought to be that soil beneath the topsoil or below plow depth.

- *Tillable soil.* Soil that is suitable for growing crops.

- *Topsoil.* Usually considered as the top, most fertile part of the soil. See Appendix F for a detailed description of different types of soils.

Classifying Soil Types and Land Categories

Real estate appraisers generally are not qualified by education and experience to analyze soils, but their clients are well served when appraisers can interpret soil maps and soil productivity reports. One level of familiarity with soils is to know the various types of soils. For example, silt clay loam soil is a soil made up of moderate amounts of fine grades of sand and moderate amounts of clay but more than 50% silt and clay, which contains more clay than silt loam. It is cloddy when dry; when wet it has the tendency to ribbon upon being squeezed between the finger and thumb. (See Appendix F.)

Capability groupings provide a general means of identifying the suitability of soils for most types of field crops. The groups are set up according to the soil limitations for field crops, risk of damage when the soils are used, and how they respond to treatment. Under this system, all soils are grouped by capability class, subclass, and unit. The capability class progresses from the least restricted soils to soils with the greatest agricultural limitations (I through VIII). *Classes* of soil types are defined as follows.

- *Class I* soils have few limitations that restrict their use.

- *Class II* soils have moderate limitations that reduce the choice of plants or require special conservation practices.

- *Class III* soils have severe limitations that reduce the choice of plants, require special conservation practices, or both.

- *Class IV* soils have very severe limitations that reduce the choice of plants, require very careful management, or both.

- *Class V* soils are not likely to erode, but have other limitations that restrict their use largely to pasture, woodland, or wildlife.

- *Class VI* soils have severe limitations that make them generally unsuited to cultivation and limit their use largely to pasture, woodland, or wildlife.

- *Class VII* soils have very severe limitations that make them unsuited to cultivation and restrict their use largely to pasture, woodland, or wildlife.

- *Class VIII* soils and land forms have limitations that preclude their use for commercial plants and restrict their use to recreation, wildlife, water supply, or esthetic purposes.[2]

Capability subclasses are soil groups within a given class and are denoted by the letters *e*, *w*, *s* or *c*, for example, IIIw. These subclasses are described as follows:

- *e* indicates that the main limitation is the risk of erosion.

- *w* indicates that water in or on the soil interferes with plant growth or cultivation.

- *s* means that the soil is limited principally due to its shallow, droughty, or stoney condition.

- *c* represents soil limitations due to climatic conditions that are either too cold or too dry; these conditions apply to only some sections of the United States.

Capability units are the third and most refined soil groups. They are designated by numerals such as IIIw-2. Each capability unit description, e.g., 2, . . . "indicates the general characteristics of the soils in the unit, their suitability for crops, and the major limitations or hazards to use for crops and pasture."[3] An example of a capability unit follows:

Capability Unit IIe-2 consists of deep, moderately well-drained, gently sloping soils of the Altavista, Angie, Bourne, and Duplin series.... Soils in this unit have an erodible plow layer, ...Available water capacity in all of the soils is medium, and the rooting zone is deep in all but Bourne soils, which have a moderately deep root zone. Reaction, except in limed

2. John W. Clay, *Soil Survey of Henrico County, Virginia* (Washington, DC: United States Department of Agriculture Soil Conservation Service in cooperation with Virginia Polytechnic Institute and State University, October 1975), p. 52.

3. Ibid. p. 53.

areas, is strongly acid to very strongly acid in the root zone. Depth to bedrock is commonly more than 5 feet.... The capacity of these soils to store and release plant nutrients for crop use is medium. Runoff on these soils is medium. The hazard of erosion is moderate if they are cultivated or if the pasture vegetation is thin.... Artificial drainage helps alleviate seasonal wetness in these soils. The soils in this unit are suited to the commonly grown field crops, hay, and pasture plants.[4]

Estimating Crop Yields

The appraiser will want to be able to judge the estimated crop yields for the different parts of an appraised parcel. Localized data is, of course, most helpful in making an appraisal. Countywide crop yield data is useful, but, actual crop yield information for the appraised parcel is more relevant. The best source of this yield information is typically from a two- or three-year record the farmer or tenant keeps. It may be necessary to divide the number of acres for each crop into the annual number of units sold, e.g., bushels, pounds, or bales. For example, one farm in Mississippi reports yields of 950 pounds of cotton per acre, 30 bushels of soybean per acre, and 50 bushels of wheat per acre. Table 20.1 shows reasonable yield expectations for farmland in a Virginia county. A local Soil Conservation Service map will show a soil conservation plan that uses optimum farming practices that develop long-term conservation results under improved management. Appraisers, however, are interested in soil yields under typical management. Of course, yields will vary from this or any table as the result of different management practices, weather, varieties of crops, insects, and diseases. These and similar soil ratings are general in nature and are not specific to a particular farm. They should not be thought of as a simplistic, fill-in-the-blanks shortcut to farmland appraisal.

Comparable Sales

Various methods of compiling information on land transfers are discussed throughout this book. In the case of rural appraising, knowing how to locate comparable sales and actually obtaining such data may be quite different.[5] In urban areas, there generally are a variety of sources of information, but in rural areas there are fewer sources, fewer transactions to analyze, and typically much longer distances must be covered in obtaining and inspecting land sales. Due to the scarcity of market data, it is important to develop and maintain good working relations with persons who can provide data. Included are buyers and sellers such as pension

---

4. Ibid., pp. 53–54.

5. A starting point, as well as a source of statewide annual value changes, is the "Agricultural Land Values" series published by the National Agricultural Statistics Service, United States Department of Agriculture. An example of average values per acre, by region and state, for cropland, pasture, and irrigated and nonirrigated cropland from March 2000 is found in Appendix G.

Table 20.1   *Estimated Average Acre Yields of Principal Crops Under Improved Management*

Mapping Unit	Corn (Bu)	Corn Silage (Tons)	Wheat (Bu)	Barley (Bu)	Soybeans (Bu)	Alfalfa (Tons)	Grass-Legume (Tons)	Pasture (Cow-acre-days)*
Abell fine sandy loam, 2 to 6 percent slopes	120	24	60	60	40	3.5	4.0	280
Altavista fine sandy loam, 0 to 2 percent slopes	120	24	60	50	40	3.5	4.0	280
Altavista fine sandy loam, 2 to 6 percent slopes	120	24	65	50	40	4.0	4.0	280
Angie loam, 0 to 2 percent slopes	110	22	60	45	40	3.5	4.0	250
Angie loam, 2 to 6 percent slopes	110	22	60	45	40	3.5	3.5	250
Angie loam, 2 to 6 percent slopes, eroded	100	20	55	40	35	3.0	3.0	240
Angie loam, 6 to 10 percent slopes, eroded	90	18	50	40	30	3.0	2.5	210
Angie loam, 10 to 25 percent slopes, eroded	55	11	35	—	—	—	2.0	120
Angie loam, concretionary subsoil variant	95	19	50	45	35	—	3.5	240
Appling fine sandy loam, 2 to 6 percent slopes	120	24	75	60	40	4.5	4.0	270
Appling fine sandy loam, 6 to 15 percent slopes, eroded	95	19	50	45	30	3.5	3.0	220
Appling fine sandy loam, 15 to 25 percent slopes, eroded	75	15	40	35	—	2.5	2.0	180
Appling clay loam, 2 to 15 percent slopes, severely eroded	75	15	35	30	—	2.5	2.0	140
Ashlar gravelly sand loam, 6 to 15 percent slopes	45	9	35	—	—	—	1.0	90
Ashlar gravelly sand loam, 15 to 45 percent slopes	—	—	—	—	—	—	–	90
Atlee very fine sandy loam	90	18	50	40	30	3.0	3.5	225

Absence of data indicates stated crop is not grown, or the soil is not suited to it.

* This term is used to express the carrying capacity of pasture. It is the number of animal units carried per acre multiplied by the number of days the pasture is grazed during a single season without injury to the sod. An acre of pasture that provides 30 days of grazing for 2 cows has a carrying capacity of 60 cow-acre-days.

Source: John W. Clay, *Soil Survey of Henrico County, Virginia* (Washington, D.C.: United States Department of Agriculture Soil Conservation Service in cooperation with Virginia Polytechnic Institute and State University, October 1975), p. 61.

funds, and life insurance companies, farm brokers, farm appraisers, farm lenders such as the Federal Land Bank, local banks that make farm loans, closing attorneys, and county agricultural agents. Of course, all sales should be verified. The appraiser should be willing to reciprocate when these sources need information that the appraiser may have. Sharing of market-based data should be a two-way street.

A story illustrates the dilemma of obtaining and analyzing land sales in some rural parts of the country, especially when the appraiser does not expand the geographic scope of his or her research. An appraiser was attending a seminar on using multiple regression analysis in the valuation of land. The instructor noticed that the appraiser had a puzzled look on his face as she explained the intricacies of properly applying this technique. She approached him and asked if he was having difficulty. He replied that although he understood this advanced analytical technique, he was not sure how to apply it to the three land sales that occurred last year in his market.

Types of Land Conveyances

Several types of conveyances may be used to sell farmland. The appraiser must carefully scrutinize each to determine its effect on the sale price. For instance, land may be sold by deed transfer, which includes such possibilities as **an all-cash sale** where no seller or third-party financing is used. Sometimes this type of land sale may cause a seller to accept a slightly lower price because the purchaser does not need to qualify for a loan and settlement can occur relatively fast. Typically, the sale of farmland is by a deed transfer that involves **third-party financing** by a lending institution. This type of sale transaction is not as desirable for a seller as an all-cash sale because of the uncertainty that the buyer will be able to obtain the necessary amount of debt financing and because delays in processing the loan may occur. No discount or premium is associated with this type of transaction beyond that which a buyer or seller may be able to negotiate.

Second-party or seller financing is another type of transaction involving a deed. A loan from the seller to a buyer may be in the form of either a first or second mortgage. These loans generally are made to facilitate the sale because the buyer may be unable to obtain a loan amount sufficient to make up the difference between the sale price and the amount of down payment the purchaser can afford. Also, they may be used when the loan terms or interest rates of the bank are unacceptable to the buyer. Alternately, the seller may prefer the annuity-type income represented by receiving mortgage payments or use an installment sale for income tax purposes. If seller-financed interest rates are atypical or below prevailing third party rates, the appraiser may need to make a downward adjustment to the sale price to estimate the price that a parcel would have realized with typical financing terms. This adjustment can be mathematically computed to reveal the amount of the discount. Although this adjustment may be mathematically correct, it could bear little relation to the actual intentions of the buyer or seller. Thus, it is always critical to interview one or both of these parties to learn the amount of the discount, if any.[6]

A **land contract or contract for deed** provides for the title to be transferred to a buyer once he or she has met certain conditions. This means of transferring land may be used when the buyer lacks the usual down payment. The buyer is accommodated, but usually at a higher-than-usual price. Title to the land may not pass to the buyer until perhaps 20% to 25% of the purchase price has been paid or the last payment is made by the buyer to the seller.[7]

The appraiser should be aware of all influences and motivations that have an effect on the price paid for farmland. During the growing season, the crops may transfer along with the land to the buyer. During the non-growing season, there would be no crops to convey, so two similar parcels could bring different per acre prices based on when they sold. Different water rights can affect sale prices. Also, it is possible that some sales will be encumbered by prior conveyance of future development rights such as a conservation easement. (See Chapter 22 for more details on this topic.) Irrigated land sales require additional analysis. The appraiser should compare the effectiveness of irrigation systems, their operating expenses, the dependability of water systems, and the priority of water rights.[8]

Allocating Value By Land Categories

Farmland typically consists of several categories or types of land. For example, there may be tillable land, pasture, meadow, woodland, mountainside, and marsh. Several methods may be used to establish the values of each of these categories. One method is to analyze and compare market sales of similar land and apply the value per acre for each land type. However, in doing so the appraiser must avoid using a per acre value of small parcel sales to estimate the value of a similar-sized part of a larger

---

6. The topic of cash equivalency or prevailing financing equivalency is covered in James H. Boykin and Alfred A. Ring, *The Valuation of Real Estate,* 4th ed. (Englewood Cliffs, NJ: Regents/Prentice Hall, Inc., 1993), pp. 168–172.

7. Additional details on types of land conveyances and financing are found in William G. Murray, *Farm Appraisal and Valuation,* 5th ed. (Ames, Iowa: The Iowa State University Press, 1969), pp.91–102 and James H. Boykin and Richard L. Haney, *Financing Real Estate* 2nd ed. (Englewood Cliffs, NJ: Regents/Prentice Hall, Inc., 1993), pp.330–336.

8. A thorough discussion of this topic is found in *The Appraisal of Rural Property,* 2d ed. (Chicago: American Society of Farm Managers and Rural Appraisers and Appraisal Institute, 2000) and *The Appraisal of Irrigated Properties* (Chicago: Appraisal Institute, 1985).

parcel. That is, the value of 20 acres of meadow would likely be overstated if a 15- to 30-acre comparable meadow sale is used to appraise a 20-acre meadow that is part of a 400-acre farm.

Another method is the algebraic approach described in Chapter 23 and later in this chapter. This method allows an appraiser to estimate the value of one category of land when the overall parcel's sale price, the per acre value of one category of land, and the acreage in each category of land are known. From this information the unknown land category per acre value can be estimated.

Still another method for estimating the values of the different land categories is paired sales analysis. This valuation technique, the subject of Chapter 10, typically would commence with identifying similar features in two sale parcels, isolating a single value-influencing difference such as tillable land, and then adjusting the unit sale prices to reflect the value of the land category of the parcel being appraised.

Comparable land sales can be analyzed based on carrying capacity when appropriate. That is, it may be appropriate to use this method for balanced, year-round livestock operations, but not when farms or ranches are used for several commercial functions such as hunting, fishing, and other recreational activities. The land breakdown method is more appropriate in these situations.

Generally, it is possible to estimate the value of a single category of land in a parcel that includes several categories.[9] In the following example, the appraiser was able to determine that tillable land (cropland), as part of a larger holding, was selling for about $2,000 per acre. The appraisal assignment involves a 400-acre farm that has 50 acres of level, tillable land, 150 acres of rolling pasture, and 200 acres of woodland. The following three land sales are analyzed. All sales are recent so no time adjustment is necessary. Sale 1 sold for $290,000, Sale 2 sold for $315,000, and Sale 3 sold for $290,000.

Land Type	Land Sale 1	Land Sale 2	Land Sale 3
Tillable land	—	60 ac.	90 ac.
Pasture	340 ac.	125 ac.	—
Wood land	130 ac.	270 ac.	260 ac.
Total acreage	470 ac.	455 ac.	370 ac.

Extracting the tillable land value of $180,000 from Sale 3's price leaves a value of $110,000 for the remaining 260 acres of woodland, which indicates a value of approximately $400 per acre for woodland. Applying the $400 per acre woodland value to Sale 1 produces a woodland value of

9. See Chapter 23 "Floodplains and Wetlands" for a procedure to estimate the value of a particular land category when there are two or more catagories.

$52,000. This figure is then deducted from the sale price of $290,000 and leaves $238,000 for the 340 acres of pasture, or $700 per acre for pastureland. Sale 3 suggests the same per acre values, except the woodland value is $423 per acre, which includes $23 for a recent reseeding. Sale 2 supports these unit values. Thus, the appraised value of the subject parcel is:

50 acres tillable land @ $2,000	$100,000
150 acres pasture @ $700	$105,000
200 acres woodland @ $400	$80,000
Total appraised value	$285,000

A further refinement of this method is to identify the land categories by soil class and indicate the presence or absence of irrigation. An example of this refinement follows.

Class I and II soils with irrigation—800 acres @ $1,650	$1,320,000
Class I and II soils without irrigation—300 acres @ $1,525	457,500
Class III soils without irrigation—500 acres @ $700	350,000
Total estimated value	$2,127,500

Allowing for Crop Allotments

For many years the federal government has controlled the quantity of land that could be used to raise crops such as tobacco and cotton. In particular, tobacco allotments have added a premium to the normal value of similar farmland. The amount of the premium has varied with the type of tobacco crop,—e.g., Burley, flue-cured, fire-cured leaf. The value premium also varies from place to place. This variation reinforces the importance of research and analysis of local sales to the accuracy of a farmland appraisal. One measure of the value of an allotment is the rent a farmer is willing to pay to cultivate an allotment on another person's land.

The following example shows how the value of an allotment (or different land categories) can be determined algebraically. For this illustration, assume that all the land that was sold and all the land being appraised is tillable land. The subject farm contains 250 tillable acres, including a 50-acre cotton allotment. Let x = per acre cropland value and y = per acre cotton allotment value. Two similar nearby parcels have recently sold. Sale 1 has 325 acres, includes a 60-acre allotment, and sold for $334,000. Sale 2 has 150 acres, includes a 30-acre allotment, and sold for $154,500. The simultaneous equation becomes:

$$265x + 60y = \$334,000$$
$$120x + 30y = \$154,500$$

Next solve for x by multiplying the second equation by -2

$$265x + 60y = \$334,000$$
$$-240x - 60y = -\$309,000$$
$$25x = \$25,000$$
$$x = \$1,000/\text{acre}$$

Substituting x into the first equation above and solving for y indicates:

$$265(\$1,000) + 60y = \$334,000$$
$$60y = \$334,000 - \$265,000$$
$$y = \$1,150/\text{acre}$$

The value of the subject farmland is:

$$\text{Value} = 200(\$1,000) + 50(\$1,150)$$
$$= \$200,000 + \$57,500, \text{ which is a total of } \$257,500, \text{ or } \$1,030/\text{acre}$$

The indicated per acre value of the cotton allotment is $150 ($1,150 – $1,000).

Animal Unit Value

Through research and agricultural reports, it may be possible to establish land value per animal units for cattle and sheep, land value per cow of capacity for dairy operations, or crop yields per acre. Even before commencing an appraisal, the appraiser should set up local records on per acre land values, per acre crop yields for different crops, and animal unit values. For example, to estimate land value for a ranch with 7,000 acres and a carrying capacity of 500 animal units that sold for $900,000, unit prices can be computed both on a per acre basis ($129) and an animal unit basis ($1,800). It is helpful to analyze the land sales by both units of comparison because one method will usually produce a more consistent value pattern than the other.

Land Value by Extraction

The extraction method often is applicable in valuing agricultural land. It is most useful when the comparable land sales have old, dilapidated buildings that contribute little to the overall property value. Such conditions exist on abandoned farms and properties whose owners have failed to maintain the structures. In using this method, which is discussed in detail in Chapter 9, the appraiser may find that the buildings enhance or impair property value.

Consider two sales that require adjustments for nominally-valued improvements. Sale 1 is a 200-acre parcel that recently sold for $600,000; it has several old farm buildings valued at $10,000. Therefore, the land value is the total sales price of $600,000 minus the $10,000 value of the buildings, or $590,000. Dividing this $590,000 residual amount by the total size of 200 acres indicates a per acre value of $2,950. Sale 2 sold recently for $760,000 and has 275 acres. Some buildings on the property are so dilapidated that they have no contributory value, but will cost $25,000 to demolish and move off the property. In this case, the total cost for the buyer to make the land usable for its intended purposes is $785,000, or $2,855 per acre ($760,000 sale price plus $25,000 demolition costs).

Income Capitalization Approach

Parties associated with farmland transfers, e.g., mortgage lenders, brokers, buyers and sellers, and some appraisers, claim that at times the income capitalization approach is inappropriate in estimating farmland value. While this may be true, the income approach does convert farmland productivity into a measure of value. If there is a discrepancy between the value indicated by the income and sales comparison approaches, it probably indicates that buyers are willing to pay a premium for the land beyond its ability to produce revenue from its agricultural productivity. When the land sales approach reveals a higher value than the income approach, it may signal that a speculative value premium has been paid. Continually rising land prices may, in time, reduce the ability of the crop earnings to pay the mortgage debt service.

Owner Operation Method

If the appraiser chooses to value farmland on an owner operation basis, he or she must have a keen knowledge of farming operations and commodity prices. Because farm commodity prices can vary significantly from year to year, it is advisable to analyze farm income-expense statements for the past three to five years. However, in doing so there is a danger of giving the same weight to the performance of the property in the earlier years as in the most recent years. An advantage of this approach is that atypical commodity prices and weather conditions can be smoothed out to approximate typical prices.

This method of appraising farmland has merit because the majority of farms are owner-operated. Management is a key ingredient in the financial performance of a farming operation. Thus, the appraiser needs to adjust for extraordinarily strong or weak management and assume that the appraised farmland is under typical management. Further, care must be taken to distinguish between a farm's business value and its real estate value.

Landlord Operation

The principal method for deriving the value of cropland is to analyze owner-tenant leases and determine farm market rental amounts for various types of land. Rental income may come from several sources. (See Chapter

22, "Scenic Land Conservation Easements.") In one arrangement, the landlord receives a part of the harvested crop, perhaps 25%. The landlord may pay a share of the expenses for irrigation and maintenance of the equipment rented to the farm tenant. The landlord also generally pays all real estate taxes and insurance. This method is somewhat difficult to use because the appraiser must analyze highly individualistic share arrangements.

The most typical arrangement is to rent farmland on a cash basis. In this case valuation is relatively easy because of the availablity of rental rates from farm tenants or lease agreements from farm management firms. Locally derived benchmarks such as those shown in Table 20.2 can provide a basis for estimating land rental rates. Local farm rental rates per acre for various land classifications are valuable information to the appraiser.

Compared to the owner operator premise, the rental income method of valuing farmland is comparatively straightforward and easier for clients to understand. Fewer assumptions are required, there is less dependence on management performance (which often is a major variable), and there tends to be a fairly consistent rental pattern within a farming community. Also, lenders readily accept rental income as the most reliable means for deriving an estimate of market value via the income capitalization approach.

Unlike owner-operator income and expense statements, cash leases and sharecrop leases generally exclude buildings and non-realty items such as farm equipment and labor. Sometimes leased irrigation equipment such as pivot systems provides extra rent in farm leases. Both cash leases and sharecrop leases typically are negotiated every year, but some may have three-year terms. Longer leases are more common and equitable because productivity and commodity prices can swing sharply from year to year.

The landlord operation method is simpler than the owner operation method of valuation since it excludes livestock operations and related income and expenses. The rental share can vary for different locations and in different years depending on the operating experience of the farmer, weather conditions (especially droughts), commodity pricing, domestic economic conditions, and foreign export markets.

Table 20.2   Gross Farm Income and Estimated Rental Income

Crop	Acres	Yield per Acre	Total Yield	Unit Price	Gross Income	Rental Share	Rental Income
Alfalfa	80	5 tons	400	$60.00	$24,000	33⅓%	$8,000
Corn	160	155 bu.	24,800	2.50	62,000	50%	31,000
Soybeans	40	35 bu.	1,400	6.00	8,400	33⅓%	2,800
Wheat	40	80 bu.	3,200	3.80	12,160	25%	3,040
Total	320				$106,560		$44,840

Source: *The Appraisal of Rural Property* (Chicago: American Institute of Real Estate Appraisers, 1983), Table 10.1, p. 178.

The farm income and rental income of a hypothetical property is shown in Table 20.2. The table shows how varying crop yields and prices can be converted into land rental income. Note that share prices may vary among different crops.

Net Operating Income

Estimates of net operating income may be made by analyzing income and expenses either on a percentage of crop or cash rental basis. It is important that the income and expenses and capitalization rate be consistently developed and applied to the appraised parcel. In using the sharecrop premise, the appraiser must determine the probable crop rotation cycle if several different crops are grown. The crop yield for each crop must be estimated, along with its likely price and, based on local practice, the percent of each crop that the landlord will receive. The appraiser must be familiar with local soil conditions and productivity as well as rotation practices.

Table 20.3 is based on the gross income data presented in Table 20.2. This income-expense statement illustrates how both owner-operator and sharecrop owner expenses are prepared. It is intended to illustrate how each method may be structured and does not depict an actual or typical situation.

Capitalization Rate Selection

Capitalization rate selection is perhaps more arduous in land appraisal than in improved property appraising. The task becomes more difficult

Table 20.3   Sample Income and Expense Statement

	Owner-Operator Gross Income	Landlord Gross Income
	$106,560	$44,840
	Owner Expenses, Owner-Operator Basis	Owner Expenses, Crop-share Basis
Expense Categories		
Taxes		
Real estate	$3,200	$3,200
Personal property	1,600	
Building insurance & maintenance	1,800	1,800
Fence maintenance	750	750
Fertilizer: corn	12,000	6,000 (corn 50%)
Other	5,600	
Production costs (including machinery)	22,000	
Labor and management	19,500	
Corn harvest/hauling	3,200	1,600 (50% corn) harvest/haul cost)
Other crop harvest/hauling cost	3,300	
Management @ 8%		3,590
Total expenses	72,950	16,940
Net income	$33,610	$27,900

Source: *The Appraisal of Rural Property* (Chicago: American Institute of Real Estate Appraisers, 1983), Table 10.1, p. 182.

when land use is changing from rural to urban use. The capitalization rate is forced down as purchasers acquire agricultural land for purposes that crop revenue does not economically support. Speculative farmland purchasers may be motivated by the prospect of long-term appreciation. As a rule, farmland values are correlated directly with population increases and the related demand for farm products. Thus, when land prices rise faster than demand for crops and crop earnings, capitalization rates will decline. Farmland rates tend to be lower than rates for most other types of real estate investments, including urban land.

Overall capitalization rates for cropland and pasture are shown in Tables 20.4 and 20.5. For example, the overall state average cash rent per acre for Kentucky cropland in 1994 was $59 and the corresponding gross capitalization rate was 5.7%. Kentucky pastureland, on average, rented for about $26 an acre while its average gross capitalization rate was 3.3%.

Rental income, operating expenses, and overall capitalization rate information is more readily available for large commercial farming operations than for small farms. This information may be obtained from farmers, farm management companies, life insurance companies, and

Table 20.4   *Gross Cash Rent per Acre and Ratio to Value for Cropland in Selected States*

State	Cash Rent per Acre ($)				Ratio of Gross Rent to Value (%)			
	1988	1990	1992	1994	1988	1990	1992	1994
CO	63.80	70.90	72.70	76.50	6.7	8.6	7.2	7.8
FL	106.90	105.00	101.50	73.10	3.0	2.0	3.0	1.9
KS	54.10	61.50	62.70	72.50	9.8	9.1	9.5	10.1
KY	52.70	47.50	52.60	59.00	6.1	6.3	5.4	5.7
LA	44.60	46.30	48.30	48.30	4.8	6.1	6.1	6.0
MO	54.70	61.90	58.20	64.80	9.1	9.9	8.0	8.6
OR	81.50	88.50	106.70	135.90	5.8	5.6	6.1	7.4
PA	42.70	43.30	42.40	41.00	2.4	2.3	1.8	1.5
WI	45.40	50.00	51.40	51.20	7.3	7.2	7.3	6.8

Source: *Cash Rents for Farms, Cropland, and Pasture,* Economic Research Service, USDA, 1997.

Table 20.5   *Gross Cash Rent per Acre and Ratio to Value for Pastureland in Selected States*

State	Cash Rent per Acre ($)				Ratio of Gross Rent to Value (%)			
	1988	1990	1992	1994	1988	1990	1992	1994
CO	11.50	6.80	8.20	9.30	3.1	5.0	3.2	5.3
FL	25.20	20.20	21.40	17.00	0.9	0.8	0.8	1.2
KS	11.80	11.50	12.00	12.80	5.5	5.2	5.0	4.8
KY	27.50	24.90	25.90	26.20	4.7	4.8	3.3	3.3
LA	14.70	18.30	17.20	15.60	1.8	3.4	2.7	2.3
MO	22.70	24.10	23.70	24.70	6.0	6.8	5.4	5.1
OR	21.50	N/A	22.60	14.50	4.8	N/A	4.0	6.8
PA	19.90	23.50	21.80	20.70	1.9	2.1	1.5	1.1
WI	21.40	25.00	25.60	22.50	7.2	6.8	7.6	6.6

Source: *Cash Rents for Farms, Cropland, and Pasture,* Economic Research Service, USDA, 1997.

pension funds for large operations. Other sources may be used as a check against less readily available income and expense data for small farming operations. One source, statewide averages, is useful but only as a starting point in deriving overall farmland capitalization rates. The income-value ratio cited relates to gross rather than the customary net operating income. Nevertheless, this ratio provides a benchmark for estimating farmland rental rates per acre and gross capitalization rates, just as published regional construction data is used in the appraisal of improved properties. The rate/value relationship has not remained constant over the years as shown in Figure 20.1. The per acre rental of dry cropland in Kansas increased at a relatively uniform rate, but value rose abruptly between 1975 and 1981 and then fell until 1987. (See Appendix G, "Agricultural Land Values.")

Figure 20.1   *Kansas Dry Crop Rent and Value*

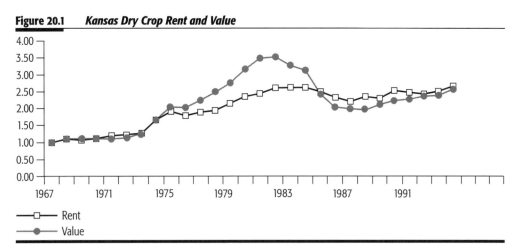

Source: *Cash Rents for Farms, Cropland, and Pasture*, Economic Research Service, USDA, 1997.

Appraising Farmland in Suburbanizing Areas

According to the U. S. Department of Agriculture, the number of farms in this country decreased between 1993 and 1997—falling from 2,201,590 to 2,190,510—while the number of acres fell from 968,845,000 to 956,010,000. The resulting average farm size changed minimally, from 440 acres to 436 acres. Of course, the amount of farmland varied among the individual states, as shown in Table 20.6. Proportionately large amounts of land were lost in Connecticut, Hawaii, Maine, Massachusetts, New York, and Virginia. An average of 5.2% of farmland was lost in these states during this five-year period. The greatest amount of land typically is lost to expanding suburbs.

The 1992 National Resources Inventory, conducted by the U.S. Department of Agriculture's Natural Resources Conservation Service, found that since 1982 cropland decreased by about 39 million acres (-9%), developed land increased by 14 million acres (+18%), and rangeland

Table 20.6 *Land in Farms: By State and the United States 1993–1997 (in Thousands of Acres)*

State	1993	1994	1995	1996	1997
AL	10,000	10,100	10,000	9,700	9,600
AK	940	930	920	920	910
AZ	28,300	28,300	28,300	28,300	28,300
AR	15,100	15,000	15,000	14,900	14,800
CA	29,900	29,600	29,300	29,000	28,700
CO	32,800	32,700	32,700	32,500	32,500
CT	400	390	380	380	380
DE	590	590	590	590	585
FL	10,800	10,800	10,700	10,700	10,600
GA	11,700	11,600	11,500	11,400	11,300
HI	1,560	1,530	1,470	1,440	1,440
ID	12,200	12,200	12,200	12,100	12,000
IL	28,100	28,100	28,000	27,900	27,800
IN	15,800	15,700	15,600	15,600	15,600
IA	33,100	33,100	33,000	33,000	33,000
KS	47,700	47,600	47,600	47,500	47,500
KY	14,100	14,100	14,000	14,000	13,900
LA	8,500	8,400	8,400	8,300	8,200
ME	1,400	1,360	1,330	1,310	1,280
MD	2,300	2,200	2,200	2,200	2,200
MA	610	590	570	570	570
MI	10,700	10,700	10,700	10,600	10,400
MN	29,700	29,500	29,400	29,200	29,100
MS	12,500	12,200	12,300	11,900	11,700
MO	30,200	30,100	30,100	30,100	30,100
MT	59,900	59,600	59,400	58,500	57,800
NE	46,500	46,500	46,400	46,400	46,400
NV	7,000	7,000	7,000	6,900	6,900
NH	430	420	420	420	420
NJ	870	860	850	840	830
NM	45,200	45,200	45,000	45,100	45,300
NY	8,100	7,900	7,900	7,800	7,800
NC	9,600	9,600	9,600	9,500	9,500
ND	40,300	40,200	39,900	39,900	39,700
OH	15,200	15,100	15,000	14,900	14,900
OK	34,000	34,000	34,000	34,000	34,000
OR	17,500	17,500	17,500	17,500	17,500
PA	7,900	800	7,700	7,600	7,700
RI	65	65	65	65	65
SC	5,150	5,100	5,050	5,000	5,000
SD	44,200	44,200	44,000	44,000	44,000
TN	12,100	12,100	12,000	12,000	12,000
TX	133,000	133,000	132,000	132,000	131,500
UT	11,200	11,200	11,400	11,400	11,600
VT	1,430	1,400	1,370	1,340	1,330
VA	8,800	8,800	8,800	8,800	8,800
WA	16,000	15,800	15,800	15,700	15,700
WV	3,700	3,700	3,700	3,700	3,700
WI	17,100	16,900	16,800	16,600	16,500
WY	34,600	34,600	34,600	34,600	34,600
US	968,845	965,935	962,515	958,675	965,010

Source: U. S. Department of Agriculture.

decreased by 10 million acres (-2.4%). Of the 50 million acres of cropland converted to other uses during this decade, about 4 million acres were converted to developed land. The 14 million acre increase in developed land came from conversion of about 5.4 million acres of forestland, 4 million acres of cropland, 2.5 million acres of pasture, and about 2 million acres of rangeland. In 1992 developed land totaled 92 million acres (less than 5% of the U.S. land base). A total of 4 million prime farmland acres were developed between 1982 and 1992. The American Farmland Trust analysis shows that every state lost some of its high-quality farmland, prime or unique, to urban development with Texas, North Carolina, Ohio, Georgia, Louisiana, Florida, Illinois, Tennessee, Indiana and California losing the most.

Some of the most difficult assignments confronting appraisers are in close-in suburban areas where residential neighborhoods, especially along main traffic arteries, are changing from single-family, detached residential land uses to commercial and retail uses. Former houses are being converted into small offices and shops. These conversions typically are interim uses until business volume increases sufficiently to justify more intense development. Then these structures will be razed, several parcels will be assembled, and larger commercial or retail buildings will be

Land Valuation: Adjustment Procedures and Assignments

constructed. Appraisers involved with these assignments must weigh market trends and sale transactions carefully to ascertain the highest and best use and value of the underlying sites and the contributory value of the improvements in accordance with the principle of consistent use. This valuation principle states that both the site and improvements must be valued for the same use. Similar concerns confront appraisers who value agricultural land in transition to different, more intensive uses.

In appraising land in an area changing from agricultural to other uses, more skill is required to select truly comparable sales that accurately reflect the value of the appraised parcel. There almost certainly will be a wide variance in unit sale prices among the market sales considered. An analysis of comparable sale parcels that have recently sold will provide the most reliable indication of value in most instances. For various reasons, including high labor costs and high real estate taxes, the capitalized net farm revenue method probably will understate the value of the land.

As the outward forces of suburban growth intensify, appraisers justifiably will place greater emphasis on sales for residential subdivision development and less reliance on farm sales. While the emphasis may shift from an earlier reliance on purely agricultural sales of perhaps $2,000 an acre to more typical sales of $30,000 an acre, it will be necessary to interpret value in this range for a particular appraised parcel. Through careful scrutiny of factors such as location, size, soil conditions, and comparative highest and best use of recent land sales, this price range can be narrowed considerably.

As the suburbanization trend in metropolitan areas progresses, older buildings designed for farm usage fall into disrepair and contribute less and less to the overall property value. As this outward growth progresses, the buildings may actually have negative value. Chapter 9 considers the analysis and adjustment of comparable land sales for improvements with nominal or negative value.

To judge the present value of farmland in transition properly, an appraiser must possess knowledge of the history of the surrounding area. Helpful in this regard is the study of aerial photographs taken at different times over a period of several years. One such photograph appears in Figure 20.2, which shows the conversion of former farmland and open space to more intensive uses. A perusal of the zoning sheet(s) covering the subject area may reveal patterns of rezoning from agricultural to nonagricultural uses. A review of the county comprehensive plan will indicate the local government's plan for future land use. Consideration of the municipal capital budget for the extension of public water and sewer lines into an area provides evidence of future growth paths. Extended and upgraded road systems in the subject area will hasten land conversion from agricultural to residential, commercial, retail, and industrial activities.

Figure 20.2   *Aerial View of a Transitional Agricultural Area*

Courtesy of Highwoods Properties, Raleigh, North Carolina.

Economic forces and trends as well as governmental policies may influence the rate of land conversion from farm uses. When prices for farm products stagnate and demand for nonagricultural land increases, farmers are pressured to sell their land. Similarly, estate taxes often force children to sell all or part of a farm to pay inheritance taxes. Changes in the highest and best use of a parcel may prompt the local real estate assessor's office to increase the tax burden to the point of forcing an owner to sell all or part of a parcel to pay these taxes.

To offset increasing real estate taxes or future inheritance taxes, some owners will voluntarily impose a conservation easement on a parcel. (See Chapter 22 for a detailed discussion of this topic.) Sometimes, landowners will donate land to charitable organizations to achieve lower real estate taxes and receive federal income tax advantages. The real estate tax burden may be reduced by farm owners applying for and receiving preferential assessments, which are based of the property's agricultural use, rather than surrounding transitional uses and values. Another method that allows farmers to retain ownership of their farms longer is deferring part of their taxes until the farm is either sold or developed for nonagricultural purposes. The appraiser should analyze why transitional land has remained in agricultural use. It may be that one of these arrangements for lowering taxes has delayed conversion of farmland to a higher and better use.

In estimating the market value of farmland located in transition zones, a thorough highest and best use analysis is imperative. If preliminary analysis suggests that the highest and best use is for large lot residential development, the appraiser should determine whether the soil conditions are conducive to the operation of septic systems. The combination of a high water table and impervious soil may prevent this type of development. Development may depend on whether the aquifer can produce an adequate supply of drinking water from individual or community wells.

In many situations, the highest and best use is to hold land until there is sufficient demand for a more valuable use. In judging the ultimate highest and best use, a discount is required for the time lag until demand catches up with the supply of competitive land. Ignoring this logic, an appraiser once testified in court that more than one mile of highway frontage on a daffodil farm had the same price per front foot as a parcel at a nearby traffic intersection recently zoned for commercial use. Another expert witness testified more realistically that the frontage had a highest and best use as potential commercial development. As part of his testimony, he described the annual rate of highway frontage absorption and then applied an appropriate discount rate to the subject road frontage to arrive at a realistic estimate of current market value.

The subdivision development valuation method is a refinement of this method. It is an appropriate valuation method when the appraised parcel has the potential to be developed in the near future, perhaps within the next five years. Through a careful study of the subject parcel and the income, expenses, and marketing periods of similarly developed tracts, the appraiser can derive an opinion of value. Chapter 17 contains a detailed discussion of the proper use of this valuation methodology.

Summary

Real estate appraisers generally are not qualified to analyze soils, but their clients are well served when appraisers can interpret soil maps and soil productivity reports. One type of soil analysis is capability grouping, which provides a general means of identifying the suitability of soils for most types of field crops. The groups are classified according to their soil limitations for field crops, risk of damage when they are used, and response to treatment. The appraiser should be able to judge the estimated crop yields for different parts of an appraised parcel.

Frequently, farmland consists of several categories of land. For example, there may be tillable land, meadow, pasture, woodland, mountainside, and marsh. Several methods can be used to establish the values of each of these categories. One method is to apply the value per acre for each land class derived from sales of similar land. Another method is the algebraic approach, which allows an appraiser to estimate the value of one category of land if the overall parcel's sale price, per acre value of one category of land, and acreage in each category are known. Another method for estimating the values of different land categories is paired sales analysis.

Several types of conveyances may be used to sell farmland. The appraiser must carefully scrutinize each to determine its effect on the sale price. Land value extraction is useful when the comparable land sales have old, dilapidated buildings that contribute relatively little to the overall property value. The capitalization of farm income is another valuation method.

In appraising land in an area that is being converted from agricultural to other uses, greater care is required in selecting comparable sales that accurately reflect the value of the appraised parcel. To judge the present value of farmland in transition properly, an appraiser must know the history of the surrounding area. Both economic trends and governmental policies may influence the rate of land conversion from farm uses. In estimating the market value of farmland in transition zones, a thorough highest and best use analysis is needed.

CHAPTER

21

Forestland

This chapter covers the appraisal of land that underlies growing timber. The value derived is known as *bare land value, cutover land value, soil expectation value,* or *land expectation value. Forestland* or *bare land* is the preferred term in the industry; *timberland* may include timber. *Forestland* is associated more readily with land used in growing timber than the term *raw land.* The terms *soil expectation value* and *land expectation value* are associated with the net present value of bare land used to produce cash flows from perpetual harvest rotations of even-aged timber. A bare land or forestland value estimate is typically based on an analysis of comparable sales.

Most real estate appraisers are not qualified through experience or education to appraise growing timber. They may require professional assistance in valuing timberland in accordance with the Competency Provision of the Uniform Standards of Professional Appraisal Practice (USPAP). The overriding concern of this provision of USPAP is that without proper knowledge and experience, an appraiser may render inaccurate or inappropriate appraisals. The provision states that if an appraiser is offered an appraisal assignment but lacks the necessary experience or knowledge to complete it competently, then "...the appraiser must disclose his or her lack of knowledge or experience to the client before accepting the assignment and then take the necessary or appropriate steps to complete the appraisal competently. This may be accomplished in various ways including but not limited to, personal study by the appraiser; association with an appraiser reasonably believed to have the necessary knowledge or experience; or retention of others who possess the required knowledge or experience."[1]

An appraiser will find it sound practice to affiliate with a forestry consultant who is familiar with local forestry practices and market

---

1.   Appraisal Standards Board, *Uniform Standards of Professional Appraisal Practice* (Washington, DC: The Appraisal Foundation, 2000), p. 5.

conditions when appraising bare timberland.[2] A knowledge of timber industry practices will enhance the appraiser's proficiency in valuing bare land and help him or her better understand the contents of timber cruises (inventories) provided by forestry consultants.

It is improper valuation methodology to appraise timberland by considering the land and the timber as a single unit. For example, it is incorrect to use comparable sales of mature mixed hardwood without having a breakdown of the timber inventory and a separate value of the bare land. When making an appraisal of timberland with premerchantable timber or merchantable timber, one must always have an inventory of the timber with the land and timber being appraised separately. Moreover, IRS regulations require separate value estimates for land and timber or young growth.

The price of timber is expected to rise in the future as more national forests are removed or greatly restricted from private commercial harvesting. Environmental concerns such as the conservation of wetlands, the use of buffer strips between streams and roadways, and the protection of threatened wildlife species and plants such as the bald eagle and the northern spotted owl in the Northwest have all reduced the amount of timberland available for harvest. Environmental concerns have sharply curtailed the extent of federal timber harvests. Also, conversion of timberland to other uses, such as residential and commercial use continues to reduce the number and size of timber tracts. Less land on which trees are grown and fewer growing trees permitted to be harvested in the future, may put upward pressure on timber and bare land prices.

Definitions

Bare land value. A timber tract's underlying land value with no value ascribed to timber of any age, not even immature timber.

Clear cutting. A harvesting method that clears all of the merchantable timber from an area in preparation for either planting or seeding to establish a new stand of trees. This method works well for understocked stands of timber, for mature stands of timber, and for clearing land of a suboptimal species of timber. Successful forestry practices call for prompt regeneration of a tract once it has been clear cut. See Figure 21.1 for an illustration of the results of this technique.

---

2. Foresters who are members of the Association of Consulting Foresters of America, Inc. (ACF) have met the educational, experience, and competency requirements of ACF and must comply with its code of ethics. A roster of ACF member foresters may be obtained by contacting ACF in Alexandria, Virginia at (703) 548-0990 (phone), (703) 548-6395 (fax), or http://www.acf-foresters.com.

Merchantable timber. A stand of timber that has reached sufficient size and maturity to economically justify its being harvested. To estimate the value of merchantable timber, "...it is necessary to first determine the volume of standing timber by species, diameter class (measured at breast height), form class (taper), and merchantable height in order to classify the inventory into the marketable product categories."[3]

Premerchantable timber. Also known as *young growth,* timber that is too small to justify economically its being harvested or even thinned. It generally is less than 15 years old.

Saw log. The harvested trunk of a tree that is of sufficient size and quality to be sawed into lumber or peeled into plywood.

Stumpage. Another term for standing or uncut timber. Stumpage, generally is harvested within six months to two years from the sale date.

Stumpage value. The price that standing timber brings in a sale, usually expressed in thousands of board feet. It is the value of merchantable timber on the stump. Factors such as distance from the tract to processing plants influence hauling costs, which influence the value of merchantable timber. Logging and weather conditions also affect value.

Timber cruise. Also known as a *timber inventory,* a statistical sampling of the timber volume and grade of each species in a particular stand of timber. The percentage of the tract area and trees included in the sample may vary widely depending on the tract size, variability of the timber, and desired precision. Computer programs are often used to extend computations from sample plots and produce an estimate of the timber volume for the entire tract. Preparing cruises requires expertise to design the location and number of sample plots accurately and to analyze and interpret the results properly. Real estate appraisers typically are not trained adequately to conduct timber cruises.

Figure 21.1   *Clear Cut of 44-Year-Old Pine Plantation*

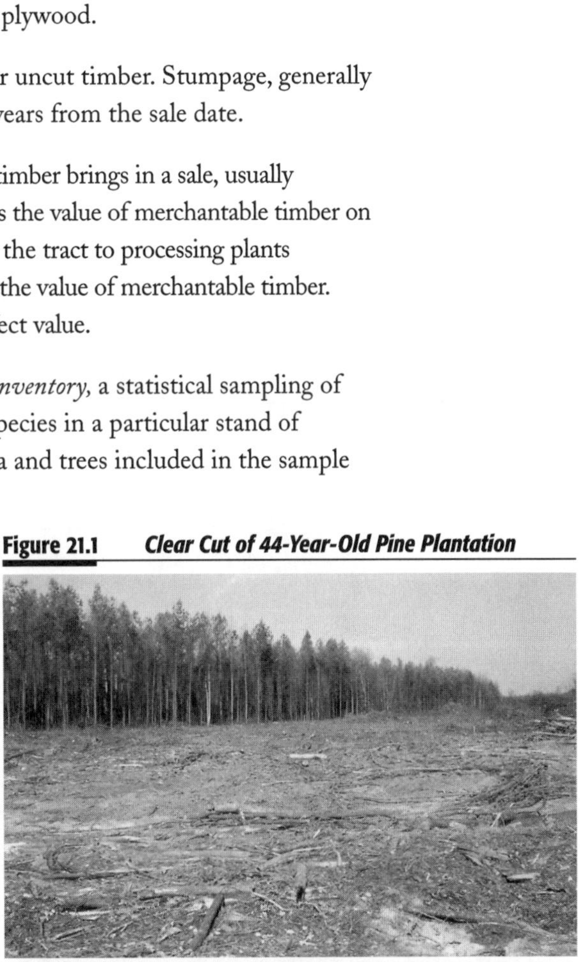

Courtesy of Forest Resources Management, Inc., King William, Virginia.

---

3.   Charles M. Tarver, "Valuation of Timberland: An Institutional Investment Perspective," presented to Real Property Law Institute, Amelia Island, Florida, May 13, 1994, pp. 2 and 3.

Influences on Timber Value

A discussion of factors that influence timber value is essential to understanding the underlying land value. Bare land value is heavily influenced by the estimated value of the crop it is capable of producing, so an appraiser must obtain a reasonable estimate of the value of the crop the land will produce. Timber (crop) value and land value are inextricably linked.

Proximity to Forest Products Mill or Log Storage Yard

Two value influences relate to proximity. First, the hauling cost of logs increases with the distance between the timber tract and the forest products mill. A higher value may be expected for a tract that is nearer to a mill. Second, in mountainous regions, "Sites at lower elevations generally have lower road building costs, superior soils, and potentially lower logging costs."[4] Competition and timber prices increase with the number of forest product mills in a vicinity.

Soil Type

As Charles Tarver points out, not all land is suitable for growing timber profitably. Both extremely dry and wet land will not be economically productive. He observes "...land that is extremely sandy, with very little nutrient content and minimal moisture-holding capacity cannot sustain sufficient tree growth. Similarly, low lying, poorly drained land may support only moderate growth of a few water tolerant species such as tupelo and cypress, and possess only marginal capacity for supporting harvesting operations."[5] It has been found that soil quality has a greater influence on the value of timberland than any other factor besides location. (See Table 21.1.) Thus, sites with good soil quality are worth more than those with poor soil.

Site Index

The site index is a measure of the soil productivity of a tract. It measures how tall a specific tree species will grow in a given time period. A period of 25 and 50 years is generally used in the southern region of the United States. Usually a site index in the range of 60 to 70 for loblolly pine in the South measured on a 25-year basis is judged to be investment grade land.

The USDA Natural Resource Conservation Service publishes soil survey maps, usually in cooperation with state universities. These survey reports can be quite useful in comparing the site indexes of comparable

---

4. Terry Gilmore and Martin J. Healy, Jr. "What is the Dirt Worth?" *The Appraisal Journal* (July 1991), p. 397.
5. Tarver, pp. 2 and 3.

sales to an appraised parcel. Table 21.1 shows the potential soil productivity, major soil limitations, erosion hazards, harvesting and management equipment limitations, seedling mortality caused by soil conditions, and windthrow hazard for two different soil categories.

Table 21.1   *Woodland Management and Productivity*

Soil Name and Map Symbol	Ordination Symbol	Management Concerns				Potential Productivity		
		Erosion Hazard	Equipment Limitation	Seedling Mortality	Windthrow Hazard	Common Trees	Site Index	Trees to Plant
2B Appling	3o	Slight	Slight	Slight	Slight	Loblolly pine	81	Eastern
						Shortleaf pine	65	red-
						Scarlet oak	68	cedar,
						Southern red oak	76	White
						Virginia pine	74	pine
						White oak	71	Loblolly
						Yellow poplar	90	pine, Yellow poplar
Wedowee	3r	Severe	Severe	Slight	Slight	Loblolly pine	80	Loblolly
						Virginia pine	70	pine,
						Shortleaf pine	70	Virginia
						Southern red oak	70	pine,
						Northern red oak	70	Eastern
						White oak	65	red cedar, Yellow poplar

Source: *Soil Survey Of Goochland County, Virginia,* USDA Soil Conservation Service and Virginia Polytechnic Institute and State University, 1980, pp. 42, 43, 96 and 97.

All soils with the same *ordination symbol* have approximately the same potential woodland productivity. The first part of the ordination symbol (the number) indicates the potential productivity of the soils for important trees. The numbers range from 1 (very high productivity) to 5 (low productivity). The second part of the symbol, a letter, indicates the major kind of soil limitation; for instance, *w* is excessive water in or on the soil, *d* is restricted root depth, *c* is clay in the upper part of the soil, *s* is sandy soil texture, *r* denotes steep slopes, and *o* means insignificant limitations. *Seedling mortality* ratings depict the degree that soil affects the expected mortality of planted tree seedlings. These rating vary from slight, where the expected mortality rate is less than 25% up to severe, where mortality is expected to exceed 50%. *Trees to plant* are the species suitable for commercial wood production and suited to the particular soils.

Timber Species and Age

Different species are prevalent in the three principal timber regions of the United States. In the Pacific Northwest, Douglas fir and western hemlock produce most of the saw timber. Southern pine, including loblolly pine, slash pine, and longleaf pine, are the predominant commercial timber species in the South. Most of the timber in the northeast comes from various softwoods, including black spruce, red spruce, and balsam fir. Also, there are major markets for hardwood in the South and Northeast, including oak, maple, cherry, and ash.

The three major categories of timber in the South are pulpwood, chip and saw (CNS), and saw timber. Pulpwood stumpage typically consists of small diameter trees, perhaps 4 to 8 inches thick at breast height, i.e., four feet above the ground. This category tends to include trees between 15 and 25 years old. Chip and saw generally includes 25- to 30-year-old timber with a minimum diameter of nine inches. Saw timber, which is much more valuable, includes large trees of over 12 inches in diameter, which are generally 30 years old and older. Pulpwood sells for the lowest price. Chip and saw may bring two to five times the pulpwood price, and saw timber is likely to command three to six times the price of pulpwood. However, because there are wide regional variations in product prices, one always must study local markets to determine local stumpage prices.

Forecast Future Timber Prices

Expected future prices are a major factor because the present value of bare land and timber is equal to the sum of the discounted future revenue that timber harvesting generates. Also influential are the anticipated timber volume, management and harvesting costs, and the potential for conversion of the land to nontimber activities such as agriculture, residential, or recreational uses.

Highest and Best Use

The same steps followed to ascertain any parcel's highest and best use are used in concluding a timber tract's highest and best use. (See Chapter 5 for a detailed discussion of this topic.) The underlying land may not have a highest and best use for timber production for two reasons: 1) governmental prohibition against logging, either to preserve old growth timber or protect endangered species or environments, such as wetlands; and 2) proximity to an urban area, scenic attractions, and extensive road or water frontage, which may indicate a higher and better use. For an example, consider the master-planned community of Stonehouse, Virginia. This land, which the Chesapeake Corporation had owned for many years, was strategically located near a major tourist and golfing destination—Williamsburg, and in the heavily traveled Interstate 64 corridor. These value-enhancing factors prompted its owner to develop it for nontimber uses.

The appraiser must exercise caution to avoid assuming that the present use is, in fact, the appraised tract's highest and best use. Rezoning, population migration, highway construction, and the extension of public utilities may enhance the appraised tract's highest and best use.

In urban fringe areas, the appraiser may need to determine if the property (land and timber) value is higher for development with the trees standing than the sum of the harvest stumpage value of the timber plus the postharvest cutover land value. Unless the highest and best use is obvious, it is necessary to have a timber cruise (inventory) and appraisal of the timber before making this determination, because timber values vary widely depending on the per-acre volumes, species, and grade and on other factors. Sometimes, especially in areas where development will be delayed for a few years, the maximum income may be derived from a development cut where the larger, high-value trees are harvested, but sufficient intermediate-size trees are left standing to maintain the wooded character of the property.

Bare Land Valuation

Market Sales Comparison

There are problems in estimating land value when the timber has not been harvested. It would seem that one could simply subtract the stumpage value of merchantable timber from the total price of the timberland sale. Unfortunately, the value of the timber is seldom known. Buyers and sellers may allocate values differently. Appraisers rely on buyers and sellers to provide allocations of the overall purchase among merchantable timber, premerchantable trees, and bare land. Often, however, allocations of value are not available from the parties to the transaction. In such cases, the appraiser either must eliminate inclusion of these sales or make his or her best estimate of the allocations.

One variation of this approach is to subtract the estimated value of the merchantable timber and young growth from the sale price. The difference should be the value of the bare land. However, another value element must be investigated. The appraiser should determine if herbicide spraying has occurred on either the comparable land sales or the appraised tract. If this cost is not recognized as part of the sale price, the price of that comparable land sale will be overstated. Spraying usually is done when the stand is about two to three years old, to eliminate competing hardwood growth. Local costs per acre can be determined.

An appraiser may need the assistance of a consulting forester to make a timber value estimate. Estimation of bare land value becomes even more difficult when dealing with uneven-aged forests. "In these cases, timber is never clear-cut and, thus, sales of bare forestland are rare. Such forests yield periodic income from partial harvests,..."[6]

Most of the value influences on timberland listed previously also influence cutover timberland value—i.e., soil type, site index, forecast

---

6. W. David Klemperer, "Segregating Land and Timber Values from Sales of Uneven-aged Forests," *The Appraisal Journal* (January 1979), p. 16.

future timber value, logging conditions (terrain), and the demand for nontimber uses. In appraising cutover timberland, it is essential that the conditions of each sale be understood fully. Also, each comparable sale and its neighborhood should be inspected to determine any unusual influences on the sale tract's highest and best use and sale price. If a comparable sale is a part of a large package transaction including several thousand acres, an adjustment may be required. Large acquisitions usually are purchased at a discounted per-acre price. (See Chapter 6 for more information on size adjustments.)

In many instances, cutover timberland may not be harvested completely due to environmental requirements. Timber along creeks and streams may be untouched to maintain the purity of these waterways. Timber on extremely severe terrain may not be harvested due to the high cost and the prospect of soil erosion from the logging operation. Also, timber may be left unharvested adjacent to roads to serve as a buffer. In some areas, timber may not be harvested if doing so threatens the habitat of threatened or endangered species under the Federal Endangered Species Act.

A reseeded tract will be worth more than a parcel that is still bare land.[7] An appraiser should be able to estimate the value of recently reseeded cutover land by adding the value of the land based on a comparative analysis of several recent, similar sales, to the cost of the reseeding work. In fact, if an appraiser has a number of recent immature timber sales (including land) available for analysis, he or she should be able to judge the value of a timber parcel accurately. A discounted cash flow analysis will provide a better estimate of value for long-term investors, while analysis of comparable sales is more acceptable for the short term. Mortgage lenders prefer the comparable sales method. The cost of reforestation may vary considerably depending on conditions of the previous stand and the condition of the tract after logging has been completed.

Once the timber reaches merchantable size, real estate appraisers usually are not equipped to estimate the value of the timber by the comparable sales method. Even experienced timber consultants shy away from using this method to estimate timber value. Instead, they conduct a timber inventory to value standing merchantable timber. This approach allows them to account for the timber volume, the species, and current pricing. When a stand first becomes merchantable (in approximately 15 years), the liquidation value as clearcut land is less than the investment value as the stand will grow into higher value products (i.e., CNS and saw

---

7. In Virginia, bare land values range around $350 to $400 per acre; in the coastal plain of Georgia and Florida, values range up to $800 or more per acre.

timber) in a few years. A discounted cash flow (DCF) analysis, discussed later in this chapter, is appropriate to help determine both the investment value and market value of stands in the early years of merchantability.

In the Pacific Northwest, it has been found that site index has a greater impact on the price of cutover land than topography, accessibility, location, weather, and soil type.[8] Another influence on cutover land value is the elevation of a tract. That is, in mountainous regions purchasers prefer parcels at lower elevations where there is less chance of soil erosion, more moderate temperature variations, deeper soils, lower road building costs, and longer logging seasons due to better weather.[9]

The four basic methods to appraise bare land (cutover) tracts are:

1. Extract bare land value by deducting the timber value, per a timber cruise, from the sale price of the timberland (timber and land). For this method to work, there must have been a timber inventory near the time of the sale.

2. Compare timberland sales in which the seller stipulates that he or she has reserved the right to harvest the timber. This type of sale is essentially a bare land sale.

3. Compare two simultaneous sales, one of timberland and the other of the standing timber. The latter transfer would convey the timber via a timber deed. The appraiser should inquire whether there is a companion timber sale for all timberland sales. The price difference suggests the value assigned to the bare land. Further investigation usually is required to determine if, in fact, this is the case.

4. Compare outright bare land sales. The local custom as to whether the buyer or seller pays the cost of reforestation should be determined.

Discounted Cash Flow Method

The present value of bare land underlying a timber tract may be estimated in a manner similar to that discussed in Chapter 17, "Prospective Subdivisions." Use of the discounted cash flow (DCF) technique for each of these types of assignments involves a number of estimates and uncertain variables. Accurate valuation results rest on in-depth research and, in the case of forestland appraising, the expertise of consulting foresters.

Because timberland often has a combination of mixed species and trees of various ages, it generally is preferable to devise a management plan

---

8. Terry Gilmore and Martin J. Healy, Jr., "What is the Dirt Worth?" *The Appraisal Journal* (July 1991), p. 396.
9. Ibid. p. 397.

that employs a single rotation of timber such as in a plantation. Typically, a complete rotation is 35 to 40 years. The use of DCF to value bare land for one rotation of timber would appear to understate land value because it fails to recognize the value of a perpetual series of future harvests. Yet, in reality, there is almost no incremental present value derived from second and subsequent rotations. One way to deal with this situation is to assume that the land will be sold at the time of the first harvest and discount this future land value back to the present. An after-tax calculation of present land value may be more meaningful for taxable investors. Anticipated future timber prices vary widely by timber type, region, market conditions, and other variables.

The necessary calculations are shown in Table 21.2, which also shows the expected annual real estate tax charge. In many parts of the country, there may be offsetting revenue from leasing land to hunt clubs. Several factors influence the stumpage value of the timber. The categories of timber are set by the tree diameter at breast height as well as other variables. The categories are pulpwood (5 inches to 9 inches), chip and saw (10 inches to 12 inches), saw timber (13 inches to 19 inches), and big saw timber (20 inches to 27 inches). Height also affects stumpage value as does form class, i.e., the degree of taper of the tree trunk or how fast the diameter decreases in relation to the height. All of these factors influence both the quantity of board feet and the stumpage value of a timber stand.

Table 21.2 reflects two harvests. The first harvest produces pulpwood and the final harvest consists of chip and saw and saw timber revenue. The discount rate selected for this example is 6%.

Table 21.2 *Calculation of Bare Land Value via DCF (in Dollars Per Acre)*

Year	Item	Amount per Acre	Present Worth of Cost/Income
0	Site preparation	($125.00)	($125.00)
0	Tree planting	($50.00)	($50.00)
19	Thinning income	$199.00	$65.77
32	Final harvest income	$2,437.00	$377.63
1–32	Real estate taxes	($2.50)	($35.21)
1–32	Hunt lease income	$4.50	$63.38
32	Land sale	$350.00	$54.24
	Present per acre value of bare land		$350.81
	Rounded to		$350

The present worth of one (reversion) equation used to compute the present value of the thinning income, final harvest income, and land sale is $1/(1 + i)^n$; it may also be solved by use of a financial calculator. For example, the keystrokes for the HP 12C calculator are 32 n 6 i 350 CHS FV PV. Also see Thomas J. Straka and Steven H. Bullard, "Land Expectation Value Calculation in Timberland Valuation," *The Appraisal Journal* (October 1996), pp. 400–401 for an alternative way to calculate bare land value.

Summary

Bare land or forestland valuation typically employs an analysis of comparable sales. Most real estate appraisers are not qualified through experience or education to appraise growing timber. When appraising bare timberland, an appraiser is generally wise to affiliate with a forestry consultant who is familiar with local forestry practices and market conditions. The estimated value of the crop that bare land is capable of producing heavily influences its value. To accurately estimate land value, an appraiser must obtain a reasonable estimate of the value of the crop the land will produce.

A higher value may be expected for a tract that is nearer to a mill than one that is more distant. Competition and timber prices increase when forest product mills are in the vicinity. The three major categories of wood products are pulpwood, chip and saw (CNS), and saw timber.

Two probable reasons that the underlying land may not have a highest and best use for timber production are 1) governmental prohibition against logging, either to preserve old growth timber or protect endangered species or environmental conditions; and 2) the land has a higher and better use due to its proximity to an urban area, scenic attractions, and extensive road or water frontage.

Four basic methods used to appraise bare land (cutover) tracts are:

1. Extract bare land value by deducting the timber value, per a timber cruise, from the sale price of the timberland (timber and land).

2. Compare timberland sales in which the seller stipulates that he or she has reserved the right to harvest the timber, which is essentially a bare land sale.

3. Compare two simultaneous sales—one of timberland and the other of the standing timber. The price difference suggests the value assigned to the bare land. Further investigation usually is required to determine if, in fact, this is the case.

4. Compare bare land sales. Local custom will dictate whether the buyer or seller pays the cost of reforestation.

Scenic Land Conservation Easements

When the word *easement* is mentioned, most people visualize a nonpossessory interest in real property that is conveyed to another party. Examples of easements are the right of one party to traverse the lands of another to gain access to a parcel or the transmission of gas, electricity, sewage, and storm water from one point to another. These easements grant certain rights to non-property owners whereas conservation easements convey the specified future development rights of a landowner to another party, which holds these rights in trust. They are easements in name only and "...should be considered restrictive covenants."[1] *Conservation easements,* also known as *open space* and *scenic easements,* restrict the use and development of a property. They are negative in that they limit a fee owner's ability to fully enjoy or develop a property rather "...than transfer to the owner of the easement (grantee, donee) any rights to use the property. Most of these easement agreements permit the grantee access to the property and authority to police the conditions of the easement ...However, the grantee has no rights to *use* the property in the normal sense of the word."[2] For instance, these easements may prohibit cutting timber, future development, or demolishing historic structures.

A conservation easement is a voluntary agreement. The donor may restrict the future use and development to whatever degree he or she desires. The value of the easement rights conveyed to the grantee increases in proportion to the extent that the easement restricts future development rights. The appraiser should note that such easements extend in perpetuity and run with the property's title, which means that future owners are bound by the terms of the easement. If designed for educational purposes, public access may be required to the property, but not necessarily continuously. The extent of public access can affect the value of the easement.

---

1. James E. Smith, "Are We Protecting The Past? Dispute Settlement and Historical Property Preservation Law," *North Dakota Law Review,* v. 71, 1995, p. 1032, quoting 3 Powell. supra note 7, Sec. 34A.01.

2. Arthur B. Daugherty, "The Economics of Federal Tax Incentives for Conservation Easement Donation," *National Tax Journal,* v. 30, no. 2, June 1977, p. 180, footnote 3.

Charitable Gift Law

In many instances, landowners donate easements to charitable [501(c)(3)] organizations to enjoy lower real estate taxes and receive a federal income tax deduction.[3] Unless the gift (easement) is properly structured, the recipient of the gift will be required to pay a gift tax. For an easement to qualify as a federal income tax deduction, two conditions must be satisfied. First, the gift must be a genuine gift and not exchanged for a benefit or proffer, such as a developer granting an easement to a governmental body in exchange for greater zoning density. Second, it must be an irrevocable gift. That is, it is not granted for a limited time period or is contingent on some future release of the donor from the agreement. The value of an easement gift is limited to the landowner's basis rather than a higher appreciated value if it is held for less than one year or if a real estate dealer, such as a land developer, holds the land.[4]

Circumstances Requiring an Appraisal

Landowners have different motivations for placing conservation easements on their property. One fundamental reason is to prevent future development of their land. It is possible to achieve this objective without encumbering the land with an easement. For instance, a landowner may lease tillable land to a farmer, lease a timber tract to a hunt club, or even lease land to a land trust. Each of these alternative strategies provides revenue, although not substantial revenue, to the owner, but creates no real estate tax or federal income tax benefits.

If a conservation easement worth less than $5,000 is donated to a qualified organization[5] an appraisal is optional. If the donated property rights exceed $5,000, an appraisal is mandatory and any of the following three situations may require an appraisal:

1. A standard easement is conveyed to a qualified organization.

2. A donor donates a remainder interest (also known as a *reserved life estate*) in his or her land. This gift occurs during one's lifetime, but the landowner reserves the right to live on and use the property until his or her death. The amount of the income tax deduction, based on the donor's age, should be determined by the donor's tax

---

3. Internal Revenue Code Sec. 170(h) is the federal statute that establishes the requirements that conservation easements must meet to qualify for federal income tax deduction.

4. Comprehensive information on the federal tax law enabling conservation easements is found in Stephen J. Small, *The Federal Tax Law of Conservation Easements,* 3d ed. (Washington, DC: Land Trust Alliance, 1994).

5. A qualified organization is a governmental unit of the United States or any political subdivision thereof, a publicly supported charitable organization, or an organization that is not publicly supported but is qualified as a public charity under Section 509(a)(3) of the IRS Code and is controlled by a government or a publicly supported charity.

advisor. This method provides the donor(s)... "income tax benefits, ad valorem tax reduction, and reduction of estate taxes..."[6]

3. If the value of the donated easement is very high in relation to a donor's income, a strategy of staged transfers may be used. Each of these gifts, known as *undivided partial interests*, requires a separate appraisal.[7]

Overvaluation Penalty

An appraiser should inform a donor of the severity of the penalty the IRS imposes for an overly aggressive valuation report. Additionally, a donor should be referred to his or her tax advisor for counseling on this matter because the donor may be liable for a penalty under IRS Code Section 6659(f). The overvaluation penalty is imposed when the IRS determines that the donor has claimed a value of 150% or more of the amount that the IRS asserts to be the correct easement value. The penalty assessed against the donor is 30% of the additional taxes due because the appraised value exceeds the correct valuation. If, for example, the additional tax due is $100,000, then the penalty is $30,000.

The IRS may waive the overvaluation penalty "...if two conditions are satisfied: 1) the taxpayer must show a reasonable basis for the claimed valuation and that the claim was made in good faith and 2) the claimed value was based on a qualified appraisal[8] from a qualified appraiser."[9] Also, the taxpayer must have made a reasonable effort to assure that the claim is reasonable.[10]

---

6. James H. Boykin, *Transfer Methods and Valuation Procedures for Conservation Easements* (Gardena, CA: Right of Way International Education Foundation, January 1998), p. 17.

7. Boykin, p.18.

8. When a donated easement has a claimed value in excess of $5,000, the Internal Revenue Service requires that a donor submit a qualified appraisal to claim a deduction [see Treasury Regulation Sec. 1.170A-13T(c)(2)(I)(A)]. The IRS defines a *qualified appraisal* as an appraisal document that relates to an appraisal that is made not earlier than 60 days before the date of contribution of the appraised property nor later than the due date of the return upon which the deduction is claimed. It should include the terms of any agreement entered into by or on behalf of the donor or donee that related to the use, sale, or other disposition of the property contributed. It further must set forth the terms of the gift, a statement that the appraisal was prepared for income tax purposes, and a description of the fee arrangement between donor and appraiser.

9. In the *Final Regulations of Appraisal Requirements* (25 CFR Ch. 1, 4-1-89 Edition), the U. S. Treasury Department defines *qualified appraiser* as an individual who includes in the appraisal summary, a declaration that: 1) the individual holds either himself or herself out to the public as an appraiser or performs appraisals on a regular basis; 2) because of the appraiser's qualifications as described in the appraisal..., the appraiser is qualified to make appraisals of the type of property being valued; 3) the appraiser is not (a) the donor or donee of the property, (b) a party to the transaction in which the donor acquired the property being appraised, (c) any person employed or related to any of the foregoing persons, (d) any appraiser who is regularly used by any person described in (a) or (b) above or who does not perform a majority of his or her appraisals made during his or her taxable year for other persons, or (e) a person who charges a fee based on a percentage of the appraised value of the property; and 4) the appraiser understands that an intentionally false or fraudulent overstatement of the value of the property described in the qualified appraisal or appraisal summary may subject the appraiser to a civil penalty... for aiding and abetting an understatement of tax liability....

10. Boykin, p. 18.

Valuation Techniques

Sales Selection via Zoning Classification

As a rule, the highest and best use of a parcel conforms with its zoning. Thus, similarly zoned sale parcels are reliable indicators of an appraised parcel's value—once the necessary adjustments have been made. To estimate the value of the donated easement, first the easement agreement must be read carefully to determine both the allowed future uses and those uses that are prohibited. Next, the appraiser can compare the prescribed uses under the conservation easement to the zoning classification that permits similar uses. Having done so, recent physically similar land sales subject to this zoning may be compiled and analyzed. This comparative analysis should produce a supportable value estimate of the subject property's easement.

Land sales in conservation zoning districts often are subject to land use restrictions similar to those of conservation easements. Thus, conservation-zoned sales may satisfactorily measure the value of these easements. As with any other type of land appraisal, adjustments are required for physical features such as access. Although both the easement area and sale parcel may have a highest and best use for passive activities, the cost and convenience to reach the parcel by road will influence the value of each.

Another important value factor that should be considered when appraising is the value of the remaining land outside of an easement that does not encumber an entire parcel. The creation of a perpetual scenic vista may be appealing and the remainder can be worth more than similar land without this amenity. This remainder situation, as well as the reduced value of land within an easement, is illustrated here.

The owners of a 400-acre parcel worth $6,000 per acre granted a 100-acre easement to a conservation group. In view of the restrictions placed on the land within the easement, it was judged to be worth $5,000 an acre. The benefits of the natural beauty being retained forever in the easement caused the remaining 300 acres to increase in value to $7,000 per acre.

Value of the entire parcel before the easement (400 ac. @ $6,000)		$2,400,000
Value of conservation easement (100 ac. @ $5,000)		$500,000
Value of remainder as part of the whole property		$1,900,000
Value of enhanced remainder (300 ac. @ $7,000)	$2,100,000	
Plus remaining value of easement (100 ac. @ $1,000)	100,000	$2,200,000
Enhancement to remainder		$300,000
Summary Calculations		
Value of conservation easement	$500,000	
Less enhancement to remainder	$300,000	
Damages (compensation due the owner)	$200,000	

Similar Easement Sales Analysis

On the surface, comparative analysis of similar easement sales seems an ideal means to ascertain the market value of an easement on an appraised parcel. Bret Vicary argues, "When sufficiently comparable easement sales exist, an appraiser must seriously consider giving greater weight to the direct comparison method than to the before and after method." He further asserts that "easement sales can be the most objective evidence of market value.... Even if some fairly significant differences exist between the sale and the subject properties, easement sales may establish a lower or upper limit of value that staves off incorrect conclusions...."[11] Moreover, this valuation method is accepted by the Internal Revenue Service in Treasury Reg. §1.170A-14(h)(3), which states, "If there is a substantial record of sales of easements comparable to the donated easement (such as purchases pursuant to a governmental program), the fair market value of the donated easement is based on the sales prices of such comparable easements."[12]

This method does have some drawbacks. Usually there is a limited number of similar easement sales to land trusts. However, there has been

11. Bret P. Vicary, "Trends in Appraising Conservation Easements," *The Appraisal Journal* (January 1994), p. 140.

12. This regulation does not specify what is a "substantial record of sales...," nor for that matter does *Uniform Standards of Professional Appraisal Practice* (1999 edition). USPAP only states that "an appraiser must develop an opinion of site value by an appropriate appraisal method or technique" [Standards Rule 1-4 (b) (i)]. "Each written or oral real property appraisal report must: contain sufficient information to enable the intended users of the appraisal to understand the report properly" [Standards Rule 2-1 (b)]. Another source, the fourth edition (1993) of Boykin and Ring's *The Valuation of Real Estate*, in the chapter "Fundamentals of Land Valuation," offers some guidance as to what is an appropriate number of sales in stating, "After a minimum of three or four comparable sales have been selected, confirmed, field inspected, and analyzed,...." It is clear to the practicing appraiser that there is no established number of land or easement sales that is universally correct. The above USPAP Standards Rule 2-1 (b) and footnote 17 provide reasonable guidance in this regard.

an increase in the use of conservation easements to conserve forests, wetlands, scenic lands, habitat for rare and endangered species, historic landscapes, and farmland and ranches. Between 1988 and 1998 land protected by these easements rose from 290,000 acres to 1,385,000 acres.[13] Also, it is reported that the market for conservation easements is expanding.[14] Land trusts often acquire easements as a bargain sale, which means that the donor only receives a partial price for an easement. The difference between market value and the sale price is treated as an income tax deduction for the donor or seller. Thus, these transfers leave the appraiser with the difficult task of determining what the full price of the easement may have been.

For example, some easement transfers may have to be eliminated completely if a conveyance was accomplished by deed of gift and no money was paid to the donor. Survey data can provide a starting point in appraising conservation easements as well as a source of individual conveyances. One California survey of 14 private land trusts and government agencies active in preserving agricultural land found that, "As a percentage of unencumbered fee value, the broad opinion is that a conservation easement can range from 25%–85%." This survey further revealed that "... the majority of easements are acquired at 40%–60% of fee."[15] In some regions, it still may be difficult to locate significant numbers of conservation easement sales, but as more of these easements are transferred, this valuation method will become more prevalent.

Before and After Easement Sales Analysis

Sometimes a conservation easement may cover a whole property. A recommended methodology for these assignments is to estimate the unencumbered value of an entire property and then deduct from that value the estimated value of the entire property that is encumbered by a conservation easement.[16] The difference between these two values is the value of the easement. The paired sales technique offers an excellent means for estimating each of these values.

For instance, suppose a group of sales for similar parcels of unencumbered land indicate a value of $10,000 per acre for the subject 400 acres. Another group of sales produce a per acre value for the easement-

---

13. Land Trust Alliance, *Summary of Data from the 1998 National Land Trust Census,* Washington, D.C., pp. 1 and 3.

14. Vicary, p. 143.

15. Janis A. Lassner, "Valuing Agricultural Conservation Easements," *The Appraisal Journal* (April 1998), pp. 147-148.

16. See also "Before and After Method Generally Used to Value an Easement," *Appraising Easements: Guidelines for Valuation of Historic Preservation and Land Conservation Easements.* (Washington, DC: National Trust for Historic Preservation and The Land Trust Alliance, 1990), pp. 19–23.

encumbered land of $4,000. The estimated market value of the easement then would be:

Value before easement	400 ac. @ $10,000	$4,000,000
Value after easement	400 ac. @ $4,000	− $1,600,000
Easement value		$2,400,000, or $6,000 per acre

This easement value could be corroborated by comparing the percentage value of other conservation easements to the value ratio for the appraised parcel, which is 60% ($2,400,000 ÷ $4,000,000) of its unencumbered value.

A more involved appraisal is required when the appraised property is only partially subject to a conservation easement. In these assignments, the appraiser needs to appraise the value of the property within and outside of the easement area. An example of this technique involves a comparable 100-acre sale, which recently sold for $1,300,000, or $13,000 an acre. No conservation easement had been donated by the owners of this property. A nearby 80-acre parcel sold for $800,000, or $10,000 an acre. Sixty acres of this second sale were donated to a qualified organization for a scenic easement before the sale of the entire parcel. No adjustments were necessary for either of these land sales.[17] The value of the 60-acre easement is computed as follows:

Total value of 80-acre sale parcel	$800,000
Unencumbered 20 acres @ $13,000	− $260,000
Value of 60-acre easement	$540,000, or $9,000per acre

There is no uniform relationship between the post-easement value of a parcel and its pre-easement value. However, a general rule is that the difference between these two values increases as the parcel's development potential increases. For example, if the pre-easement highest and best use is for residential subdivision development and after imposition of a conservation easement the parcel is restricted to agricultural purposes, then there will be a substantial difference in the two values. Also, as an easement becomes more restrictive, its value increases and the donor is entitled to more compensation and/or income tax benefits. These restrictions may prohibit or limit new development, prohibit or limit

---

17. In practice, an appraiser probably would analyze a minimum of five to eight sales of parcels affected by conservation easements and a like number of unaffected sale parcels. Moreover, several adjustments for differences in the sales and the appraised parcel would be expected. However, this example is simplified to focus the reader's attention on the valuation procedure explained.

timber cutting, and require that the property be open to the public.[18] In reaching a value conclusion, it is imperative that the appraiser be familiar with local growth trends and land values as well as the restrictions a particular conservation easement imposes.

Capitalized Income via Sales and Rentals

The technique used to derive a capitalization rate from comparable land sales and rentals is the same as that applied to improved properties. That is, the land capitalization rate for the appraised parcel usually is based on an analysis of the net operating income of several recent, similar parcels[19] divided by their respective sale prices. Sometimes, when sales of leased land are scarce, it is acceptable to use several similar, but different, rental and sale parcels to develop a land capitalization rate. That is, the appraiser examines some parcels that have sold recently and other, similar parcels that have not sold, but are currently leased. Often ground leases are used for urban/suburban office and retail properties. However, scenic easements typically are found in outer suburban and rural areas where commercial ground leases are rare. Hence, most leases used in developing capitalization rates in outlying areas are for agricultural, timber, or seasonal hunt club purposes.

Some sources of land leases and capitalization rates include rural banks, timber companies, county agricultural extension agents, state university agriculture departments, the Farmers Home Administration, the Farm Credit Association, county real estate assessors, life insurance companies with farm investments, brokers specializing in outlying properties, and land trusts and agricultural conservation organizations. Members of the American Society of Farm Manager and Rural Appraisers and Accredited Land Consultants of the Realtors Land Institute also may provide land value-related information.

Cropland usually is valued by analyzing owner-tenant leases. The most typical and simplest lease to study relates to farmland (usually tillable land) that is rented on a cash basis.[20] In estimating the value of agricultural land via capitalized income, it is necessary to ascertain both a typical per-acre value and rental and the amount of annual expenses borne by farm owners. (This may be only the real estate taxes and some

---

18. A more detailed listing of these restrictions is found in Judith Reynolds, *Historic Properties: Preservation and the Valuation Process,* 2d. ed. (Chicago: Appraisal Institute, 1997), pp. 108–110.

19. Similar sale parcels are those that have equivalent or nearly the same size, location, access, soil productivity and crop allotments (for agricultural land), terrain, water rights, zoning, frontage to depth ratio, and shape.

20. This and other alternative farmland lease practices are discussed in Robert C. Sutter, "The Earnings or Income Capitalization Approach to Value," *The Appraisal of Farm Real Estate,* 3d ed. (West Lafayette, IN: Retus, Inc., 1992).

insurance if the fertilizer and other crop-related expenses are paid by the tenant.)

For example, suppose that the typical per-acre price for tillable land is $1,500; per-acre annual rent is $70; annual real estate taxes are 0.75% of assessed value; similar land is assessed at 40% of market value on an agricultural use basis; and the subject tract is renting currently for $60 an acre, which is fair considering its location and soil productivity. The estimated value for the subject 200-acre tract is:

Typical per-acre rental	$70.00
Less real estate taxes ($1,500 × 0.40 × 0.0075)	− $4.50
Net operating income per acre	$65.50
Divided by typical value	$1,500
Indicated land capitalization rate	4.37%
Divided into subject's per-acre rental ($60/4.37%)	$1,373
Rounded to $1,375 per acre	
Indicated value of the subject cropland: 200 ac. × $1,375 =	$275,000

Subdivision Development Method

The discounted cash flow method may be applicable in deriving an estimate of the market value of a property prior to the owner granting a conservation easement and even afterward if the easement does not severely restrict future development of the entire parcel, or if it encumbers only part of the entire property. Yet, it should be noted that this method is best applied as a means for estimating the bulk sale value of improved subdivision lots rather than raw land.[21] To properly apply this valuation method, the appraiser must be familiar with the land development process and thoroughly understand all aspects of the market in which the appraised property is situated. Every input in this discounting process must be market-derived because this method is intended to depict market reality. Of course, this market portrayal requirement governs every valuation technique. But, improper application of this valuation technique can more easily result in a highly unrealistic indication of market value due to the assumptions about future conditions and the comparatively high number of variables that must be considered.

At the pre-easement stage, the value of a property can be estimated based on the extent of development permitted by the physical constraints on the parcel, availability and capacity of public utilities, uses allowed by zoning, and degree of present and scheduled competitive developments. The present value also is governed by lot pricing, annual sales revenue, and

---

21. A detailed discussion of this subject is found in Douglas D. Lovell and Robert S. Martin, *Subdivision Analysis* (Chicago: Appraisal Institute, 1993). Especially helpful is the Forest Oaks Subdivision case study on pages 64 to 114.

the expected lot sell-off period. Expenses that must be taken into account are development, marketing and promotion, and loan interest as well as the developer's expected yield. This valuation method provides an answer to the question: How much can a party justify paying for a property in view of its market potential and development expenditures? As its name implies, this method is well suited to appraising parcels with development potential. Its usefulness diminishes as an easement curtails the prospect for future land development. Usually, in fact, it is not applicable to the post-easement value when an entire property is subject to an easement because most, if not all, development rights will have been donated via the conservation easement. On the other hand, if a conservation easement encumbers only part of a property, this valuation method is applicable in valuing both the pre- and post-easement property.

Summary

Conservation easements differ from nonpossessory easements whereby a property owner grants another party the right to traverse his or her lands. Instead, conservation easements, also known as *open space* and *scenic easements,* restrict the use and development of a property. A conservation easement is a voluntary easement in which the donor restricts the future use and development of a property. In many instances, landowners donate land to charitable organizations to enjoy lower real estate taxes and receive federal tax benefits. If the value of the donated property exceeds $5,000, an appraisal is mandatory. An appraiser should inform a donor of the severity of the penalty the IRS imposes for an overly aggressive valuation report. The different valuation methods that are potentially applicable in appraising conservation easements include sales of parcels with zoning restrictions that are similar to those of conservation easements, similar easement sales, and before and after easement sales analysis. (This approach involves estimating the unencumbered value of the property and then deducting from that value the estimated value of the property encumbered by the conservation easement. The difference between these values is the value of the easement.)

A variation of the before and after easement method is the valuation of a property when only part of it is subject to a conservation easement. In this case, the value of agricultural land can be estimated via capitalized rental income or the subdivision development method. This latter method is most applicable when estimating the value of a property prior to an owner granting a conservation easement. It does not work as well for valuing land at the post-easement stage because most, if not all, development rights will have been donated in the conservation easement. However, when a conservation easement encumbers only part of a property, this method is suitable for estimating both its pre- and post-easement values.

Floodplains and Wetlands

There are similarities, differences, and even confusion between the terms *floodplain* and *wetlands*. A *floodplain* is level land (plain) adjacent to a river, creek, or stream that periodically overflows. This zone sometime is known as *bottomland* and generally is covered with rich soil deposited during floods. *Wetlands* are defined as areas that are flooded or saturated by surface or ground water at a frequency and duration that support vegetation typically adapted for life in saturated soil conditions. Thus, principal differences between floodplains and wetlands are the frequency and duration of flooding, the height of the water table, and the type of vegetation. A wetland that meets certain specifications pertaining to hydrology, vegetation, and soils is classified as a *jurisdictional wetland*. The U.S. Army Corps of Engineers or another government agency takes jurisdiction over land that is so classified. To do anything on the land (i.e., fill, drain, or dispose of waste) permission must be granted from the jurisdictional authority.

Detection of Floodplains

Floodplains may be detected by checking municipal zoning maps, determining the outer limits of floodplains, interviewing local people, or examining FEMA flood insurance rate maps.

- *Check municipal zoning maps.* Floodplain districts typically overlap underlying zoning districts; that is, they are superimposed over districts zoned as industrial or residential. Floodplains take precedent over these other land use districts. The general purpose of floodplain districts is to encourage the retention of open land and protect areas that are subject to flooding. The boundaries of these districts tend to coincide with the outer limits of the 100-year floodplain, as delineated by the U. S. Department of Housing and Urban Development's Federal Insurance Administration.

    Permitted uses may include agricultural uses for pasture, grazing, and sod farming; residential accessory uses such as gardens; hunting and fishing; wildlife preserves and conservation areas; golf courses, private recreation and public parks; and commercial campgrounds. Generally, floodplain districts prohibit the filling in of land with dirt or gravel that may obstruct or interfere with water flow and flow patterns during flooding.

- *Determine floodplain outer limits.* Floodplain outer limits are generally at the same elevation, i.e., the same number of feet above sea level, and are depicted on topographical maps by a contour line (isoline). For example, they may include land up to 25 feet above sea level. Land above this height would be outside of the floodplain. A particular elevation may be identified on a quadrangle map. (See Appendix C for source.)

- *Interview local persons who are familiar with flooding history.* Former and present owners, real estate agents, county agricultural agents, and farmers may provide useful information. In one assignment, an appraiser spoke to a farmer who farmed a particular floodplain parcel. He noted that the parcel already had flooded five times during the first six months of the year and that, so far, no crops had been planted. Water had risen as high as 12 feet, preventing the planting of crops and blocking access to the parcel. Figure 23.1 shows this parcel during the dry season.

- *Examine FEMA flood insurance rate maps.* FEMA maps cover flood-prone areas where there is a risk of serious flooding at least once every 100 years. (See Figure 23.2, a FEMA map, and Appendix C for the map source.) A FEMA flood insurance rate map will denote the most severely affected flood areas as special flood hazard areas.[1] These are within the 100-year flood boundary where there is a 1% probability (1/100) of land flooding annually. Some maps are further broken down into two zones. The first zone is the floodplain situated between the 100- and 500-year flood frequency; this zone is known as a *moderate flood hazard area.* A less severely

Figure 23.1   *Floodplain During Summer Season*

---

1. According to the Office of Hydrology in the U.S. Department of Commerce, total damages suffered in fiscal year 1995 were $5.11 billion with 78% being property damages and the balance being agricultural damages; 103 lives were lost. Major losses occurred in Louisiana (61% of total) and California (29% of total); Texas and Virginia were next in losses, at 1.7% and 1.3%, respectively.

Figure 23.2 *Flood Insurance Rate Map City of Grand Rapids, Michigan*

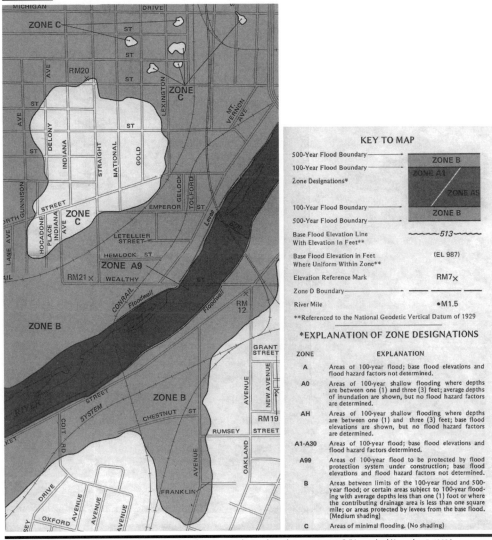

Source: Federal Emergency Management Agency, Panel 15 of 25, Community-Panel Number 260106 0015 C (Map revised November 5, 1982.)

affected area is the *minimal flood hazard area,* where flooding is not expected more frequently than every 500 years. Flood maps can be used to spot floodplains visually when inspecting appraised and comparable sale parcels. The maps are helpful especially during dry seasons when floodplain boundaries are not so readily apparent.

Appraisal of Floodplains

The adage that real estate values are local in nature probably is best exemplified by floodplains. Generalizations regarding the market value of such land likely will lead to erroneous value estimates. Key factors influencing the value of floodplains are access, zoning, frequency and severity of flooding, and availability of flood insurance. (See also Chapter 18 "Residential Waterfront Property.") Typically the sales comparison method is used in appraising floodplains and wetlands, but there are some instances in which the income approach may be applicable. (Examples of this technique are presented in Chapters 17, 20, 22, and 24.)

As in all types of real estate valuation, highest and best use dictates the means for supporting the estimated value of a particular parcel. For example, if an appraised parcel is situated in a floodplain and therefore its highest and best uses are agricultural and private recreational, then sales with similar zoning and land uses should be analyzed to estimate value. Ideally, such sales will be completely within floodplains. Table 23.1 compares land sales that are solely floodplain and, while the uses are different, they are reasonably similar. The per acre values derived form a tight range of indicated values.

Sales Comparison Approach

The four sales shown in the table indicate a range of adjusted unit prices from $1,570 to $1,650 and an average value of $1,627. Because only one adjustment was required for Sale 3, it is given the most weight as a value indicator. Sales 2 and 4 produced slightly lower indications of value. The final per acre value estimate selected was $1,650. Some of the specific value factors considered in making these adjustments were:

- *Market conditions.* There had been only a nominal increase in the value of this type of land.[2]

- *Location.* The subject parcel was in a developing residential corridor and on a small creek, while Sales 1 and 2 fronted on a navigable river and Sale 4 was in a remote agricultural area.

Table 23.1 *Floodplain Comparable Land Sales Adjustment Table*

Land Sale No.	Size (Acres)	Sale Date	Price per Acre	Mkt. Cond.	Location	Use	Access	Net Adjust.	Adjust. Price
				Adjustments					
Subject	52.56								
1	113.04	10/93	$1,642	+8%	-5%	+5%	+7%	+1%	$1,658
2	42.00	8/94	$1,463	+5%	-5%	+5%	+7%	+12%	$1,638
3	32.87	11/97	$1,563	—	—	+5%	—	+5%	$1,641
4	63.88	6/98	$1,308	—	+10%	—	+10%	+20%	$1,570

2. Another adjustment sequence is to adjust first for nonstandard financing terms, conditions of sale, and changes in market conditions between when the comparable sale occurred and the appraisal date. This adjusted price then can be further adjusted for location, physical and economic characteristics, and use. An example of this adjustment sequence is found in *The Appraisal of Real Estate,* 11th ed. (Chicago: Appraisal Institute, 1996), p. 421.

- *Use.* The subject parcel abutted residentially developed land while Sales 1 and 2 were used for occasional recreational purposes and Sale 3 was cropland.

- *Access.* The subject parcel had access from a deeded easement relatively close to a paved road, but Sales 1 and 2 were reached over a longer graveled road beyond a railroad right of way.

Frequently, all or at least some of the comparable sales considered will contain a combination of upland (also known as *highland*) and floodplain.[3] In these situations, it is necessary to extract the value of both categories of land in each land sale to estimate the value of the floodplain. One method is use of the paired sales technique explained in Chapter 10. Another method is to use algebra. Suppose that in a given floodplain valuation assignment, only one or two similar land sales are available. From these two sales it is concluded that the appropriate per acre value of the subject parcel's 52.56 acres is $1,550. By comparing these floodplain sales to similar upland sales, it is determined that floodplain land is worth approximately 25% of upland with the same zoning as the appraised parcel.

Next, two recent land sales with both upland and floodplain are found. Their per-acre sale prices fall between the expected values of these two land categories, but in this form the prices are of no help in judging the value of the appraised parcel's flood land. The next step is to relate the flood land value ratio to upland value to estimate the value of the two sale parcel's upland value. Sale 1 contains 40 acres with 35 acres of upland and 5 acres of floodplain. It sold three months ago for $220,000 an acre. Sale 2, containing 51 acres, sold six months ago for $275,000 an acre; it has 41 acres of upland and 10 acres of floodplain. The per-acre sale price of upland in each of these two land sales is computed by use of the following algebraic equation:

$$P_o = (A_u \times P/A_u) + (R \times P/A_u)(A_f)$$

where:

P_o = Overall sale price
A_u = Upland acreage
A_f = Acres of floodplain
P/A_u = Computed per-acre price of upland
R = Ratio of flood land price to upland price

---

3. Upland may be further subclassified as pasture, meadow, and woodlot. The appraiser must be cautious in assigning values to wetlands as part of an overall parcel's sale price. In some instances, especially in industrial and commercial land sales, parcels may have sold on a net usable basis, with virtually no value having been assigned to the wetland portion. Sometimes it will be given credit as ratio land in establishing a site coverage ratio for the proposed building.

Using this equation, the per-acre price for Sale 1's upland is:

$$P_o = (35 \times P/A_u) + (0.25 \times P/A_u)(5)$$
$$\$220,000 = 35 \ P/A_u + 1.25 \ P/A_u$$
$$\$220,000 = 36.25 \ P/A_u$$
$$P/A_u = \frac{\$220,000}{36.25 \ \text{ac.}} \ \text{or}$$
$$P/A_u = \$6,069$$

Thus, the flood land is indicated to be worth $\$6,069 \times 25\%$, or $\$1,517$ per acre.

Similarly, the value of Sale 2's floodplain is:

$$\$275,000 = (41 \times P/A_u) + (.25 \times P/A_u)(10)$$
$$= 43.5 \ P/A_u$$
$$P/A_u = \frac{\$275,000}{43.5 \ \text{ac.}} \ \text{or}$$
$$P/A_u = \$6,321$$

The per acre value of the floodplain of $\$1,580$ ($\$6,321 \times 25\%$). These two algebraic solutions corroborate the per acre value of the subject's floodplain indicated by the four floodplain sales analyzed in Table 23.1. Assuming that the appropriate adjustments have been made between these two sales and the subject parcel's floodplain, then these indicated prices would measure the subject's floodplain value.

The appraiser could be confident about the value of the upland, but uncertain of the floodplain's value. Using the same information on Sale 1, the value of the floodplain could be computed as follows, assuming that the upland is worth $\$6,069$ per acre:

$$P_o = (35 \times 6,069) + (R \times 6,069)(5)$$
$$\$220,000 = 212,415 + 30,345R$$
$$R = 7,585/30,345$$
$$R = 25\%$$
$$\text{Value of floodplain} = (25\%)(\$6,069), \text{ or } \$1,517.$$

Wetland Trends and Significance

At the time of the American Revolution, there were approximately 221 million acres of wetlands in the continental United States. In 1980, only 104 million acres remained, a loss of over one-half of the original acreage, or 1.17 million acres per year. During the period between the mid-1950s and the late 1970s, 11 million acres of wetlands were lost,[4] for an annual loss of approximately one-half million acres. The rate of loss should have declined after President Jimmy Carter signed Executive Order 11990 on

---

4. Jean Watts, Curtis Bohlen, and Ray Bahr, *Wetlands Regulation and Resource Manual for Virginia,* 2d ed. (Richmond, Va: Chesapeake Bay Foundation, 1992), p. 7.

May 24, 1977, to provide protection for wetlands, and President George Bush set a 1989 national goal of no overall net loss of wetlands.[5] Yet, an additional 4.25 million acres is expected to have been lost between 1990 and 2000,[6] or 425,000 acres annually, which is not a substantial improvement on the annual rate of decline experienced from the mid-1950s to the late 1970s. The U. S. Fish and Wildlife Service estimates, "...wetlands are being lost in the conterminous United States at a rate approximately 20 times greater than they are being gained. An estimated 400,000 acres are being lost while only about 25,000 acres are gained on an annual basis."[7]

In the past, swamps generally were thought of as areas to be avoided or improved by draining and filling to make them useful. The conversion of swampland was widespread, especially in Florida where dredging created canals with the spoil used for building sites. Gradually, this attitude changed as people gained an understanding of the ecological merits of saving wetlands. A greater appreciation of the expansive views of scenery and wildlife followed and, more recently, developers have learned that proximity to wetlands can add appeal and value to land developments. Some of the important benefits of wetlands are described below.

- *Water quality.* Wetlands protect and improve water quality by removing pollutants, such as the nutrients found in fertilizers, sewage, and industrial effluent and sediments, before they can reach streams, lakes, and rivers. Wetlands are so effective in enhancing water quality that they are now built to treat industrial, agricultural, and municipal wastewater.

- *Flood control.* Wetlands reduce flooding by temporarily storing flood waters, decreasing water velocity, and delaying and reducing peak flood flowage. It has been estimated that the presence of wetlands along rivers can reduce water velocities by one-half.

- *Groundwater discharge and recharge.* When water in wetlands seeps to the surface, it aids stream flow and helps to assure water quality. Recharge occurs when water seeps into the ground, thereby replenishing groundwater supplies, which can be used for drinking water and irrigation.

- *Shoreline erosion control.* Wetlands have an excellent dampening effect on erosion and have been found to be an inexpensive and ecologically superior alternative to man-made, fixed structures

---

5. *Wetlands: Meeting the President's Challenge* (Washington, D.C.: U.S. Department of the Interior, Fish and Wildlife Service, 1990), pp. 11 and 55.

6. Ibid, p. 6.

7. Ibid., p. 16.

such as bulkheads. At times, wetlands retain more wave- and current-born sediment than they lose to erosion, expanding wetlands or raising their elevation.

- *Food chain support.* Dead plants and partially decayed organic matter in wetlands form an important part of the food chain. Microorganisms and small aquatic invertebrates feed on these decaying plants. In turn, they become food for aquatic insects, fish, birds, and mammals.

- *Fish and wildlife.* Waterfowl have long used wetlands for nesting areas and food as well as wintering grounds, breeding areas, and stopovers for migratory waterfowl. Wading birds, such as herons and egrets, feed in and build nesting colonies in wetlands. They also provide nurseries for many fish and shellfish.

- *Threatened and endangered species.* Although wetlands make up only 5% of the land mass in the United States, they shelter over 20% of our threatened and endangered plants and animals.

- *Recreation and aesthetic values.* While wetlands have long been important for fishing, hunting, and trapping, an expanded group of visitors now visit wetlands for boating and birdwatching.[8]

Identification of Wetlands

Wetlands are fairly obvious in such places as swamps, marshes, and bogs. They are less obvious when situated in bottomland hardwood forests, pine savannas, and wet meadows.[9] They are transitional zones between open water and upland where water is near or above the ground surface for part or all of the growing season. Water sources may be precipitation, groundwater, tides, or a combination of all three. A good starting point for identifying wetlands is use of wetlands, topographic, soil, and floodplain maps. Description of these maps and instructions for ordering them can be found in Appendix C.

Most appraisers are not trained to detect wetlands and typically include a disclaimer in the limiting conditions section of their reports such as this: "There may or may not be wetlands on the appraised property. Identification of wetlands and determining their impact on value is beyond the scope of this assignment. For the purpose of this appraisal, it is assumed that there are no wetlands." For some assignments, wetlands may

---

8. Much of this section is based on "Wetland Values," *Wetlands Regulation and Resource Manual for Virginia,* 2d ed. (Richmond: Chesapeake Bay Foundation, 1992), pp. 9–11.

9. The terms *swamp, marsh,* and *bog* are interchangeable. Marshes tend to have stands of course grasses. A pine savanna is low-lying damp or marshy ground in which pines are the prevailing trees. A wet meadow is a low grassland that is near a stream, lake, or other body of water and generally is wet.

have been delineated for the appraiser. The U. S. Army Corps of Engineers considers the following three factors in determining whether a particular area is a wetland: hydrology, vegetation, and soils. The most emphasis is given to soils. Wetlands are associated with any combination of the following factors.

- *Hydrology.* Hydrology refers to the presence of water on or in the soil sufficiently long enough to influence the types of plant life. It is revealed by waterlogged soil; standing or flowing water for seven or more consecutive days during the growing season; drift lines or small piles of debris oriented in the direction of water movement through an area; debris lodged by the water in or against trees or other objects; water marks on trees or other erect objects; and thin layers of sediment deposits on leaves or other plants.

- *Vegetation.* Plants may include cattails, bulrushes, willows, mangroves, and sphagnum moss. Also, trees with shallow root systems, swollen trunks, or roots growing above the ground are good indications of wetlands.

- *Soil.* Hydric soil may be indicated by an abundance of decomposed plant material on the soil's surface; bluish-gray, brownish-black, or black soil 10 to 12 inches below the surface; and an odor like rotten eggs.[10]

Estimating the Value of Wetlands

Generally, wetlands may be expected to have a similar or lower value than floodplains because they are more limited from an agricultural, building construction, and regulatory perspective. One of the methods that may be used in appraising wetlands is the comparative sales analysis method, which was discussed in the prior section, "Appraisal of Floodplains." This method is based on analysis of a reasonable number of similar, recent wetland sales. The usual adjustments are made for such factors as access, size, market conditions, and type of wetlands. Differences in these factors may require adjustments in paired sales analysis. This valuation method is satisfactory if there is a small proportion of upland. It also may be used if there is no requirement to account for the individual land categories of value and the comparable sales and appraised parcels have similar ratios of wetlands and uplands. In valuing wetlands, unlike land with development potential, the presence of public utilities, size and shape, and zoning are less important because the highest and best uses of this type of land are quite limited.

---

10. James H. Boykin and Alfred A. Ring, *The Valuation of Real Estate* (Englewood Cliffs, NJ: Regents/Prentice Hall, 1993), p. 135, citing Richard S. Hawrylak, "What You Should Know About Wetlands," *The Practical Lawyer* (January 1991), pp. 60–61.

Sources of Comparable Sales

Sales of wetlands and floodplain are limited, but, with more commercial wetland banks being created for persons who need to compensate for wetland damage, the number of transactions is increasing. Sources of sales data familiar to appraisers and customarily used for land appraisal assignments include other appraisers and land brokers who specialize in land valuation or brokerage. Other sources of information include timber companies, real estate assessor's offices, municipal planning offices, local and state parks and recreation departments, state game and fish departments, federal agencies such as the U.S. Fish and Wildlife Service, and various land protection groups, such as state outdoors foundations and land trusts and the Nature Conservancy. Environmental consultants often can provide information on land transfers as well.

Sales Comparison Approach

It is not always possible to find land sales that are limited to just one category of land such as wetlands. Appraised parcels are likely to have a mix of land classifications, such as wetlands, floodplain, and upland. Thus, a variation of the second method explained in the "Appraisal of Floodplains" section may be used. This technique, sometimes called *sum-of-the-parts analysis*,[11] is based on the following steps:

- Compile and analyze recent comparable land sales for each land category present in the appraised parcel, making all required adjustments.

- Multiply the number of acres in each land category on the appraised parcel by its corresponding unit value (usually value per acre).

- Sum the value of each land category to find the total estimated value of the appraised parcel.

These steps are illustrated in the following example in which the subject upland is estimated to be worth $10,000 an acre and wetlands are worth $800 an acre. The subject parcel contains a total of 100 acres, of which 80 acres are upland and 20 acres are wetlands. Great care should be taken to avoid overestimating the value of the entire parcel by adding the smaller land components without adjusting downward to reflect the overall large size of the whole parcel. (See the "Court Rulings" section in Chapter 6, which deals with size adjustments.)

The sum-of-the-parts method is expressed in the following equation:

---

11. See discussion of this method and of residual analysis in David Michael Keating, MAI, *The Valuation of Wetlands* (Chicago: Appraisal Institute, 1995), pp. 31–33.

$$V_o = V_w + V_u$$

where

V_o = market value of whole parcel
V_w = market value of wetlands
V_u = market value of uplands

To show the per acre value and acreage of wetlands and uplands, the following equation is used:

$$V_o = (A_w \times V/A_w) + (A_u \times V/A_u)$$

where

V_o = market value of whole parcel
A_w = number of acres of wetlands
V/A_w = market value per acre of wetlands
A_u = number of acres of uplands
V/A_u = market value per acre of uplands

Thus, the subject parcel's overall estimated value is calculated as follows:

$$V_o = (20 \text{ ac.} \times \$800) + (80 \text{ ac.} \times \$10,000)$$
$$V_o = \$16,000 + \$800,000$$
$$V_o = \$816,000 \text{ or } \$8,160 \text{ per acre}$$

If the adjusted sale prices (market value) of comparable land sales have been estimated and the per acre value of uplands has been established, a variation of this equation can be used to compute the value of the appraised parcel's wetlands. (See the previous example used to compute the value of floodplain, which converts to the following equation.)

$$V/A_w = \frac{V_o - (A_u \times V/A_u)}{A_w}$$
$$V/A_w = \frac{\$816,000 - \$800,000}{20}$$
$$V/A_w = \$800$$

Of course, the computation could have been concluded at the total value of the wetlands, which would have been $16,000 ($816,000 − $800,000).

Cost of Mitigation

If wetland destruction cannot be avoided or minimized when land is developed, the U.S. Army Corps of Engineers can allow the property owner four forms of compensatory mitigation. These choices are wetland restoration, creation, enhancement, or preservation. These acts of mitigation are applied to other wetlands to offset the amount of wetlands that have been diminished. *Mitigation* is defined as making a condition less severe or harsh. It may be thought of as a means of alleviating or moderating the negative effects of losing wetlands through human activities. Any of these four actions may

Figure 23.3 *Man-made Wetlands Constructed as Part of a New Shopping Center*

indicate the cost to create or maintain wetlands, but they may not correlate with the value of such lands.

In development situations involving valuable commercial land, the cost to create substitute wetlands may approximate their value. On the other hand, when wetlands are destroyed in connection with a less valuable development or construction project, the landowner will be required to acquire and permanently conserve other wetlands that may cost more than the value of the destroyed wetlands. Although the ratio of acquired wetlands to damaged wetlands may be 1 to 1, it often is a much higher ratio. These acquisitions, while not indicating the market value of a particular damaged wetlands, may be an excellent source of wetlands comparable sales. A created wetland which is part of a newly developed regional shopping center is shown in Figure 23.3.

Summary

A floodplain is the level land adjacent a river, creek, or stream that periodically overflows. This zone sometime is known as *bottomland* and is covered generally with rich soil deposited during floods. Wetlands are defined as areas that are flooded or saturated by surface or groundwater at a frequency and duration that support vegetation typically adapted for life in saturated soil conditions. Some ways in which floodplains may be detected include checking municipal zoning maps, determining floodplain outer limits, interviewing local persons who are familiar with flooding history, and examining FEMA flood insurance rate maps.

Key factors influencing the value of floodplains are access, zoning, frequency and severity of flooding, and availability of flood insurance. Important benefits of wetlands include improved water quality, flood control, groundwater discharge and recharge, shoreline erosion control, food chain support, fish and wildlife preservation, protection of threatened and endangered species, and recreation and aesthetic values. Wetlands are fairly obvious in such places as swamps, marshes, and bogs. They are less obvious when situated in bottomland hardwood forests, pine savannas, and wet meadows. Generally, wetlands may be expected to have similar or lower values than floodplains because they are more limited from agricultural, building construction, and regulatory perspectives.

Contaminated Sites

Causes of contamination, or environmental impairment, always will emanate from a *source property*. This is the property on which a hazardous substance[1] has been released. It is this property owner who bears liability under the Comprehensive Environmental Response, Compensation and Liability Act (CERCLA). Another category of property may also require an appraisal, a *nonsource property*. While no liability attaches to this property, its value may have been eroded severely from the release of an environmentally hazardous substance on another property that has migrated to the nonsource property.

Most of the environmental regulations now in force grew out of the pro-environment movement of the 1970s. The growing concern with polluted rivers, streams, land, and air led to a maze of laws and regulations. The Federal Water Pollution Control Act in 1972 was followed by the Clear Air Act, the Resource Conservation and Recovery Act, Toxic Substance Control Act, and, in 1980, the Comprehensive Environmental Response, Compensation and Liability Act (also known as CERCLA or the Superfund Act). Of all the state and federal laws pertaining to environmental liability, CERCLA is the most significant law governing remediation of hazardous contamination. It provides a broad legal framework for cleaning up contamination. The breadth of these cleanup costs extends to current and past owners of a contaminated property, current and past business operators who occupied the property, entities that disposed of hazardous substances at the property, and entities that transported hazardous substances to the property.

Appraiser's Responsibilities

Ideally an appraiser will commence his or her valuation of an environmentally impaired parcel after having received the results of an inspection by a qualified environmental professional. However, frequently

---

1. A hazardous substance is any material within, around, or near a property that may have a negative impact on its value.

the appraiser is the first real estate professional to inspect an affected property and its immediate neighborhood. Appraisers are trained observers and researchers, so their initial observations of a tract may serve the client by pointing out suspect conditions or identifying prior users or uses of the parcel. Nevertheless, it must always be prominently noted in the appraisal report that the appraiser is not technically trained or experienced in the detection of potential environmental problems. The Appraisal Institute has prepared a property observation checklist for this purpose. (See Appendix H.) Several caveats must be taken into account when an appraiser uses this or a similar environmental checklist:

- A mere "yes" or "no" answer may be insufficient and even misleading. The appraiser should supplement his or her one-word answer with an explanation of both the information on which the response was based and the scope of his or her (or another investigator's) research.

- Questions should be answered only if the appraiser is able to do so competently.

- Before responding to the questions in a checklist, the appraiser should state in the scope of his or her valuation services the extent of his or her inspection and investigation.

Contingent Conditions

In their text on the subject, Colangelo and Miller suggest the following phrasing:

> This is a limited scope appraisal prepared by the appraiser during the course of his/her inspection of the property in preparation of a real estate appraisal. In completing the checklist, only a visual observation was performed. The appraiser did not search title, interview the current or prior owners, or do any research beyond that normally associated with the appraisal process unless otherwise stated. The user of this checklist is reminded that the responses to the questions are being provided by an appraiser who is not trained or qualified to identify potential environmental problems; therefore, it should only be used to assist the users in their own determination of whether an environmental professional is required for further study. Since the appraiser is not an environmental professional, the appraiser cannot be held liable for the lack of detection or identification of possible environmental problems. The appraisal report and/or any environmental checklist must not be considered an environmental assessment of the property, as would be performed by an environmental professional.[2]

Other examples of statements of purpose, final opinion of value, and disclaimers can be found in the Appraisal Institute's Guide Note 8:

> The purpose of this appraisal is to estimate the market value of the subject property, as if unaffected by hazardous substances, as of January 1, 2xxx.

---

2. Robert V. Colangelo and Ronald D. Miller, *Environmental Site Assessments and Their Impact on Property Value: The Appraiser's Role* (Chicago: Appraisal Institute, 1995), p. 24.

The final estimate of the market value of the subject property, as if unaffected by hazardous substances, as of January 1, 2xxx is....

Unless otherwise stated in this report, the existence of hazardous substances, including without limitation asbestos, polychlorinated biphenyls, petroleum leakage, or agricultural chemicals, which may or may not be present on the property were not called to the attention of nor did the appraiser become aware of such during the appraiser's inspection. The appraiser has no knowledge of the existence of such materials on or in the property unless otherwise stated. The appraiser, however, is not qualified to test for such substances. The presence of such hazardous substances may affect the value of the property. The value estimated herein is predicated on the assumption that no such hazardous substances exist on or in the property or in such proximity thereto which would cause a loss in value. No responsibility is assumed for any such hazardous substances, nor for any expertise or knowledge required to discover them.

If the appraiser has received a Phase I, Phase II, or Phase III environmental assessment report indicating no evidence of contamination, then he or she should state so in the appraisal report, giving the name of the firm and the date of assessment. He or she should encourage the client to thoroughly read the environmental assessment. If no Phase I report has been provided to the appraiser and there is no reason to suspect the existence of hazardous substances, it is appropriate for the appraiser to note in his appraisal that no report has been received and the appraisal is based on the assumption that a Phase I assessment would have indicated no contamination. Finally, if an environmental assessment (Phase I, II, and/or III) has been prepared and received by the appraiser and it indicates the possibility of contamination, the client should be encouraged to review the entire environmental assessment and request a higher phase assessment.

The Property Observation Checklist has three sections (see Appendix H.) The first section, "Extent of Appraiser's Inspection of the Property," calls for the appraiser to describe his or her on- and off-site inspection. Section 2 contains 13 questions dealing with possible environmental factors the appraiser may have observed. These questions cover such items as prior or current industrial uses of the property; the presence of suspect containers, stained soil, or distressed vegetation; pits and lagoons; evidence of storage tanks (aboveground or underground); water discharges; indication of dumping or burning; electrical or microwave transmission towers on or near the parcel; rivers, streams, or marshes on the appraised or adjoining properties; and any other factors that might require an investigation by environmental professionals. This section also includes questions about structures, which are pertinent in the appraisal of land where structures either have a contributory value or encumber a parcel's highest and best use. In these instances, the appraiser would be concerned with floors, drains, or walls that are stained or emit unusual odors;

chipped, blistered, or peeled paint; and any sprayed-on insulation or pipe wrapping.

Section 3 concentrates on "Possible Environmental Factors Reported By Others." The client, owner, owner's agent, or any other person may have provided this information. The appraiser is asked to comment on whether he or she has been informed about government records indicating environmentally sensitive sites on the subject or adjoining properties, knowledge of violations of environmental laws on the property, environmental lawsuits concerning the subject property, and tests for lead-based paint or other lead hazards, asbestos-containing materials, radon, or soil or groundwater contamination on the subject property. Finally, the appraiser is asked whether he or she has been informed about other professional environmental site assessment(s) of the subject property.

The following points also could be used as a partial checklist for an appraiser who realizes the limitations of his or her expertise, but nevertheless wants to provide assistance to the client by noting the following possible indicators of environmental degradation:

- Damaged landscaping
- Sickly or dead vegetation
- Discolored or disturbed soil
- Discolored or polluted water
- Depressed areas or pits
- Mounds of dirt
- Drainage ditches
- Discharge/seepage of water or fluids
- Noxious or unusual odors
- Soil borings holes
- Storage tanks—aboveground or underground

Responsibility Concerning Toxic or Hazardous Substance Contamination

The two most authoritative guidelines on how appraisers should deal with the possible presence of hazardous substances on appraised parcels are Advisory Opinion 9 of the 2000 *Uniform Standards of Professional Appraisal Practice* (see Appendix I) and the Appraisal Institute's Guide Note 8, "The Consideration of Hazardous Substances in the Appraisal Process" (see Appendix J).

The USPAP Advisory Opinion concentrates on recognition of contamination, remediation and compliance cost estimation, and value estimates of interests in impacted real estate. It asserts that "recognizing, detecting or measuring contamination is often beyond the scope of the appraiser's expertise." Further, an appraiser, when requested to complete a checklist, should answer only those questions within the scope of his or her expertise. Specialized expertise is required to assess the proper processes and expenditures to remediate environmental damages and comply with state and federal compliance requirements. In some instances an appraiser may be requested to appraise a possibly contaminated parcel as if it is free of contamination. Acceptance of an assignment under such hypothetical conditions is warranted "...when (1) the resulting appraisal is not misleading, (2) the client has been advised of the limitation, and (3) the Ethics Provision of the USPAP is satisfied."[3]

Guide Note 8 points out the growing necessity for appraisers to consider hazardous substances that may impact property value, even to the extent of leaving a property with a negative value after remediation expenses. Because real estate appraisers are not expected or qualified to detect or measure the impact of hazardous substances, this guide note largely alerts appraisers "...to disclose the lack of knowledge or experience to the client, take all steps necessary or appropriate to complete the assignment competently and describe in the report the lack of knowledge or experience and the steps taken to competently complete the assignment."[4] Lacking the required experience or knowledge to analyze the consequences of hazardous substances, an appraiser may associate with a party who possesses the necessary knowledge and experience. It is recommended that the appraiser have the client retain this environmental professional directly.

The proper valuation of parcels that may be adversely affected by hazardous substances obligates the appraiser to consider any possible influence on property value such as on- and off-site factors, changes in highest and best use, and stigma. An appraisal assignment may be accepted and a consideration of hazardous substances may be omitted if the results are not misleading, the client has been advised of this limitation, and the report is qualified to reflect this limitation. In all reports, care must be exercised to prevent misuse and misleading readers. If there are no known hazardous substances on a parcel, then it is advisable for the appraiser to include a limiting condition that the appraisal is based on the assumption that no hazardous substances are present. However, if hazardous substances affect the appraised property or there is cause to suspect their presence, the appraiser cannot exclude a consideration of such material without limiting the scope of the appraisal report.

---

3. Appraisal Standards Board, *Uniform Standards of Professional Appraisal Practice* (Washington, DC: The Appraisal Foundation, 2000), pp. 114–115.

4. Appraisal Institute, "Guide Note 8, The Consideration of Hazardous Substances in the Appraisal Process," amended by the Board of Directors, January 28, 1994.

Unacceptable Appraisal Practices

As noted in Appendix J, Guide Note 8 deems the following actions to be unacceptable in appraising property that requires consideration of hazardous substances:

- Failure to disclose to the client the appraiser's lack of knowledge and experience with respect to the detection and measurement of hazardous substances.

- Failure to take the necessary steps to complete the assignment competently such as personal study by the appraiser, association with another appraiser who has the required knowledge and experience or obtaining the professional assistance of others who possess the required knowledge and experience.

- When appraising an affected property as if unaffected by hazardous substances, failure to include in the report a qualification that reflects the limited scope of the appraisal, a limiting condition that clearly reveals the fact that the property is appraised as if unaffected by hazardous substances, or an appropriate statement of purpose and properly qualified conclusions.

- Failure to report known hazardous substances affecting the property when appraising affected property as if unaffected by hazardous substances.

- Failure to acknowledge the professional assistance of others and to name the persons providing the assistance in the certification when appraising affected property if the appraiser relies on the findings of other professionals with respect to the presence of, and probable effect of, hazardous substances.

Working with Environmental Professionals

Appraisers will want to be familiar with and be able to work with such professionals as environmental lawyers, soil specialists, and environmental engineers. Of course, appraisers always must clearly and fully recognize the contributions of these professionals in their appraisal reports. At times, the services of several environmental specialists may be required in the valuation of contaminated parcels.

Environmental Site Assessment

Evidence of onsite pollutants generally can be detected in a Phase I environmental site assessment. This survey will include a site inspection, review of regulatory agency files, and review of aerial photographs taken over several years. It also includes an initial description of site conditions, including past and present uses of the appraised property and adjacent properties; information on local soil and groundwater conditions; detection of any hazardous substances; charting of probable routes through which these substances may have entered or exited the site; identification of probable sources of hazardous materials affecting the site such as landfills; and an evaluation of all probable risks to humans from site contamination. This assessment is conducted to determine if there is a reasonable basis for an environmental risk and whether these risks, if present, impair the highest and best use of the parcel.

If the Phase I assessment finds that there is a reasonable basis for an environmental risk, a Phase II environmental site assessment may be requested. This phase involves additional research, physical testing, and chemical analysis. The location of any underground storage tanks is determined and they are tested for leakage. Soil and groundwater testing also may be necessary.

A Phase III environmental site assessment is called for if the Phase II assessment reveals an environmental risk. Generally, the Phase III effort includes a cleanup plan. It measures the nature and degree of the environmental risk and prepares an acceptable remediation plan and budget for accomplishing the cleanup.

Stigma

In the context of real estate appraising, *stigma* is defined as the adverse effect on value of environmental-related uncertainty and risk. A purchaser who acquires a parcel that has experienced environmental problems will incur these risks. A prospective buyer or tenant of a previously contaminated property may be concerned about the extent of the contamination, whether its effects have been adequately remediated, and his or her possible financial and legal exposure.

Most stigma losses arise from perceived ownership risks and usually are measured by use of higher capitalization rates. Uncertainty and risk can be reduced if the seller provides a buyer with sufficient warranties or indemnifications. Experience has revealed the following findings: "Properties that are in demand and are hard to find in the market generally experience less stigma than those with many substitutes." "...unimproved land generally suffers a greater stigma loss than improved property." Improved property tends to suffer less stigma loss than vacant land because "...most improved properties have an income stream or some type of value in use that tends to place a floor under its contaminated value."[5]

---

5.   Peter J. Patchin, "Contaminated Properties and the Sales Comparison Approach," *The Appraisal Journal* (July 1994), p. 408.

One may think that if a property was worth $1,000,000 prior to contamination and the cost of remediation was $200,000, then the post-contamination value would be $800,000. However, if it is worth only $500,000 afterward, then the $300,000 loss is the result of stigma ($800,000 − $500,000). The additional $300,000 loss in value is due to prospective buyers who will discount the remediated value because of their concern about any lingering contamination problems that they may be forced to cure. As market participants' concern over safety and the financial risk of ownership and use of a remediated parcel abates over a period of time, the amount of buyer price or rent discount diminishes.

Specifying the Problem

As is true in any real estate appraisal assignment, it is necessary to specify the nature and scope of the problem. Usually this is rather straightforward when a client has retained an appraiser to report his or her estimate of the subject property's current market value. However, an assignment involving an environmentally contaminated parcel may be considerably more complex than an ordinary appraisal. Through property inspection and familiarity with the parcel and its environs, the appraiser may observe certain signs that a parcel is contaminated. To analyze the probable adverse impact of contamination, the appraiser will need the expertise of an environmental engineer or a similar professional. If the client did not hire an environmentalist before engaging the services of the appraiser, he or she should do so before the appraiser continues his work. Without an understanding of the nature and extent of the contamination and remediation or the cost estimated for cleanup, it is premature for the appraiser to estimate the impact of contamination on the property's value.

Some of the pollutants that may be discovered on a parcel include oil, gasoline, toxic substances, chemicals, asbestos, nuclear waste, animal feces (from poultry and hog operations), septic tank cleansers, creosote (from wood treatment plants), fertilizers, polychlorinated biphenyls (PBCs used in electrical transformers), and sanitary landfills. Figure 24.1 illustrates the appropriate steps in the investigative, risk evaluation, estimate of direct cost, and determination of the risk premium phases of analysis.

Contaminated Property Market Data

The United States Environmental Protection Agency (EPA) is a starting point in the search for information on contaminated sites. Visit the EPA's Web site at http://www.epa.gov. One part of this search should be a map search called "Environmental Profiles," which can telescope down from a particular state and county to the preferred location by clicking the mouse. Alternatively, zip codes may be used to locate a given neighborhood.

Figure 24.1   *Value Estimation Model for Environmental Contamination*

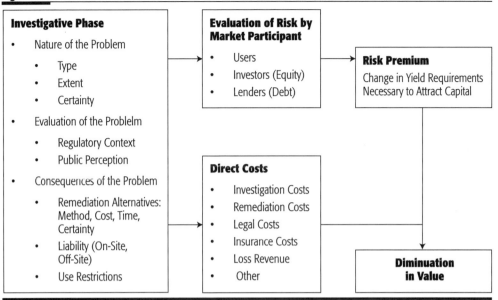

Source: James A. Chalmers and Thomas O. Jackson, "Risk Factors in the Appraisal of Contaminated Property," *The Appraisal Journal* (January 1996), p. 46.

Another EPA source is its "EnviroMapper," which has an easy-to-use zoom and location feature. An example of one of these maps is shown in Figure 24.2. This Dayton, Ohio map shows three waste-handler sites on Dorothy Road and another near the western terminus of Cardington, with a Superfund site at the end of that road. Other features are shown in the legend. Another source of maps from the EPA website is its Envirofacts' "Maps on Demand" feature. This

Figure 24.2   *EPA-Identified Environmental Problem Sites*

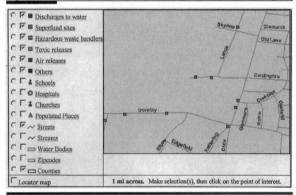

Source: US Environmental Protection Agency Internet Web site http://www.epa.gov

feature allows an appraiser to customize a computer-generated map of a specific, small area with the information sought. Once the requirements are specified on the computer, there is a turnaround time of one to 24 hours, depending on the map's complexity. The computer will e-mail the appraiser when the map is ready to be downloaded or printed. Another database is the Envirofacts Warehouse, which has lists of facilities in different localities that are releasing pollutants or legally handling hazardous materials; the locations of Superfund sites and their cleanup status; and, in some cases, information about the chemicals involved at the listed sites and whether they are potentially harmful.

Past uses of a comparable sale parcel can reveal whether it was contaminated. For instance, it may have been used for chemical storage, wood preservation processes, bulk fuel storage, a sanitary landfill, a dry cleaning operation, or a service station site. Persons familiar with the parcel can be helpful. These may include neighborhood residents or business owners, former owners, and real estate agents familiar with the parcel and neighborhood. Agents may also remember sales that fell through because of contamination problems. Patchin holds "...that the deal that did not happen is often as important as the deal that did happen."[6] That is, an unconsummated sale may provide information on the listing price before contamination was discovered.

In addition to the EPA, state and local environmental agencies may be able to provide useful information on the history of a property, its former uses, and the extent of the contamination and cleanup efforts.

Measures of Impaired Value

Rent Loss

Rent loss is a gauge of tenant resistance to leasing contaminated property. Another consequence of contamination is diminished demand in the form of reduced tenant occupancy. Many tenants are unwilling to lease such property at any price. Even when rented, income is reduced as a result of increased operating expenses. Ongoing monitoring and remediation will further reduce the net operating income. Also, it may cost more to market an affected parcel.

Remediation

The term *remediation* essentially means to provide a remedy, cure, or relief. Remediation, as associated with environmentally contaminated property, includes testing, cleanup, disposal of contaminated soil, and post-cleanup monitoring. In some instances, contaminated parcels have negative value because the cleanup costs exceed the uncontaminated value. Severely contaminated sites have virtually no marketability due to the threat of continuing future legal and financial liability that a buyer assumes plus the availability of unimpaired parcels. Future liability (and increased operating costs) includes the cost of monitoring contamination levels with wells, instrumentation, and testing.

Indemnification Costs

An *indemnity* is a financial warranty a seller of a contaminated property provides stating that a buyer will be relieved of any future costs and liabilities attributed to the specified contamination. An appraiser should

---

6.   Patchin, p. 403.

determine if indemnification exists for a property known to be contaminated and obtain assurance at to whether the indemnification has value. Patchin has found that, to have value, a financially secure organization must issue the indemnity. Only large insurance or bonding companies and governmental bodies generally meet this requirement. Insurance companies probably will not underwrite indemnity insurance for parcels with a history of contamination. Local governments may issue an indemnity to encourage the creation of jobs and increase tax revenue by putting unproductive parcels back into use.[7]

Increased Marketing Time

Typically, the amount of time required to market a contaminated parcel increases with the severity of the problem, publicity, and the immediacy of the public's awareness of the contamination. Once the public learns that the problem is not as acute as initially publicized, time has passed, remedial action has been taken, or perhaps some development and construction has occurred, the pace of property leasing or sales improves. The additional marketing time necessary to sell off the product costs the investor through added debt service and slower rental and sales activity. Both of these factors depress the value of a parcel and such losses can be reflected in the discounted cash flow valuation method. Revenue during the marketing phase of land development is also deferred while the cleanup takes place. Comparatively little revenue will be earned during the cleanup stage.

Valuation Techniques

Comparable Sales Method

Arguably the most reliable and most often used method of valuing land is the comparative analysis of recent, similar land sales. Two sources of difficulty in applying this valuation approach to contaminated parcels are the lack of these transfers and the ability of appraisers to detect with a high degree of certainty the value distinctions among affected sales and an appraised parcel. An environmental specialist can more accurately discern the implications of the nature and severity of contamination for each parcel. The appraiser then must analyze this information to judge its value implications.

If the problem is acute, then the likelihood of a sale occurring is fairly remote. In fact, if sales of contaminated parcels have occurred, it will be necessary to determine at what stage of contamination or remediation they occurred. It may have been prior to discovery of contaminants; post-

---

7.   Peter J. Patchin, "Valuation of Contaminated Properties," *The Appraisal Journal* (January 1988), pp. 10-11.

discovery but prior to approval of a remediation plan; after remediation costs have been estimated; or after remediation has been completed. Other problems in using this valuation approach are buyers' inability to provide complete information on the nature and extent of the contamination and the complicated nature of these parcel sales. Thus, the information needed for a comparative analysis derived from land sales may be incomplete and misleading. The appraiser should consider analyzing sales of parcels that sold prior to becoming contaminated and then resales of the same parcels after having been contaminated. Adjustments may be required for off-site market influences as well as changes in value between the sale date and appraisal date. This sale-resale type of analysis becomes even more useful when the extent of the contamination and remediation costs can be determined reliably.

Due to the considerable disparity in the nature and degree of contamination, its remediation cost, and market reaction to a previously contaminated parcel, a more reliable indication of a subject parcel's market value may be achieved through a variation of the market comparison approach. This more reliable estimate can be accomplished by comparatively analyzing the pre-contamination values of the comparable sales; identifying, if possible, the areas of remediation and the accompanying costs; and then accounting for any stigma effect. The resulting adjustments may appear as follows:[8]

Pre-contamination value		$1,000,000
Remediation cost	– $350,000	
Additional vacancy loss	– 20,000	
Additional financing cost	– 10,000	
Additional insurance cost	– 5,000	
Stigma effect	– 70,000	455,000
Post-contamination value		$545,000

Single-Year Capitalized Income

In judging the value of a contaminated parcel, several options are available. One approach is to estimate an overall capitalization rate through interviews with informed investors and corporate real estate department managers. This rate can then be applied to the estimated net operating income of a parcel once allowance has been made for all relevant ongoing, usual expenses and those unique to a contaminated parcel. In any attempt to measure the value consequences of contamination, two factors must be noted. First, the cleanup cost estimate will already have been made or will

---

8.   For a more detailed discussion on this topic, see Scott B. Arens, "The Valuation of Defective Properties: A Common Sense Approach," *The Appraisal Journal* (April 1997), pp. 143–148.

need to be made by an environmental engineer because the appraiser is not capable of making this determination. Most important to the appraiser's valuation are the extent of the cleanup, the nature of the contamination, and the perceived ownership liability of prospective purchasers. Second, the stage of remediation at which the appraisal occurs must be noted. Timing is important because it identifies the facts that may be available for analysis by the appraiser. Also, market participants react differently to a contaminated parcel at each stage (discovery, remediation, and post-remediation). Different price discounts apply as prospective participants' risk perceptions of a parcel change. The following example illustrates this method:

Net land rental before contamination		$100,000
Land cap rate before contamination	8%	
Land value before contamination	($100,000/8%)	$1,250,000
Net land rental after contamination	$80,000	
Land cap rate after contamination	10%	
Land value after contamination	($80,000/10%)	$800,000
Value loss (damages) due to contamination		$450,000

In some situations, the pre-contamination land value may not be an issue. Even if it is not, the appraiser should know as much as possible about the appraised parcel, including any prior leases on it.

Mortgage Equity Capitalization Approach

A variation of the comparable sales method is the *mortgage equity capitalization approach*. This method offers certain advantages over the previous approach, but is used primarily for improved leased properties. Derivation of an overall capitalization rate requires information on current equity and debt investors' attitudes and practices toward environmentally contaminated property. Several surveys have been published that reveal these attitudes, but the survey results are inconsistent and appear to vary for different sections of the country.

Some lenders will not make loans on contaminated property even with an indemnification agreement or if it has been certified clean. Other mortgage lenders are not as concerned about previously contaminated parcels. One of the surveys indicates that lenders sometimes require additional indemnification, personal guarantees, lower loan-to-value ratios, and higher interest rates. When developing capitalization rates, either for the band-of-investment or mortgage equity methods, the most dependable method of determining loan terms is to inquire of local lenders who loan funds on contaminated parcels similar to the one being appraised. Some lenders will not originate any type of land loans except for individual house construction.

Equity investors may require much higher yield rates for contaminated parcels than for similar, unaffected parcels. The best source of this information usually will be investor surveys. In their interviews Chalmers and Jackson found that equity investors required overall yields "...as much as 30% or more for a serious contamination problem relative to the unimpaired value of the property, and with less than 'bulletproof' indemnifications."[9]

The mortgage equity capitalization approach permits analysis of the expectations of both the equity and debt positions in regard to environmentally unimpaired and impaired parcels. The appraiser may use the Ellwood or Ellwood without algebra (Akerson) methods or employ mortgage equity computer software. The following examples will illustrate how the values may be estimated. This method is familiar and it has been used for many years in eminent domain appraising to measure the extent of damages to properties affected by partial takings.

There are problems in applying this method to unimproved land. There may be no foreseeable income stream for the land. Alternatively, market conditions may support an interim use of the land, agricultural uses, possibly a long-term land lease, or even subdivision of the parcel into a number of building sites. These future sites may be for residential, commercial, or resort activities. It usually is difficult to secure financing for land unless a specific end product is planned. If it is a single improvement, the loan likely will be a short-term acquisition and construction loan. A line-of-credit loan may be used for one year or less and for a longer-term loan of up to three years with annual renewals. This type of debt funding or a loan collateralized by the land probably will be interest-only, with a balloon payment at the end of the loan term. Unimpaired and impaired parcel valuations are outlined in the following examples.

The valuation methodology demonstrated may be thought of as having three tiers. The first tier is similar to the band-of-investment method of developing an overall capitalization rate, except it uses equity yield instead of the equity dividend rate. The second tier allows for equity buildup via mortgage amortization. Finally, the third tier accounts for anticipated changes in the property value. These steps are outlined below, where:

L/V is mortgage loan-to-property value ratio

R_M is mortgage annual constant rate

E/V is equity-to-property value ratio

Y_E is equity yield rate

SFF is sinking fund factor at yield rate for projection period

9. James A. Chalmers and Scott A. Roehr, "Risk Factors in the Appraisal of Contaminated Property," *The Appraisal Journal* (January 1996), p. 52.

p is percent of loan paid off at end of projection period

ΔV is projected change in value for projection period

Tier 1	$L/V \times R_M$
	$+ E/V \times Y_E$
Tier 2	$- L/V \times SFF \times p$
Tier 3	$- \Delta V \times SFF$

Unimpaired Condition Valuation

Annual net operating income from 5-year ground lease:	$20,000
Land loan terms:	50% loan to value, 8% interest only with a 7-year balloon, monthly installments
Equity investor expectation:	15% annual yield
Expected change in land value over 5-year projection period:	+20%
$0.50 \times 0.08 =$	0.0400
$+ 0.50 \times 0.15 =$	0.0750
	0.1150
$- 0.50 \times 0.1483 \times 0 =$	0.0000
	0.1150
$- 0.20 \times 0.1483 =$	0.0297
$R_L =$	0.0853
$V_L =$	$234,466, say $234,500

Impaired Condition Valuation

In the post-contamination phase, an investor would expect a yield of 25%, the loan interest would rise to 10%, the net operating income would decline to $15,000, and the value would be expected to decline 10%. The resulting land value under this premise is calculated as follows:

$0.50 \times 0.10 =$	0.05000
$+ 0.50 \times 0.25 =$	0.12500
	0.1750
$- 0.50 \times 0.1218 \times 0 =$	0.0000
	0.1750
$+ 0.10 \times 0.1218 =$	0.0122
$R_L =$	0.1872
$V_L =$	$80,128, say $80,000
Damages due to contamination ($234,500 − $80,000) =	$154,500

Discounted Cash Flow Analysis

The unimpaired and impaired values of a parcel may be estimated using the discounted cash flow (DCF) method if the parcel's highest and best use lends itself to this approach. That is, it may be used if the parcel's highest and best use supports it being subdivided into several sites. This method is illustrated in Table 24.1. The unimpaired value of the 40-acre parcel is $1,000,000. In estimating the value of the impaired tract, the lot development rate is 30 in Year 1, 50 in Year 2, and 15 in Year 3. Several adjustments were required. Due to subdivision redesign, five lots were lost, lot prices were lowered, miscellaneous expenses were increased to 15% to allow for periodic monitoring of any residual contamination, loan interest was raised 100 basis points to 10.0%, and the developer's yield was raised from 30% to 35%. These adjustments resulted in an impaired value of $700,000, a reduction of $300,000 from the pre-contamination value.

Table 24.1   ***Present Value of Proposed Subdivision***

	Year 1	Year 2	Year 3	Year 4
Lot sales:				
8 @ $37,500	$300,000			
28 @ $40,000		$1,120,000		
39 @ $42,000			$1,638,000	
20 @ $45,000				$900,000
Less:				
Development costs:				
1. Streets & drainage				
@ $6,000/lot	$180,000	$300,000	$90,000	
2. Sewer lines				
@ $3,500/lot	105,000	175,000	52,500	
3. Water system				
@ $2,500/lot	75,000	125,000	37,500	
4. Engineering & surveying				
@ $1,500/lot	45,000	75,000	22,500	
Miscellaneous expenses*	54,000	90,000	27,000	6,500
Loan interest & points				
@10.0%†	45,900	76,500	22,950	650
Sales commission/ management				
@6%	18,000	67,200	98,280	54,000
Marketing & promotion	15,000	25,000	20,000	10,000
Total expenses	$537,900	$933,700	$370,730	$71,150
Net sales revenue	($237,900)	$186,300	$1,267,270	$828,850
Discounted @ 35%	($176,222)	$102,222	$515,072	$249,540
Total present value of 40-acre tract:				$690,612
rounded to				$700,000

* 15% of items 1, 2, and 3 to allow for rock, hardpan, inspection fees, bonds, real estate taxes, soil studies, closing costs, contamination monitoring, etc. except in Year 4, which is limited to real estate taxes and closing costs.

† The loan funds all development and miscellaneous expenses.

Contingent Valuation Method

The contingent valuation method (CVM) is an alternative valuation methodology that may offer a reasoned approach to measuring the diminished value of contaminated properties according to Chalmers and Roehr.[10] They point out that appraisers are accustomed to interviewing parties who are familiar with market behavior. These same interview techniques can be applied to valuing contaminated properties, especially when there is a dearth of similar contaminated land sale transactions. The contingent value method expands on the usual valuation interview methodology in using more formalized "...procedures to select interviewees, to determine the number of interviewees, and to set other interview conditions. Also, ...much effort has been expended to develop questioning techniques in terms of a hypothetical choice that will have maximum reliability for actual choices."[11]

10.   Chalmers and Roehr, "Issues in the Valuation of Contaminated Property," *The Appraisal Journal* (January 1993), p. 37.

11.   Ibid., p. 38.

Cummings quotes Randall's definition of the contingent valuation method as "asking individuals, in survey or experimental settings, to reveal their personal valuations of increments (or decrements) in unpriced goods by using contingent markets.... Contingent markets are highly structured to confront respondents upon the occurrence of the posited situation."[12] The CVM method essentially asks a respondent, "If a certain event occurred, how much would you be willing to pay?" Criticism of the method, particularly among economists, seems to relate to the reliability and accuracy of the responses given. The more hypothetical the question, the less incentive for accurate responses.[13] A familiar example of this method is found in the U.S. Bureau of the Census, *Annual Housing Survey and Census of Population*, which asks for an estimate of value under a hypothetical situation: "What is the value of this property, that is, how much *do you think* this property would sell for if it were for sale?"[14]

In the case of contaminated land, not only must the value situation be defined clearly, but the respondents should be chosen from persons who have considerable knowledge of the implications of the contamination and are financially qualified to acquire such property. It may be difficult to find fully informed prospective buyers of contaminated property because the underlying circumstances are complex. Thus, a respondent may require technical assistance in explaining the degree of risk before being able to respond to the survey.

Summary

Most of the environmental regulations now in force grew out of the pro-environment movement of the 1970s. The growing concern with polluted rivers, streams, land, and air led to a maze of laws and regulations. Of all the laws pertaining to environmental liability, the most significant law governing remediation of hazardous contamination is CERCLA. It provides a broad legal framework for cleaning up contamination.

Frequently appraisers are the first real estate professionals to inspect a property and its immediate neighborhood. Thus, their initial observations of a tract may serve the client by pointing out suspect conditions or identifying prior users or uses of a parcel. Nevertheless, it must always be noted prominently in the appraisal report that the appraiser is not technically trained or experienced in the detection of potential environmental problems.

---

12. R. G. Cummings, D. S. Brookshire, and W. D. Schulze and contributors, *Valuing Environmental Goods: An Assessment of the Contingent Valuation Method* (Totowa, NJ: Rowman & Allanheld, 1986), p. 3.

13. Cummings, et al, p. 5.

14. Cummings, et al, Table 11.1, p. 167.

To value parcels that may be adversely affected by hazardous substances, the appraiser must consider any possible influence on property value such as on- and off-site factors, changes in highest and best use, and stigma. Evidence of on-site pollutants generally can be detected in a Phase I environmental site assessment. A Phase II environmental site assessment involves additional research, physical testing, and chemical analysis. A Phase III environmental site assessment includes a cleanup plan. In the context of real estate, stigma is defined as the adverse effect on value of environmental-related uncertainty and risk. A purchaser who acquires a parcel that has experienced environmental problems will incur these risks.

Past uses of a comparable sale parcel can reveal whether it was contaminated. For instance, it may have been used for chemical storage, wood preservation processes, bulk fuel storage, a sanitary landfill, a dry cleaning operation, or a service station site. Impaired value may be measured by considering rent loss, remediation, indemnification costs, and increased marketing time.

Valuation methods include the comparable sales method; a single-year capitalization rate applied to the pre- and post-contamination condition; the mortgage equity capitalization approach, which permits analysis of the expectations of both the equity and debt positions in environmentally unimpaired and impaired parcels; discounted cash flow analysis (if the parcel's highest and best use lends itself to this approach); and the contingent valuation method. The last method employs interviews, especially when there is a lack of similar contaminated land sales. In the case of contaminated land, the value situation must be defined clearly and respondents should have some knowledge of the implications of the contamination and be qualified to acquire such property.

Eminent Domain: Partial Takings

Before discussing partial takings under the power of eminent domain, this chapter will review the legal concept of bundle of rights, which is defined as all the rights of ownership inherent in fee title to real property. This bundle includes the right either to use or not to use a property, the right to lease all or part of the property (rights or physical division), and the right to sell or to convey property interests to other parties via a will, life estate, or other means. The full enjoyment of these property rights is limited by certain public and private constraints, such as the police power of government and the right of eminent domain.

Police power is the sovereign power of government to restrict the use of a property to protect the well-being of its citizens. The police powers of a community are exercised through planning, zoning, building codes, and traffic and subdivision controls. *Eminent domain* allows a government or its agency to acquire all or part of a parcel for the common benefit of its citizens by due process of law. Reasonable compensation to the owner is required but consent is not necessary for the acquisition. *Condemnation* is the process that authorized units of government and public utility companies use to take private property for public benefit upon payment of just compensation to the property owner.

This chapter focuses on partial takings in which there is severance of the property rights. The full acquisition of a property under eminent domain is no different than appraising for other purposes such as for a sale or mortgage loan.

Distinction Between Compensable and Nocompensable Actions

The government exercise of its police powers for the protection of the general health, safety, morals and welfare of citizens is not a compensable action. Generally, when the safety of citizens is protected by installing a traffic control such as a median strip in a street, creating a one-way street, prohibiting left turns, or creating a cul-de-sac by closing a road, compensation is not paid to the property owner. Also, compensation seldom is paid to an owner when no property is taken and traffic is diverted to relocate a highway (sometimes referred to as *circuitous travel*). On the other hand, when there is a physical taking of a property or property rights via eminent domain, the affected property owner is entitled to compensation from the condemning agency. This payment is called *just compensation*.

Just compensation is provided for in the Fifth and Fourteenth Amendments to the U.S. Constitution. The logic behind the payment of just compensation is to make the affected property owner financially whole. It would be virtually impossible to replace the property taken with other equivalent property so a monetary award is substituted. The amount awarded the property owner should offset any loss in value to the property resulting from the eminent domain action. This objective of making the condemnee financially whole is also the goal if the appraisal report. The value should be the same whether the appraiser is representing the condemnor or the condemnee.

Basis for Payment of Just Compensation

The two elements of just compensation are payment for that part of a property physically acquired as part of a public project, such as construction of a highway, and payment for any loss in value to the remainder property. The principal causes for loss in value to the remainder are diminished utility and reduction of the highest and best use from the use enjoyed prior to the taking. Some specific causes for loss in value discussed in this chapter are odd-shaped remainders, superadequate remainder improvements, isolated remainders, land-locked remainders, road grade change, and impaired access. This chapter also discusses how to properly appraise the value of trees and landscaping in partial takings and how an appraiser should prepare and present expert testimony.

Valuation Procedure

There are two basic valuation procedures used to estimate the total just compensation due to a landowner in partial takings. The federal rule, used in some states, is known as the *before and after rule*. It holds that the measure of just compensation is the difference between the value of the whole property before the taking and the value of the remainder after the taking. Under this set-off rule, special benefits are allowed to offset both the value of the land acquired by the condemnor and any damages to the residue. Thus, it is possible that the landowner may receive no compensation even though a condemnor has taken property. In some states, however, special benefits may be applied only against damages to the residue. In still other states, the law is unclear as to which value elements benefits may be applied against. It is essential that an appraiser understand clearly if the federal before and after rule applies or if a modified before and after rule is applicable.

The second valuation procedure described in this section pertains to partial takings of property under the modified before and after premise. The following steps may be used to estimate the total just compensation that a property owner should receive.

1. Estimate the value of the whole property based on market evidence. The whole property, sometimes called the *larger* or *greater parcel*, is a continuous, unbroken tract under the same ownership. This value estimate is not influenced by the effect of the proposed facility on property use.

2. Estimate the value of the part taken. This includes any fee acquisition and permanent and temporary easements. The usual method applied is the equal-unit-value method. This method assigns the same unit value used in the estimated value of the whole property. For example, assume that 0.50 acre is acquired from a property containing 5.0 acre and worth $20,000 per acre. The value of the part taken would be 0.50 acre times $20,000, or $10,000.

3. Deduct the value estimated in Step 2 from the value estimated in Step 1. This amount represents the value of the remainder, without any consideration of enhancement (special benefits) or severance damages resulting from the proposed public improvement.

4. Estimate the value of the remainder parcel, taking into account the value influence of the proposed improvement and the utility of the remainder.

5. Estimate damages to the remainder, if any. This calculation is made by comparing the values estimated in Steps 3 and 4. If the value reported in Step 4 is less than shown in Step 3, severance damages have occurred. If the value in Step 4 exceeds the value in Step 3, there are no damages and the landowner's just compensation is the amount estimated in Step 2.

6. Compute the total just compensation, if there are damages, by adding the value of the part taken (Step 2) to the severance damages suffered by the remainder (Step 5).

These steps are illustrated in the following example, which is based on the commercial property shown in Figure 25.1.

1.	Value of the whole property	$500,000
2.	Less value of the part taken	100,000
3.	Equals value of remainder, unaffected by taking	$400,000
4.	Value of remainder as affected by taking	350,000
5.	Severance damages due to impaired highest and best use	$50,000
6.	Total just compensation (item 2 + item 5)	$150,000

Odd-Shaped Remainders

Frequently, odd-shaped residue parcels are a product of highway construction. A fundamental question that the appraiser must raise is, "What can be done with this remainder?" Imbedded in this question are other related queries such as: What is the highest and best use? Does the parcel fulfill the requisite setback and minimum area requirements for this use? If public utilities are not available, will the site permit installation of a well and septic system with ample distance between the well and drain field, and is there ample area for a reserve drain field, as required by the locality? and How strong is demand for the remainder site? The demand for an irregular-shaped parcel often comes from an adjoining owner who can use the site for additional parking, storage, advertising, maintaining a clear view of the business for travelers, or achieving density requirements for the present or prospective uses. Typically, these parcels suffer a loss in value.

The highest and best use of the remainder will be influenced strongly by its shape and its ability to meet the zoning ordinance requirements. Once highest and best use is determined, it is necessary to consider if the parcel will need to be rezoned to achieve this use and if it is likely that rezoning will be allowed. Whatever the outcome of this analysis, the appraiser must obtain recent land sales that are reasonably similar in shape and highest and best use.

One prospect available when appraising remainder parcels like the one shown in Figure 25.2 is to locate regular-shaped sales and then make an adjustment to reflect either the additional land at the rear (Lot 1) or proportionately more road frontage (Lot 2). Any

Figure 25.1 *Strip Taking for Street Widening Project*

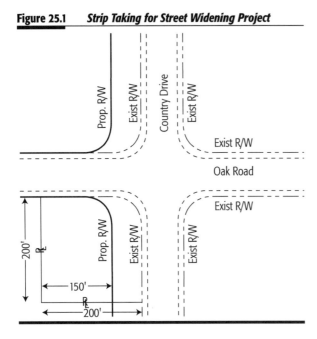

adjustment should be market-derived, but a relatively higher unit value would be assigned to the lot with the triangular base on the street. A proportionately lower value would apply to a site that had its triangular base at the rear of the lot. For example, 65% of the regular-shaped lot's value would apply to the triangular part with its base fronting the street and perhaps 35% of the normal unit price would be assigned to the triangular-shaped part with its base along the rear property line.

Figure 25.2 *Lots with Different Frontage and Rear Dimensions*

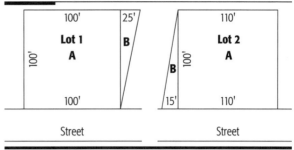

Lot 1			Lot 2		
(A) 100 feet @ $1,000		= $100,000	(A) 110 feet @ $1,000		= $110,000
(B) 25 feet @ $1,000 × .35	=	8,750	(B) 15 feet @ $1,000 × .65	=	9,750
Total value of Lot 1		$108,750	Total value of Lot 2		$119,750

Diminished Size and Road Frontage

Diminished size and road frontage damages occur when the functional balance between the parcel size and the size of prospective improvements on the parcel is disturbed. Although the site is vacant, the nature and amount of the right-of-way taking may leave the remainder parcel too small or narrow to satisfy its former highest and best use. A modern three-bay service station operation can be used to illustrate this situation. A 200-ft. by 200-ft. site has sufficient parking, braking space, and turning radius for prospective customers' vehicles. A street widening project reduces the frontage of this corner site to 150 feet, greatly reducing parking for vehicles being serviced, limiting the turning space for cars, and diminishing the space for underground fuel storage tanks. After the taking, the reduced site is incapable of supporting its former highest and best use. Consequently, its value is reduced sharply. In fact, the site will no longer support an auto service operation and the gasoline trade will also be reduced significantly. Further proof of the after value can be obtained through analysis of similarly zoned, narrow sale sites. Also, study of former service stations that have reverted to lesser uses such as repair shops and small engine repair businesses will further corroborate the diminished value due to loss of road frontage.

Isolated Remainders

Damages to a remainder can also be caused by an isolated remainder, as in the case of a large operating dairy farm. Over the years, a farm owner has increased his herd with a proportionate increase in barns, silos, milking parlors, and implement sheds. A proposed limited-access interstate highway will sever this 600-acre farm. Prior to the right-of-way acquisition, the farm's pastures and cropland supported 200 cows[1]; afterward, there was only enough accessible acreage to support 100 cows. The dairy-related buildings were affected negatively in this same proportion. The apparent damages due to excessive operational capacity totaled $250,000.

In an attempt to minimize the loss to the farmer, the appraiser asked the state highway department to price the cost of building a cattle tunnel under the interstate highway. The $83,000 cost of this facility (a 200-ft. long, 5-ft. by 7-ft. concrete box culvert with concrete wing walls) was much less than the initial value loss to the remainder. If access to the land-locked remainder was needed for farm equipment, then this cost to cure damage estimate would be insufficient to compensate the landowner fully. In this situation, the condemnor may request that the appraiser provide two appraisals—one that shows the total just compensation without the cattle tunnel and another that includes the added costs and lower amount of damages. Then, the condemnor's agents can negotiate with the owner on the basis of the least expensive basis.

Landlocked Remainders

A severe form of severance damage occurs when a parcel is severed in such a way that it becomes landlocked. The only access to and from a landlocked parcel is over the lands of other, adjoining property owners. The acquisition greatly diminishes the utility of the property.

A landlocked remainder's value is diminished because the land is no longer contiguous with the original larger parcel. Who would want to buy a landlocked tract? Without access to the parcel or the possibility of gaining an easement for access purposes, most people would not be interested.

The market for landlocked tracts is limited essentially to one or more adjoining property owners. The degree of motivation must be considered when viewing this limited number of prospective buyers. The value of the remainder parcel declines in inverse relationship to the number of adjoining owners. A landlocked parcel has a certain nuisance value if one

---

1. Depending on the soil and climatic conditions, 2½ acres of pasture may be required to support a mature dairy cow weighing approximately 1,500 pounds and 1 acre of cropland per cow is needed to produce corn silage, which is stored in silos.

adjoining property owner is fearful about how another owner may use it. However, if there is only one adjoining owner who has no intention of granting access to the landlocked parcel, then there is little incentive for him or her to purchase the land. He or she can continue using it as a buffer. It may be worth more to him or her if it has a beneficial use, permitting timber harvesting or business expansion onto the land.

As estimate of value is best achieved by locating sales of similar landlocked parcels or properties with severe terrain or wetlands which cannot be accessed readily or used for any economic purpose. Insight can be gained by studying highway before and after sales of land affected by right-of-way construction and severance, even if the parcels are of a different type with different zoning. For example, if there is a pattern of landlocked parcels selling for 30%–40% of their former unit price, this price relationship can be used to temper the value indication derived by other means. Similarly, landlocked sales may be compared to nearby unencumbered land sales to derive the percentage of price reduction.

Impaired Access

There are several possible scenarios concerning impaired access for a remainder property. This issue generally relates to limited-access highways such as interstate highways or urban expressways. In one situation a limited access road may traverse the rear of a property. The owner is not deprived of road access because none existed before the construction. A second example is the construction of a limited-access road that severs a parcel, leaving part of it landlocked. A third situation occurs when a property loses frontage on an existing primary road and, after construction of the limited-access highway, is left with access on a service road. Several factors enter into this after-value equation. What is the highest and best use now versus the use before the taking? Has the remainder been enhanced in value due to its proximity to a new interchange and increased traffic flow on the mainline road? How does the traffic flow on the proposed service road compare to traffic on the previous road frontage? In some states, neither circuity of travel caused by dividing a highway or rerouting of traffic are considered legally compensable damages.

The following example is based on an appraisal and demonstrates how impaired access can reduce the value of a remainder parcel. The subject property is on Route 1, a two-lane road. The highest and best use of the property prior to the acquisition was to hold the property until there is ample demand for additional retail activities, public water and sewer are available, and the narrow, two-lane road is upgraded. Zoning was tourist commercial. A new highway, Route 2, is planned. After construction of Route 2, the existing Route 1 will become a service road along the northwestern line of Route 2.

Another service road will be constructed on the opposite side of Route 2. The distance from the subject remainder property to the nearest intersection will be approximately 5,400 feet, or 1.02 mile.

The average daily traffic volume on Route 1 in front of the subject parcel was 8,130 vehicles in the year of the appraisal. A traffic consulting firm survey conducted on behalf of the condemnor projected a daily traffic flow on Route 2 of 12,700, which is expected to increase to 19,000 vehicles a day in 10 years. The projected traffic flow per day on the service road once the road is open to traffic is estimated to be 3,700 vehicles. Thus, the amount of traffic directly in front of the property will decrease 54%, but it will increase 56% on Route 2 over the present Route 1.

The appraiser concluded that the remainder has essentially the same proposed uses as it had previously. It will benefit from the increased traffic flow along the new Route 2. However, it will not be as attractive as it was prior to the road construction because it will not be as accessible. It will take prospective customers longer to reach the remainder site. Thus, the remainder was estimated to have suffered a 35% loss in value.

Grade Change

A change in road grade occurs when a proposed highway is to be built either below or above the existing grade of an appraised property. Whether a change of grade is compensable is a controversial topic. The prevailing judicial view holds that an owner of an affected property can receive payment for damages due to a grade change. However, before an appraiser can estimate the extent of damages experienced, if any, he or she must determine if the grade change has diminished the highest and best use of the remainder property. For some uses, such as agricultural, it is possible that no damages occur as a result of a grade change.

Of course, the extent of the grade change will determine the amount of diminished utility and value experienced by a remainder parcel. The highest and best use and present activities on a site will influence the amount of damages, if any, resulting from a change in grade. Residential uses, which benefit from privacy and minimized traffic noise, would suffer less value loss from abutting a depressed roadbed than an elevated one. Commercial users generally prefer being either at road grade or slightly below it to gain an advertising advantage and visual exposure to vehicular traffic. Any value change should be judged from an analysis of similar sales. In some instances, a cost-to-cure approach may be used. A qualified engineer can estimate the cost to provide access to the site and any additional site preparation costs caused by the grade change.

Because highway construction generally will not have begun when the appraisal is conducted, the appraiser must rely on the right-of-way plans, especially the profile sheets which will show the extent of the grade change once the road has been constructed. Figures 25.3 and 25.4 illustrate the adverse effects of a change of grade. Assume that the appraised parcel is the land situated between the existing roads (right and left) in Figure 25.3, and the secondary right of way at the top and an existing subdivision at the bottom of the figure. The developer-owner planned to develop the tract as a continuation of the residential subdivision at the lower end of the parcel. As shown in this figure, the parcel is severed by a proposed right of way. Figure 25.4 is the companion profile sheet for this project. The two existing rights of way will remain at grade with the proposed road passing over them. Thus, approximately 24 to 30 feet of fill material will be used to elevate the proposed roadway.

Trees and Landscaping

In partial takings some landscaping is usually within the proposed right of way. There are two basic schools of thought on how to assign values to landscaping. One approach is to obtain an estimate from a landscaper or tree nursery as to the cost of replacing landscaping elements. The second approach is to determine the contributory value of any trees and landscaping the proposed construction acquires.

The appraiser is advised to use the contributory approach. First, ascertain the value of the entire property then allocate the value of the building(s), other on-site improvements such as fencing,

Figure 25.3   *Proposed Right of Way Bisecting Parcel*

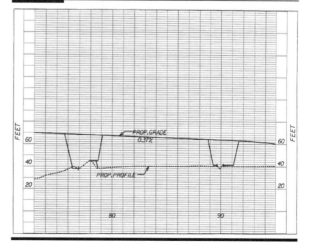

Figure 25.4   *Profile of Proposed Right of Way*

parking areas, accessory buildings, trees, and landscaping. In one particular road-widening project, several mature trees were to be lost because they were in the proposed right of way. The appraiser contacted a nursery to get an estimate of how much it would cost to replace these trees with similar ones. The total estimate to replace approximately one-third of the trees on the property exceeded the price paid for the parcel just two years earlier, including all of the trees.

Sometimes it is possible to locate similar land sales with and without landscaping and trees. While some adjustments invariably must be made, this approach can provide a basis for estimating how much these elements contribute to the overall value of the subject property. For example, suppose that the total value of a residential property is $500,000; the depreciated cost of the dwelling is $300,000; and the swimming pool, pool house, garden shed, driveway, walks, and fencing are worth $75,000. Now assume that comparable lots with trees and no landscaping in the same development sell for $100,000. Thus, the total value of the improvements and lot is $475,000, indicating a $25,000 value contribution for the landscaping. The contributory value of the trees is not so clear. However, it was discovered that two, open-field lots had sold recently for $90,000, implying that the trees contribute $10,000 to the value of the property.

Now suppose that a strip of the same property was being taken for a street-widening project and approximately 10% of the landscaping and 15% of the trees were within the proposed right of way. Further, the nature and maturity of the landscaping and trees within the proposed right of way were similar to the overall landscaping on the property. In this case, the owner would be entitled to receive a pro rata value of that part of the lot acquired, any damages to the remainder, plus $2,500 (10% × $25,000) for landscaping and $1,500 (15% × $10,000) for the trees lost to the street-widening project.

There will be instances in which an appraiser must retain experts to assist in valuing complex or large-scale landscaping components. Also, professional foresters may be required in appraising timber or ornamental trees.

Temporary Easements

Not all eminent domain acquisitions are fee takings or even permanent easements. Right-of-way construction projects generally require temporary space for storing equipment and access roads to get the heavy construction equipment to the construction site. In effect, the condemning authority is renting the land temporarily. There are several ways to appraise temporary easements. Two methods frequently used are value of rental loss and value of expected return. In applying either methods, the appraiser must be thoroughly familiar with the characteristics of the defined easement area and determine if the temporary easement disrupts adjacent business operations or causes value losses beyond the easement area. In the examples considered here, the easements have no adverse effect on adjacent operations or property value.

Value of Rental Loss

It is determined that one acre of a parcel will be subject to a temporary easement. A representative of the condemnor's engineering department expects the clearing and construction project will take two years. This temporary easement site is on the edge of cultivated fields that presently rent for $75 an acre per year. Other neighboring farms rent for a similar amount. Thus, the amount due the landowner in this case would be $150 (2 × $75). While it would be mathematically correct to compute the present value of the rental loss, it is judged to be an unnecessary, and even complicating, step with no appreciable effect on the total amount. In this situation, the easement is for a short period and a modest annual rental amount is involved.

Value of Expected Return

In estimating the value of the part the condemnor acquires the appraiser would have estimated the per-acre value of the adjoining land. If the land underlying the temporary easement is similar to the land acquired, the same unit value could be used. In this example, suppose that three-quarters of an acre will be needed for two years. The land is worth $3.00 per square foot and investors expect to earn 12% on similar commercial land. The landowner is due the following amount if the payments are not discounted:

$$(0.75 \text{ ac.})(43,560 \text{ sq. ft.})(\$3.00)(12\%)(2 \text{ years}) = \$23,522.$$

If two equal, annual payments are discounted 12% annually, the amount payable to the landowner on a present value basis is:

For Year 1 paid in arrears	$11,761 × 0.8929 = $10,501
For Year 2 paid in arrears	$11,761 × 0.7972 = 9,376
Total compensation for temporary easement	$19,877

The appraiser should be familiar with local and state policy concerning discounting. In states such as Utah, compensation to a landowner is not discounted to a present value.

Analysis of Benefits from Public Improvements

As mentioned previously, the justification for a public or quasi-public body taking all or part of an individual property is to benefit the overall community. In appraising an affected property remainder, it must be determined whether the benefits accrue to the community as a whole (general benefits) or specifically to the appraised property (special benefits) for which severance damages are claimed. In most states, general benefits cannot be considered to offset the value of the part taken or any damages claimed for the remainder parcel. In some states special benefits may be used to offset the estimated value of the part taken and damages to the remainder parcel. In other states special benefits accruing from the public improvements may be used to offset damages to the remainder.

Trial Preparation and Testimony

Eminent domain valuation assignments can be intellectually stimulating and professionally satisfying. Before accepting an assignment, the appraiser must make it abundantly clear to the client that he or she will make an objective analysis and, throughout the assignment, resist pressure from the client or its legal counsel to become an advocate for the client or produce a desired value estimate. The appraiser's fee must be based on the time and expenses incurred; it must not be contingent on the outcome of the case or the amount of the award. In accepting eminent domain appraisal assignments, an appraiser must accept that he or she may have to present expert testimony in a court of law. The late George Schmutz, an early leader in the Appraisal Institute and in the development of appraisal methodology, defined an expert witness as:

> one who is possessed of peculiar knowledge and experience that are not common to persons generally, and who has an opinion based upon such knowledge and experience that is peculiarly fitted for assisting in court, or jury, in determining an issue, such as the amount of damage measured in terms of dollars.[2]

Expert witness testimony should be supported by a detailed appraisal report in which the value conclusions reached are fully documented. The report need not be, and generally is not, submitted as a court exhibit, and the opposing counsel cannot demand it for inspection unless the report is referred to and used as a basis for testifying under direct examination. Comprehensive preparation will allow the client's lawyer to become familiar with the factual details of the appraisal and the technical terminology peculiar to the case. Visual aids should be employed where possible. Subdivision plats, photographs, plot plans, comparable sale tables, depreciated costs, and capitalized income summary sheets should be submitted as court exhibits to facilitate the appraiser's testimony during the trial.

Direct Examination

Where permissible, the expert opinion given may relate directly to the value of the entire property before the taking and the value of the

---

2. George L. Schmutz, revised by Edwin M. Rams, *Condemnation Appraisal Handbook* (Englewood Cliffs, N.J.: Prentice-Hall, Inc., 1963), p. 360.

remainder after the taking. This simplifies the proceedings and indicates the amount of compensation (the difference between the before-and-after values as a result of condemnation) to which the owner is entitled. Compensation should cover both the taking of a part of the property and the severance damages, if any, suffered by the remainder. Of course, the appraiser must be prepared to testify as to the extent and possible effects of potential special benefits caused by the public improvements, provided such questions are raised with the permission of the court (and undoubtedly over the objection of the counsel for the condemnee).

After stating the value opinion, the expert witness generally is called on to give reasons for the conclusions reached, either as to the value of the property as a whole or the allocation of this value to the parts and the severance damages resulting from the taking. The answer is merely a summary of the important conclusions reached as a result of the appraisal investigation and a reemphasis of the sales comparison, depreciated cost, or income capitalization approaches which support the expert opinion.

To ensure a successful performance, the appraiser and trial attorney must agree on the order of data presentation and outline the questions and answers to be asked and given during direct examination. The sequence of questions asked generally falls these categories:

1. Qualifications of the witness
2. Inspection of subject property
3. Methods used in arriving at the estimate of value
4. Opinion of value

Care should be taken to present the qualifications of the expert witness in a simple, but impressive manner. Even when opposing counsel stipulates that, in the interest of time, he or she accepts the witness as qualified to testify as an expert, the client's lawyer should—for the court's benefit—qualify the witness as an expert in his or her field. It is the jury or court that sets the award, and the testimony of the witness has greater weight if his or her extensive experience and knowledge of the field of property appraising backs up the findings.

Expert's Background

Qualifying questions should inform the court as to the expert's background and experience relating to

- Occupation
- Place and geographic extent of business or profession
- Education and degrees earned
- Membership in professional associations and state licensure

- Years of experience as an appraiser
- Types of clients served
- Types of properties appraised
- Appraisal courses completed or taught
- Publication of appraisal articles
- Experience in related fields such as brokerage, property management, and lending

Demonstrated Familiarity with Property
Questions pertaining to the examination of the subject property should establish the appraiser's thorough knowledge of the details of the land and site improvements. Here the direct testimony should answer questions such as:

- Can you describe and clearly identify the subject property?
- When did you last inspect the property?
- Have you examined the building plans and specifications in estimating the reproduction cost of the improvements?
- What is the age of the structure and what methods were used to determine the accrued depreciation?
- Have you compared the subject property with other similar properties that have sold recently?
- Did you verify the income experience of this property? Have expenditures been verified?
- What is the present and foreseeable future highest and best use of the subject property?

The next group of questions under direct examination explores the methods used in deriving an estimate of value. Because any testimony offered at this stage of the court proceedings is subject to rebuttal during cross-examination, the appraiser should be careful not to present unnecessary details that later may be questioned to pinpoint errors of judgment or of fact. Care must be taken not to testify that the value was derived solely by the summation method—i.e., estimating the value of the lot separately and adding the value of the improvements less accrued depreciation. Land and buildings are considered a single operating unit and any division of the whole into arbitrary parts may be challenged in some states as constituting hypothetical appraising, which is contrary to accepted valuation theory and practice.

It is best to generalize and explain in simple, nontechnical words the methods used in estimating value. The appraiser, for instance, may state, "I have examined the property; considered its location within the neighborhood; inspected the site; checked public records for the legal description and zoning, deed restrictions, and assessment data; studied comparable sales; and analyzed other general and specific factual data essential to the formation of a professional opinion of value."

It is advisable at this point for counsel to request that the witness describe and explain the comparable sales that he or she considered in formulating an estimate of market value. The witness should ask permission to refer to a large subdivision or area map, which should be marked for identification as a court exhibit so jurors may study and refer to it during their deliberations. On this map the subject property should be marked prominently in color and the sale properties should be clearly numbered and marked in different colors. As each sale property is identified, the transaction price should be stated, the seller and buyer named, the date of sale specified, and the terms of sale for the transaction given. The appraiser should make certain that each sale was verified with the purchaser, seller, or real estate broker as to the date of sale, transaction price, and terms of sale.

It is never wise to rely on the state transfer tax, if the state has one, as evidence of the prices paid for comparable sale properties. Even if the tax information posted in the deed book is accurate, the jury or court may be adversely influenced by the lack of sale confirmation and by an admission from the witness that revenue stamps can readily and legally be overstated or understated to mislead those who rely on such evidence as a guide to market value. The witness may be discredited by failing to learn through his or her interviews that there were circumstances that distorted the price paid for the property.

The final category of questions concerns the opinion of value. As a rule counsel asks: "As a result of your investigation, and by reason of your experience, have you formed an opinion of value for the subject. Identify by name the property as of a specified date (date of the taking)." The witness, of course, answers in the affirmative. Counsel then may ask the witness to state his or her professional opinion concerning:

1. Value of the entire property as a whole

2. Value of the part taken when considered as a part of the whole or as a separate parcel (when such testimony is deemed advantageous to the interests of the condemnee)

3. Value of the remainder considered as part of the property as a whole

4. Value of the remainder as a separate parcel after the taking of a part of the whole property

5. Severance damage attributable to the remainder property, if any (Item 3 less Item 4)

6. Total compensation due the landowner (Item 2 plus Item 5)

Cross-Examination

It is during cross-examination that the competence of the appraiser and his or her ability as an expert witness come to light. Many appraisers are thorough, diligent, and accurate in their value findings, but lack experience on the witness stand and the ease that comes from a broad educational background. Such witnesses, through indecision, lack of confidence, and the inability to think quickly on their feet, may undo the work of many days or weeks of preparation. Other witnesses have oversized egos, which cause them to falter or to explode when—directly or by implication—their integrity or competence is questioned. In court, appraisers will have their findings exposed to ruthless analysis and their community reputations jolted by lawyers who will go all out to destroy the effectiveness of a witness's testimony. This adversareal atmosphere keeps many otherwise qualified professional appraisers from accepting assignments that require them to defend their findings in court.

Those who enter the appraisal profession should be trained to take the stand as expert witnesses. As a first step, personal fear must be overcome and confidence must be acquired by undertaking a thorough analysis and seeing the estimate of value as a means of aiding the court in reaching a just decision. The court and jurors usually frown on personal abuse and tricky behavior unbecoming to the legal profession. Witnesses should remind themselves that, while giving testimony, their counsel is a sort of partner and that unfair or misleading questions will be objected to when raised. Further, the court and jurors are intelligent observers seeking truth, not entertainment through a display of legal skill.

The witness should listen to questions earnestly and carefully. When the intent of the question is not clear, clarification should be requested. Answers should be short, simple, polite, and directed to the jury or court. When "yes" or "no" answers are requested, the witness should comply but ask permission to explain an answer when clarification is essential. To illustrate, a series of "yes" or "no" questions may be asked as follows:

1. Are you representing the condemnee?

2. Have you served him or her previously?

3. Are you paid by him or her for your services?

4. You would not be testifying without the promise of pay, would you?

5. Your opinion of value is bought, is it not?

Certainly, Questions 4 and 5 should be explained because bias is implied and that may influence the court's decision. In replying to Question 4, the witness should add that as a member of the appraisal profession he or she is not accustomed to volunteering his or her services, and that as a professional appraiser he or she gladly serves all who seek professional aid. To Question 5, the witness should answer "no" and state that although his or her services are paid for, his or her opinion of value is based on facts gathered and studied during the course of the investigation. The findings and opinions stated would be the same no matter who engaged his or her services.

The cross-examiner can be expected to do all in his or her power to weaken or even discredit the value testimony of the opposing expert witness. The questions asked are generally designed to cast doubt on the appraiser's

1. Experience or education
2. Familiarity with the subject property or subject area and neighborhood
3. Preparation or omission of relevant data
4. Freedom from bias or incompetence
5. Computations or the validity of the valuation premises

In preparing his or her valuation report and in planning the sequence of testimony, the appraiser, with the aid of a lawyer, should anticipate the questions that may be raised during cross-examination and be ready to offer clear and convincing answers. The following 13 guidelines can be invaluable to appraisers giving expert testimony in court:

1. Never lie or be evasive.
2. Never exaggerate the highest and best use.
3. Never testify to a dictated appraisal.
4. Carefully examine and evaluate all comparable sales.
5. Avoid capitalizing the hypothetical income of vacant land.
6. Judiciously exercise your right to explain your answer.
7. Avoid giving the false appearance of infallibility.
8. Always remember that you are an impartial witness, not an advocate.
9. Your testimony should be the same if you were appearing for the opposing party.
10. Think carefully before you respond to questions.

11. If you do not know the answer to a question, say so. In other words, neither guess nor answer questions in areas in which you have no expertise.

12. Always avoid allowing an opposing attorney to put words in your mouth. Restate the attorney's questions so that they accurately describe the issue being examined.

12. Always remember to control your temper on cross-examination and retain a sense of humor. Likewise, do not argue with opposing counsel.[3]

Summary

Eminent domain allows a government or its agency to acquire all or part of a parcel for the common benefit of its citizens by due process of law. Reasonable compensation to the owner is required, but consent is not necessary for the acquisition. Condemnation is the process through which authorized units of government and public utility companies take private property for public benefit and use upon payment of just compensation to the property owner. When there is a physical taking of a property or property rights via eminent domain, the affected property owner is entitled to compensation from the condemning agency; this payment is called just compensation.

There are two basic valuation methods used in estimating total just compensation to a landowner in partial takings. The federal rule, used in some states as well, is known as the before and after rule. It holds that the measure of just compensation is the difference between the value of the whole property before the taking and the value of the remainder after the taking. Under this set-off rule, special benefits are allowed to offset both the value of the land acquired by the condemnor and any damages to the residue. Under the second method, the modified before and after premise, the following steps are used in arriving at the total just compensation that a property owner receives: 1) estimate the value of the whole property; 2) estimate the value of the part taken; 3) deduct the value of the part taken from the value of the whole property; 4) estimate the value of the remainder parcel, taking into effect the value influence of the proposed improvement and the utility of the remainder; 5) estimate damages to the remainder, if any; and 6) compute the total just compensation if there are damages by adding the value of the part taken to the severance damages suffered by the remainder.

Damages to a remainder parcel may result from any of the following circumstances: odd-shaped remainder, superadequate remainder

---

3.   Much of this section is taken from pages 422–427 of James H. Boykin and Alfred A. Ring *The Valuation of Real Estate* (Englewood Cliffs, NJ: Regents/Prentice Hall, 1993).

improvements, isolated remainders, landlocked remainders, impaired access, and grade change. In partial takings, there typically will be landscaping within the proposed right of way. Its value should be estimated by its contributory value to the whole property. Right-of-way construction projects generally require temporary space for storing equipment and access roads to get the heavy equipment to the construction site. In effect, this amounts to the condemnor renting the land temporarily.

In accepting eminent domain appraisal assignments, an appraiser must accept the prospect of having to present expert testimony in a court of law. A detailed report in which the value conclusions reached are documented fully should support the appraiser's testimony. During the first phase of testimony, the appraiser is questioned by his or her client's attorney. The attorney generally will ask the appraiser to inform the court about his or her professional background, to demonstrate familiarity with the appraised property, and then to outline the steps taken to reach a conclusion of just compensation. Following this phase, the opposing attorney will conduct the cross-examination. It is during this phase that the competence of the appraiser and his or her ability as an expert witness is tested rigorously.

Appendices

Glossary

Affirmative easement grants a right to a nonowner to perform a particular action on a specific parcel or part of a parcel. The fee owner gives up some of his or her rights as a result of the easement. The right may or may not be an exclusive right.

Animal unit (AU) A unit of measurement that provides a benchmark against which different sizes of cattle, sheep, or horses can be measured.

Armor stone is a large stone that when combined with other such stones preserves beach frontage from erosion.

Bare land value is a value that relates solely to a timber tract's underlying land with no value ascribed to timber of any age, not even immature timber.

Bundle of rights is all the rights of ownership inherent in fee title to real property.

Capability grouping provides a general means of identifying the suitability of soils for most types of field crops.

Cash crop is raised for sale to customers rather than as feed for livestock on the farm.

Clear cutting is a harvesting technique that clears all of the merchantable timber from an area in preparation for either planting, seeding, or sprouting to establish a new stand of trees. It works well especially for understocked stands or mature stands of timber, or clearing land of a suboptimal species.

Comparative land sales method involves a comparison of recent sales of similar parcels to an appraised parcel as a means of estimating its value.

Condemnation is the process by which authorized units of government and public utility companies may take private property for public benefit and use upon payment of just compensation to a property owner.

Contribution, principle of asserts that the value of a particular component is measured in terms of its contribution to the value of the whole property, or as the amount that its absence would detract from the value of the whole.

Crop allotment is that number of acres the federal government allots to a farm such as a Burley tobacco allotment.

Deep-water lot is a lot that provides water of sufficient depth to accommodate a pier for deep-draft boats such as cabin cruisers and sail and shrimp boats.

Dry farming is a type of farming associated with semiarid areas in the southwestern United States. It generally involves water conservation and harvesting crops once every two years.

Easement is a nonpossessory interest in another party's real property that benefits the second party.

Eminent domain allows a government or its agency to acquire all or part of a parcel by due process of law for the common benefit of its citizens.

Excess land is land that is not needed to support the use of existing or probable future improvements.

Exposure time is the time required to sell a parcel before the date of the appraisal.

Farm is defined by the USDA as any establishment from which $1,000 or more of agricultural products were sold or would normally be sold during the year.

Farmland is agricultural land associated with a farming operation; it includes all categories of tillable and untillable land as well as woodlots.

Farmstead is that part of a farm where the farm buildings and house are located.

Fee simple estate is the full, unimpaired estate, but both governmental and private limitations may restrict the full use and enjoyment of a parcel. These governmental limitations are police power, escheat, eminent domain, and taxation. Private constraints include leases, easements, mortgages, and restrictive covenants.

Financing adjustment is made as of the date the comparable sale occurred to reveal the price that the sale parcel would have achieved if it had sold subject to typical financing terms at that time.

Floodplain is level land (plain) adjacent a river, creek, or stream that periodically overflows.

Floor area ratio (FAR) governs the quantity of building area that may be built on a site. It is computed by dividing the area of the building by the site area.

Golf course hot spots are lots located around such areas as tees, greens, and landing areas and usually bring higher premiums than lots on fairways or most any other part of a development.

Hazardous substance is any material within, around, or near a property that may negatively impact its value.

High tide access is an important value issue for low-lying parcels and peninsulas; it may be affected adversely by a section of road leading to the property that is subject to flooding during high tides.

Highest and best use for appraisal purposes is defined as that use or succession of available, legal, and physically-permitted uses for which there is sufficient demand that produces the most probable present site value.

Hydrology is the science of water and its properties; regarding wetlands, it refers to the presence of water on or in the soil sufficiently long as to influence the types of plant life.

Indemnity is a financial warranty a seller of a contaminated property provides that a buyer will be relieved of any future costs and liabilities attributed to the specified contamination.

Interim use is a short-term existing or future use.

Land contract is also known as contract for deed; it provides for a deed being delivered to a buyer once he or she has met certain conditions, such as having made payments equal to a typical down payment.

Land value extraction method produces an indication of the land value of a sale property that has improvements of relatively modest value. The value of the improvements is deducted from the sale price to indicate the underlying land value.

Legal access relates mainly to easements and rights-of-way over the lands of others.

Location adjustment is made to determine the influence that different locations have on comparable sales. It is sound valuation policy whenever possible to avoid using sales distant from or in significantly different locations from the appraised parcel.

Market conditions (time) adjustment is made before adjusting for physical, legal, or conditions of sale. It answers the question, "What price would the sale parcel probably have brought at the date of the subject parcel's appraisal?"

Merchantable timber is a stand of timber that has reached sufficient size and maturity to justify its being harvested.

Mineral interests relate to ownership of minerals in place as well as access, exploration, extraction, processing, and transport rights.

Minimal flood hazard area is a flood plain where flooding is not expected more frequently than every 500 years.

Mitigation is the act of making a condition less severe or harsh. It is a means of alleviating or moderating the negative effects of losing wetlands through human activities.

Moderate flood hazard area is a flood plain situated between the 100- and 500-year flood frequency.

Most probable use is defined as the use to which a site will most likely be placed.

Multiple regression analysis is a statistical technique that involves correlating each value determinant (called independent variable) with the estimated value (known as dependent variable). During this process the rest of the variables are held constant to learn how much each variable contributes to the overall site value.

Negative easement prohibits a land owner from using his or her land for zoned uses, such as land within an avigation easement.

Nonsource property is a property having no environmental liability, but whose value may have been eroded severely from the release and migration of an environmentally hazardous substance from another property.

Paired sales analysis is a valuation technique where several pairs of sales, which are similar in all respects except one, are comparatively analyzed to estimate the value contribution of a particular feature.

Police power is a sovereign power of government to restrict the use of a property to protect the well-being of its citizens.

Pre-merchantable timber, also known as *young growth*, is timber that is too small to economically justify its being harvested or even thinned. It generally is less than 15 years old.

Production valuation method is a present value method for an oil well operation which accounts for annual production revenue less royalties and other operating expenses discounted over a forecast production period.

Reasonable marketing time is an estimate of the amount of time it might take to sell a property interest in real estate at the estimated market value level during the period immediately after the effective date of the appraisal.

Remediation is a means to provide a remedy, cure, or relief. As associated with environmentally contaminated property, it includes testing, cleanup, disposal of contaminated soil, and post-cleanup monitoring.

Riparian rights are a form of water rights. Property owners whose land abuts a body of water such as a stream or river enjoy riparian rights.

Rough terrain access relates to a site user physically being able to reach a site and may require substantial road building expense and the additional cost of having to acquire a four-wheel vehicle

Royalty income method for appraising minerals is similar to estimating the present worth of an annuity plus the present worth of the residual at the end of the projection period.

Royalty interests are concerned with the right to receive revenue from the extraction of minerals, with neither the right to extract nor the financial burden to do so.

Saw log is the harvested trunk of a tree that is of sufficient size and quality to be sawed into lumber or peeled into plywood.

Shape adjustment takes into account zoning setback requirements, frontage and capability of a site to permit sufficient space for a building, onsite parking, and sufficient separation of future well and septic system drain field.

Sharecrop rent is an agreement between a farm owner and a tenant who works the land. A variety of share arrangements may be used, including respective contributions by each party for the purchase of fertilizer, seed, irrigation, and harvesting costs.

Site index is a measure of the soil productivity of a tract. It measures how tall a specific tree species will grow in a given time period, such as 25 or 50 years.

Size adjustment is made to reflect the market value of an appraised parcel. The appraiser must take care to choose comparable sales that have the same highest and best use and similar size.

Source property is the property on which a hazardous substance has been released.

Special flood hazard area is within the 100-year flood boundary where there is a one percent probability of land therein flooding annually.

Stigma is the adverse effect on value of environmental-related uncertainty and risk.

Stumpage is another term for standing or uncut timber. Generally, it is sold for harvest within six months to two years from the sale date.

Stumpage value is the price that standing timber brings in a sale; this value usually is expressed as value per thousand board feet.

Subsoil is generally thought to be that soil beneath the topsoil or below plow depth.

Tillable soil is land that is suitable for growing crops.

Timber cruise, also known as a timber inventory, it is a statistical sampling of the timber volume and grade of each species in a particular stand of timber.

Topsoil is usually considered as the top, most-fertile part of the soil. (See Appendix F for a detailed description of different types of soils.)

Wetlands are areas that are flooded or saturated by surface or ground water at a frequency and duration that supports vegetation typically adapted for life in saturated soil conditions.

Winter access may affect the desirability and value of parcels that are not accessible readily during the winter months.

Internet Web Site Addresses

Title	Address
American Real Estate Exchange	www.amrex.com
American Resort Development Association (ADRA)	www.arda.org
American Society of Civil Engineers	www.asce.org
Anywho Directories— National Telephone Directory	www.anywho.com
Appraisal Institute	www.appraisalinstitute.org
Appraisal Institute of Canada	www.appraisalinstitute.org
ARGUS Technologies Homepage	www.argus.com
Association of Consulting Foresters of America, Inc.	www.acf-foresters.com
Association of Environmental and Resource Economists (AERE)	www.ecu.edu/econ/aere
Building Officials and Code Administrators (BOCA)	www.bocai.org
Building Owners and Managers Association	www.boma.org
Bureau of Land Management	www.blm.gov
Census Bureau	www.census.gov
Commercial Investment Real Estate Institute	www.ccim.com

Consumer Price Index	stats.bls.gov/news.release/ cpi.toc.htm
Counselors of Real Estate	www.cre.org
DeLorme	www.delorme.com
EnviroLink Library	www.library.envirolink.org
EPA	www.epa.gov/epahome
ERE Yarmouth	www.ereyarmouth.com
Geographic Information Systems	www.usgs.gov/research/gis/ title.html
Housing and Urban Development, U.S. Dept. of	www.hud.gov
International Association of Assessing Officers (IAAO)	www.iaao.org
International Council of Shopping Centers (ICSC)	www.icsc.org
Korpacz	www.korpacz.com
LEXIS-NEXIS	www.lexis-nexis.com
Loopnet	www.loopnet.com
MapBlast	www.mapblast.com
MapQuest	www.mapquest.com
Map Stats	www.census.gov/datamap/www/ index.html
Map Unit Interpretation Database	www.statlab.iastate.edu/soils/muir
Marshall & Swift	www.marshallswift.com/ costrev.html
Mortgage Bankers Association of America (MBAA)	www.mbaa.org

Mortgage Market Information Systems	www.interest.com
National Association of Environmental Professionals (NAEP)	www.enfo.com/NAEP
National Association of Home Builders (NAHB)	www.nahb.com
National Association of Industrial and Office Parks (NAIOP)	www.naiop.org
National Association of Real Estate Investment Trusts (NAREIT)	www.nareit.com
National Association of Realtors (NAR)	www.realtor.com
National Parks and Recreation Association (NPRA)	www.nrpa.org
The Nature Conservancy	www.tnc.org
Plants, Sites and Parks	www.bizsites.com
Scorecard—An Environmental Information Service	www.scorecard.org
The Sierra Club	www.sierraclub.org
Society of Industrial and Office Realtors	www.sior.com
Site Net	www.sitenet.com
State Soil Geographic (STATSGO) Data Base	www.ncg.nrcs.usda.gov/
Tiger Map Server Browser	tiger.census.gov/cgi-bin/ mapbrowse-tbl
USADATA Local Market Data Resource	www.usadata.com
US Geological Survey	www.usgs.gov/
US Government Printing Office	www.access.gpo.gov

USDA	www.usda.gov
USDA Economic Research Service	www.ers.usda.gov
USDA Economics and Statistics System	www.mannlib.cornell.edu
WebAppraiser	www.webappraiser.com

Maps

Federal Emergency Management Agency Map Service Center

The Map Service Center (MSC) distributes National Flood Insurance Program (NFIP) materials to a broad range of customers. Its products include hard-copy maps, data products and insurance manuals, and the newly developed *digital Q3 Flood Data* product. Paper Flood Insurance Rate maps may be ordered by phone or fax, Monday through Friday from 8:00 a.m. to 8:00 p.m., eastern time.

> Map Service Center
> P.O. Box 1038
> Jessup, MD 20794-1038
> Tel: (800) 358-9616
> Fax: (800) 358-9620

Each map panel and index map is $0.50 plus $2.50 for shipping and handling per order. Each Flood Insurance Study is $2.50 plus $2.50 for shipping and handling per order. Orders should be prepaid by check, made payable to *NFIP,* and mailed to the above address, or charged to your VISA, MasterCard, or deposit account.

Maps may be ordered by community or county number, which can be obtained by calling MSC's toll-free number. If you are interested in one particular part of a community or county, it is recommended that an index map be ordered for the area. Panel numbers for specific areas are clearly indicated on the index map and should be referenced when placing an order. Another source of community panel numbers is your local public works department, zoning department, or local public or university library.

Digital Q3 Flood Data are available on CD-ROM for more than 900 counties. These may be ordered by calling the Map Service Center. All counties for a single state are on one CD-ROM; however, some CD-ROMs may have more than one state, while Florida, New York, and

Pennsylvania are on two separate CD-ROMs. Each CD-ROM is $50 + $2.50 shipping. (Effective July 6, 1999).

FEMA flood maps also are available on CD. This technology allows an appraiser to scroll from county to town to subject area to identify the presence of flood plains. Minimum use requirements are 486 - 8 megs of Ram, Windows program, and 256 color or higher graphics card. CD packages are available for individual areas from $89.95 to $245.00 from

Digital Media Services
PO Box 417
353 Sweetmans Lane, Suite 1A,
Perrineville, NJ 08535
Phone (732) 446-2211; Fax (732) 446-3445
Email: dms@injersey.com, and Internet http://www.floodmaps.com

U.S. Department of Interior, Geological Survey

Information about topographical maps produced by USGS is available at 1-800-USA-MAPS.

A list of State Earth Science Information Centers that offer information and sales service for USGS map products and earth science publications, including geologic, hydrologic, topographic, and land use maps, books and reports: aerial, satellite, and radar images and related products; earth science and map data in digital format and related applications software; and geodetic data can be obtained by calling the above telephone or by visiting the ESIC Internet site at:

www.usgs.gov.

ESICs can fill orders for custom products such as aerial photographs and orthophotoquads, digital cartographic data, and geographic names data.

National Oceanic and Atmospheric Administration
National Ocean Service Coast Survey

Charts and related publications are available from the Distribution Division, (N/ACC 3), National Ocean Service, Riverdale, MD 20737-1199. Telephone orders may be placed (VISA or Mastercard accepted) by calling (301) 436-6990 or 1-800-638-8972. The following four catalogs cover the entire coast of the United States: United States Atlantic and Gulf Coasts; United States Pacific Coast, including Hawaiian, Mariana, and Samoa Islands; Alaska, and U. S. Great Lakes and adjacent waterways. Also available on CD-ROMS and IBM compatible 3.5-inch disks are tidal current charts, tide tables, and tidal current tables.

U.S. Army Corps of Engineers

Great Lakes and Ohio River Division
P.O. Box 1159 (550 East Main Street)
Cincinnati, OH 45201-1159
(502) 582-5010

Mississippi Valley Division
P.O. Box 80
Vicksburg, MS 39181-0080
(601) 634-5750

North Atlantic Division
USACE
Building 301
Fort Hamilton Military Community
Brooklyn, NY 11252-6700
(718) 491-8707

Northwestern Division
220 NW 8th Avenue
Portland, OR 97208-2870
(503) 808-3700

Pacific Ocean Division
Bldg. 230
Fort Shafter, HI 96858-5440
(808) 438-1500

South Atlantic Division
60 Forsyth St. S.W.
Atlanta, GA 30303-8801
(404) 562-5011

South Pacific Division
333 Market Street
San Francisco, CA 94105-2195
(415) 977-8001

Southwestern Division
1100 Commerce Street
Dallas, TX 75242-0216
(214) 767-2502

Soil Maps in County Units (by Bureau of Plant Industry)

Division of Public Documents
U.S. Government Printing Office
Washington D.C. 20402

These maps may be available in book form in many counties from the Soil Conservation Service.

U.S. Fish and Wildlife Service Maps
National Wetlands Inventory

The U. S. Fish and Wildlife Service can provide nationwide data on the characteristics and extent of wetlands. These maps reveal the approximate location, shape, and types of wetlands. In using these maps, it should be remembered that wetlands smaller than five acres, thin bands along waterways, and farmed wetlands may not be shown. The maps may contain errors because they are derived from high-altitude photography and are not always field checked for accuracy. Because the photographs used depict hydrologic conditions at a given time, such as during the summer dry season, they may either not show or minimize wetlands. The photography may be several years old and not accurately show the effects on wetlands of change conditions, such as beaver dams, drainage, filling, or road and parking lots construction.

Information on ordering National Wetland Inventory maps may be obtained from state offices or from:

USGS/ESIC
National Headquarters
507 National Center
Reston, VA 22092
Telephone: 1-888-275-8747 or 1-800-872-6277
www.wetlands.fws.gov/order__maps.htm

National MUIR Database Data Access

The National MUIR (Map Unit Interpretation Database) of the USDA-NRCS Survey Division has data available for most counties in the United States. MUIR data is a collection of soil and soil-related properties, interpretations, and performance data for a soil survey area and its map units, map unit components, and component layers. These include available water capacity, soil erodibility factors, hydric soil ratings, flooding, water table depth, building site development, cropland, woodland, and recreational development; and yields for common crops, site indices of common trees, and potential production of rangeland plants.

MUIR data should be used in conjunction with soil survey maps and are not intended to be used for site-specific land use suitability determinations, such as approval, siting, and sizing of septic tank absorption fields.

Additional information may be obtained from

www.statlab.iastate.edu/soils/muir

Orders may be made by contacting:

USDA-Natural Resources Conservation Service
National Cartography and Geospatial Center
501 Felix St., Bldg. 23 (P.O. Mail 6567)
Fort Worth, TX 76115
Telephone: 1-800-672-5559.

Current price is $50.00 for single CD-ROM disk.

Map Stats

The US Census Bureau through Map Stats provides Census data by city and county on such topics as population, demographics, and housing from the 1990 Census, 1998 county population estimates, 1995 income and poverty estimates, 1992 Economic Census, County Business Patterns Economic Profile for 1993 through 1996, and USA Counties General Profile for 1994 and 1996.

Data may be accessed via: http://www.census.gov/datamap/www/index.html.

U.S. Census Bureau TIGER Mapping Service

The main purpose of the TIGER Map Service is to provide a good quality, national scale, street-level map to users of the World Wide Web. This service is accessible freely to the public and based on an open architecture that allows other Web developers and publishers to use public domain maps generated by this service in their own applications and documents. This service provides legend components; areas can be accessed by entering precise map coordinates or by entering a city or town, state or even a zip code.

Information is available at: http://tiger.census.gov/

USGS Node of the National Geospatial Data Clearinghouse

This federal agency can provide Geographical Information Systems (GIS) technology, which is data identified according to their locations. This GIS makes it possible to perform complex analyses, such as informational retrieval, topological modeling, overlay and it can be applied in the form of mapmaking, site selection, and simulating environmental effects.

Information is available at: http://www/usgs/gov/research/gis/title.html

DeLorme

DeLorme provides a topographical map (DeLorme Topo 2.0 National Edition). This and its other products allow a user to obtain topographic data of all 50 states at 20-foot contour intervals, detailed street information, precision controls to view and print customized maps, and route directions.

Product and price information may be obtained from telephone 1-800-569-8313 or fax 1-800-575-2244; its web site is: www.delorme.com

Aerial Photography

There are a variety of sources for aerial photography. Possible sources include state highway departments, private companies that often can fly a particular route to provide custom-work for a given valuation assignment, and the U.S. Geological Survey which may be reached via 1-900-USA-MAPS or its Internet site at: http://edcwww.cr.usgs.gov/webglis

USGS can provide high quality, cloud-free aerial photography that is flown 20,000 feet above a particular area. This photography would be useful for showing a metropolitan area or area that would fit within a five square mile photograph. Also available is satellite imagery of defined areas, but these views contain 1,000 square miles (100 miles per side).

Land Measurement and Conversion Tables

Acreage

Acres	Square Feet	One-acre rectangles can have these dimensions:	
		Width	Length
1	43,560	16.5	2,640.0
2	87,120	33.0	1,320.0
3	130,680	50.0	871.2
4	174,240	66.0	660.0
5	217,800	75.0	580.8
6	261,360	100.0	435.6
7	304,920	132.0	330.0
8	348,480	150.0	290.4
9	392,040	208.71	208.71
10	435,600		

Linear Measurement

12 inches equal 1 foot
3 feet equal 1 yard
$5^1/_2$ yards or $16^1/_2$ feet equal 1 rod
40 rods equal 1 furlong
8 furlongs, 32 rods, or 5,280 feet equal 1 statute mile

Square Measurement

144 square inches equal 1 square foot
9 square feet equal 1 square yard
$30^1/_4$ square yards equal 1 square rod
160 square rods or 43,560 square feet equal 1 acre
640 acres equal 1 square mile

Surveyor's Linear Measurement

7.92 inches equal 1 link
25 links equal 1 rod
4 rods or 66 feet equal 1 chain
80 chains equal 1 mile

Surveyor's Square Measurement

625 square links equal 1 pole
16 poles equal 1 square chain
10 square chains equal 1 acre
640 acres equal 1 square mile
36 square miles equal 1 township

Conversion of Chains to Rods and Feet

Chains	Rods	Feet	Chains	Rods	Feet
1	4	66	21	84	1386
2	8	132	22	88	1452
3	12	198	23	92	1518
4	16	264	24	96	1584
5	20	330	25	100	1650
6	24	396	26	104	1716
7	28	462	27	108	1782
8	32	528	28	112	1848
9	36	594	29	116	1914
10	40	660	30	120	1980
11	44	726	31	124	2046
12	48	792	32	128	2112
13	52	858	33	132	2178
14	56	924	34	136	2244
15	60	990	35	140	2310
16	64	1056	36	144	2376
17	68	1122	37	148	2442
18	72	1188	38	152	2508
19	76	1254	39	156	2574
20	80	1320	40	160	2640

Engineer's Chain

12 inches equal 1 link
100 links or 100 feet equal 1 chain
52.8 chains equal 1 mile

Board Measurement

1 board foot equals 144 cubic inches

1 board foot equals 1 ft. × 1 ft. 1 ft.

1 ton round timber equals 40 cubic feet

1 ton hewn timber equals 40 cubic feet

Metric Conversions

Conversion from metric

1 kilometer equals	0.62137 mile
1 meter equals	39.37 inches
	3.28083 feet
	1.0936 yards
1 centimeter equals	0.3937 inch
1 millimeter equals	0.03937 inch, or approximately 1/25 inch

Conversion to metric

1 mile equals	1.6093 kilometers
1 rod equals	5.029 meters
1 yard equals	0.9144 meter
1 foot equals	0.3048 meter
1 inch equals	2.54 centimeters
	25.4 millimeters

Types of Soils

Acid soil—A soil that has an acid reaction; more particularly it is a soil which has a preponderance of hydrogen ions over hydroxyl ion in the soil solution. A pH of 7 represents the neutral point in soil solution and any value below is acid.

Adobe—A term describing a soil which cracks deeply upon drying and breaks into irregular but roughly cubical blocks. Adobe soils are usually heavy textured and have a content high in colloidal clay.

Aeloian soil—The opposite of acid soil. Any soil which is alkaline in reaction. It has a pH above 7.

Alluvial soil—An azonal soil forming from materials (alluvion) transported by flowing water. Such soil is unstable.

Azonal soil—A soil without horizons, one insufficiently developed, thus lacking a definite soil profile.

Bog soil—An intrazonal group of marshy or swampy soils underlain with peat, common to humid or subhumid climates.

Calcareous soil—One containing carbonate of calcium (limestone).

Catena—A group of soils within one zonal region developed from similar parent material but different in solum characteristics owning to differences in relief/or drainage.

Chernozem—A zonal group of soils having a deep, dark, colored to nearly black surface horizon, rich in organic matter, which grades into lighter colored soils and finally into a layer of lime accumulation; developed under tall and mixed grasses in a temperate to cool subhumid climate.

Clay—Small mineral soil grain, less than 0.005 mm. In diameter; plastic when moist but hard when baked or fired.

Clay loam—A textural term describing a soil which contains a moderate amount of fine material mixed with coarser soil grains. When the moist soil is pinched between the thumb and finger, it will form a thin ribbon that will break readily, barely sustaining its own weight. The moist soil is plastic and will form a cast that will bear much handling. When kneaded in the hand it does not crumble readily but tends to work in a heavy, compact mass.

Claypan—A dense and heavy soil horizon underlying the upper part of the soil, which because of the characteristics of clay, interferes with water movement or root development.

Coarse textured soil—A soil that contains a preponderance of soil grains larger than 0.25 mm. Sandy loams, gravelly sandy loams, and loamy sands are classed as coarse-textured soils.

Colluvial soil—Soil material found at the base of a steep hill or slope that has been transported by gravity or water.

Desert soil—A zonal group of soils having a light-colored surface soil usually underlain by calcareous material and frequently by a hardpan. They develop under scant shrub vegetation in areas having warm to cool arid climates.

Drouthy soil—A loose-textured soil with poor water holding capacity due to such conditions as sand or gravel subsoil.

Fine sandy loam—A soil with a fine sandy loam texture containing much sand but that has enough silt and clay to make it coherent. The sands contain 50% or more of fine sand, or less than 25% fine gravel, coarse, and medium sand. Thus, the fine sandy loam type contains a larger percentage of fine sand than does the sandy loam type.

Fine textured soil—A soil that contains a high percentage of fine particles 0.005 mm. in diameter or less. Such soils are also referred to as clays.

Glacial soil—Parent material of soil that has been moved and redeposited by glacial activity.

Gumbo soil—A silty, fine textured soil that becomes sticky when wet and has a greasy appearance.

Hardpan—A lay of silt, clay, or any soil material cemented together. A hardened soil horizon which will not dissolve to any appreciable extent in water. The soil may have any texture and be compacted or cemented by iron oxide, organic material, silica, calcium carbonate, or other substances.

Heavy soil—A term sometimes used to describe a clay soil. A term sometimes used to describe a clay soil. See, Clay; Fine Textured Soil.

Immature soil—A young or imperfectly-developed soil; one lacking individual horizons.

Impervious soil—Not allowing the passage of water, air, or plant roots.

Lacustrine soil—Soils formed from materials deposited by the waters of lakes and ponds, usually fine textured and heavy.

Light textured soil—A term sometimes used to denote a sandy or coarse-textured soil.

Loam—A soil having a mixture of different grades of sand, silt, and clay in such proportions that the characteristics of no one predominate. It is mellow with a gritty feel, and when moist is slightly plastic. Squeezed when dry, it will form a cast that will require careful handling. The cast formed by squeezing when moist can be handled freely without breaking. See also, Clay Loam, Fine Sandy Loam, Sandy Loam, Silt Clay Loam, Silt Loam.

Loess—Wind blown material. It differs from till and water sediment in that it is uniformly silty.

Marine soil—A soil formed from materials deposited by the oceans and seas and later exposed by upward movement; for example, the coastal plain soils of Maryland and Virginia

Medium textured soil—Sometimes used to designate loams, fine sandy loams, and clay loams.

Mellow—A soil is termed mellow when it can be worked easily due to its friable and loamy characteristics.

Muck—Fairly well decomposed organic soil material, relatively high in mineral content, dark in color, and accumulated under conditions of imperfect drainage.

Neutral soil—A soil that is not significantly acid or alkaline which is a desirable condition. It has a pH between 6.6 and 7.3.

Organic soil—A general term used in reference to any soil, the solid part of which is predominantly organic matter.

Peat soil—Unconsolidated soil material consisting largely of undecomposed or slightly decomposed organic matter accumulated under conditions of excessive moisture.

Pedalfers soil—A soil in which there has been a shifting of alumina and iron oxide downward in the soil profile but with no horizon or carbonate accumulation.

Pedocal soil—A soil with a horizon of accumulated carbonates in the soil profile.

Phase soil—That part of a soil unit or soil type having minor variations in characteristics used in soil classification from the characteristics normal for the type, although they may be of great importance. The variations are chiefly in such external characteristics as relief, stoniness, or accelerated erosion.

Podsol—A zonal group of soils having an organic mat and a thin organic-mineral layer above a gray leached layer which rests upon an alluvial dark brown horizon, developed under the coniferous or mixed forest, or under vegetation in a temperate to cold moist climate.

Prairie soils—The zonal group of soils having a dark brown or grayish brown surface horizon, grading through brown soil to the lighter colored parent material at two to five feet, developed under tall grasses, in a temperate, relatively humid climate. The term has a restricted meaning in soil science and is not applied to all dark colored soils of the treeless plains but only to those in which carbonates have not been concentrated in any part of the profile by soil-forming processes.

Primary soil—A soil formed in place from the weathering of the underlying rock and minerals.

Recent soil—A secondary soil of such recent deposition that the weathering or aging processes have made little or no change in the profile.

Residual soil—Soil formed in place by the weathering of mineral material or, in other words, by the disintegration and decomposition of rock in place.

Saline soil—A soil containing enough common alkali salts to injuriously affect plant growth.

Sandy loam—A soil containing much sand and enough silt and clay to make it somewhat coherent; the sand grains can be felt. It will form a weak cast when dry and squeezed in the hand.

Secondary soils—A soil that has been transported by water or wind and redeposited; alluvial soil.

Silt clay loam—A soil made up of moderate amounts of fine grades of sand and moderate amounts of clay but more than 50% silt and clay, and contains more clay than silt loam. It is cloddy when dry; when wet it has the tendency to ribbon upon being squeezed between finger and thumb.

Silt loam—A soil made up of moderate amounts of the fine grades of sand, small amounts of clay, and one-half or more silt. It appears cloddy when dry but has a smooth feel when wet and will not ribbon.

Transported soil—Secondary soils; soils that have been moved and redeposited by water or wind.

Upland soil—Soils developed through the disintegration and decomposition of rocks in place and the weathering of the resulting debris; primary soils; usually occupying hilly to mountainous terrain.

Source: Byrl N. Boyce (compiler and editor), *Real Estate Terminology,* American Institute of Real Estate Appraisers and Society of Real Estate Appraisers (Cambridge, MA: Ballinger Publishing Company, 1981), pp. 351–354.

Agricultural Land Values

Cropland: Average Value per Acre, by Region and State, January 1, 1997-00

State	1997	1998	1999	2000	Change 99-00
	Dollars	Dollars	Dollars	Dollars	Percent
Northeast:	**2,590**	**2,620**	**2,700**	**2,820**	**4.4**
DE	2,500	2,620	2,700	2,800	3.7
MD	3,050	3,100	3,200	3,400	6.3
NJ	8,500	8,000	7,800	7,900	1.3
NY	1,020	1,040	1,100	1,160	5.5
PA	2,650	2,740	2,870	3,020	5.2
Oth Sts [1]	4,260	4,290	4,360	4,490	3.0
Lake States:	**1,130**	**1,220**	**1,340**	**1,440**	**7.5**
MI	1,360	1,480	1,670	1,920	15.0
MN	1,090	1,160	1,230	1,270	3.3
WI	1,040	1,130	1,300	1,450	11.5
Corn Belt:	**1,760**	**1,910**	**2,030**	**2,010**	**-1.0**
IL	2,070	2,240	2,370	2,320	-2.1
IN	1,900	2,100	2,270	2,250	-0.9
IA	1,700	1,860	1,930	1,890	-2.1
MO	1,040	1,130	1,190	1,250	5.0
OH	1,990	2,150	2,350	2,380	1.3
Northern Plains:	**633**	**648**	**658**	**668**	**1.5**
KS	649	655	659	666	1.1
NE	1,020	1,040	1,080	1,110	2.8
ND	427	440	435	425	-2.3
SD	456	480	491	510	3.9
Appalachian:	**1,730**	**1,830**	**1,930**	**1,980**	**2.6**
KY	1,500	1,620	1,630	1,630	0.0
NC	1,880	1,950	2,130	2,300	8.0
TN	1,830	1,970	2,100	2,150	2.4
VA	1,820	1,880	1,980	1,980	0.0
WV	1,540	1,600	1,570	1,500	-4.5
Southeast:	**1,610**	**1,670**	**1,720**	**1,850**	**7.6**
AL	1,200	1,260	1,320	1,460	10.6
FL	3,280	3,230	3,190	3,340	4.7
GA	1,060	1,140	1,250	1,400	12.0
SC	1,090	1,160	1,200	1,240	3.3
Delta States:	**956**	**996**	**1,030**	**1,060**	**2.9**
AR	968	1,030	1,080	1,080	0.0
LA	1,080	1,060	1,060	1,110	4.7
MS	821	878	925	983	6.3
Southern Plains:	**641**	**667**	**681**	**708**	**4.0**
OK	553	577	558	548	-1.8
TX	674	701	728	770	5.8
Mountain:	**904**	**936**	**968**	**993**	**2.6**
AZ [2]	3,700	3,800	4,100	4,300	4.9
CO	772	809	833	852	2.3
ID	1,320	1,370	1,420	1,490	4.9
MT	458	463	461	458	-0.7
NV [2]	1,700	1,850	1,900	1,900	0.0
NM [2]	1,330	1,380	1,420	1,370	-3.5
UT [2]	2,300	2,390	2,610	2,740	5.0
WY	744	777	781	815	4.4
Pacific:	**3,030**	**3,150**	**3,350**	**3,460**	**3.3**
CA	5,080	5,260	5,700	5,960	4.6
OR	1,430	1,430	1,520	1,570	3.3
WA	1,340	1,430	1,410	1,340	-5.0
48 Sts	**1,270**	**1,340**	**1,410**	**1,440**	**2.1**

[1] Includes: CT, ME, MA, NH, RI, and VT.
[2] Excludes Native American Reservation Land.

Source: United States Department of Agriculture, National Agricultural Statistics Service (March 2000).
http://www.usda.gov/nass/

Pasture: Average Value per Acre, by Region and State, January 1, 1997-00

State	1997	1998	1999	2000	Change 99-00
	Dollars	*Dollars*	*Dollars*	*Dollars*	*Percent*
Northeast:	**1,990**	**2,030**	**2,060**	**2,090**	**1.5**
MD	3,300	3,350	3,400	3,400	0.0
NJ	9,100	8,800	8,800	8,900	1.1
NY	515	530	550	560	1.8
PA	1,630	1,740	1,790	1,820	1.7
Oth Sts [1]	3,910	3,900	3,910	3,990	2.0
Lake States:	**486**	**520**	**574**	**629**	**9.6**
MI	800	890	980	1,080	10.2
MN	360	380	400	410	2.5
WI	520	550	630	720	14.3
Corn Belt:	**756**	**813**	**859**	**883**	**2.8**
IL	870	940	1,000	1,040	4.0
IN	1,160	1,270	1,400	1,440	2.9
IA	615	665	660	650	-1.5
MO	660	700	750	790	5.3
OH	1,280	1,410	1,480	1,450	-2.0
Northern Plains:	**206**	**216**	**222**	**231**	**4.1**
KS	365	367	370	375	1.4
NE	200	210	220	230	4.5
ND	141	144	146	155	6.2
SD	155	173	180	190	5.6
Appalachian:	**1,510**	**1,600**	**1,700**	**1,800**	**5.9**
KY	1,210	1,320	1,400	1,450	3.6
NC	2,020	2,100	2,270	2,400	5.7
TN	1,720	1,860	2,000	2,150	7.5
VA	1,780	1,800	1,900	2,050	7.9
WV	840	860	825	820	-0.6
Southeast:	**1,340**	**1,410**	**1,490**	**1,600**	**7.4**
AL	990	1,100	1,170	1,300	11.1
FL	1,430	1,450	1,500	1,570	4.7
GA	1,650	1,770	1,950	2,150	10.3
SC	1,220	1,340	1,380	1,450	5.1
Delta States:	**955**	**971**	**992**	**1,030**	**3.8**
AR	890	910	960	1,000	4.2
LA	1,210	1,200	1,160	1,150	-0.9
MS	860	890	910	1,000	9.9
Southern Plains:	**484**	**523**	**533**	**543**	**1.9**
OK	361	395	410	415	1.2
TX	510	550	560	570	1.8
Mountain:	**219**	**231**	**233**	**241**	**3.4**
AZ [2]	300	320	340	360	5.9
CO	320	335	340	345	1.5
ID	640	700	780	850	9.0
MT	190	197	200	205	2.5
NV [2]	220	230	250	270	8.0
NM [2]	150	160	155	150	-3.2
UT [2]	395	400	400	420	5.0
WY	150	160	150	160	6.7
Pacific:	**754**	**731**	**729**	**698**	**4.3**
CA	1,100	1,050	1,050	1,000	-4.8
OR	400	400	400	405	1.3
WA	550	550	540	490	-9.3
48 Sts	**466**	**489**	**503**	**517**	**2.8**

[1] Includes: CT, DE, ME, MA, NH, RI, and VT.
[2] Excludes Native American Reservation Land.

Source: United States Department of Agriculture, National Agricultural Statistics Service (March 2000).
http://www.usda.gov/nass/

**Irrigated and Non-Irrigated Cropland: Average Value per Acre,
by State, January 1, 1997-00 [1]**

State	1997	1998	1999	2000	Change 99-00
	Dollars	*Dollars*	*Dollars*	*Dollars*	*Percent*
Corn Belt:					
MO Cropland	1,040	1,130	1,190	1,250	5.0
Irrigated	1,600	1,670	1,820	1,900	4.4
Non-Irrigated	1,000	1,090	1,150	1,210	5.2
Northern Plains:					
KS Cropland	649	655	659	666	1.1
Irrigated	990,	1,010	1,020	1,030	1.0
Non-Irrigated	615	620	623	630	1.1
NE Cropland	1,020	1,040	1,080	1,110	2.8
Irrigated	1,500	1,510	1,550	1,580	1.9
Non-Irrigated	775	799	840	860	2.4
SD Cropland	456	480	491	510	3.9
Irrigated	710	810	770	740	-3.9
Non-Irrigated	451	473	485	505	4.1
Southeast:					
FL Cropland	3,280	3,230	3,190	3,340	4.7
Irrigated	4,100	4,000	3,950	4,120	4.3
Non-Irrigated	1,550	1,600	1,600	1,680	5.0
GA Cropland	1,060	1,140	1,250	1,400	12.0
Irrigated	1,230	1,290	1,380	1,500	8.7
Non-Irrigated	1,020	1,110	1,220	1,380	13.1
Delta States:					
AR Cropland	968	1,030	1,080	1,080	0.0
Irrigated	1,070	1,140	1,180	1,190	0.8
Non-Irrigated	880	940	1,000	980	-2.0
LA Cropland	1,080	1,060	1,060	1,110	4.7
Irrigated	920	928	990	1,060	7.1
Non-Irrigated	1,120	1,100	1,080	1,120	3.7
MS Cropland	821	878	925	983	6.3
Irrigated	964	1,010	1,080	1,100	1.9
Non-Irrigated	780	840	880	950	8.0
Southern Plains:					
OK Cropland	553	577	558	548	-1.8
Irrigated	800	810	790	780	-1.3
Non-Irrigated	540	564	545	535	-1.8
TX Cropland	674	701	728	770	5.8
Irrigated	800	780	830	880	6.0
Non-Irrigated	540	564	545	535	-1.8
Mountain:					
AZ Cropland	3,700	3,800	4,100	4,300	4.9
Irrigated	3,700	3,800	4,100	4,300	4.9
CO Cropland	772	809	833	852	2.3
Irrigated	1,500	1,580	1,600	1,600	0.0
Non-Irrigated	380	395	420	450	7.1

[1] States not listed make all cropland estimates only.   --continued

Source: United States Department of Agriculture, National Agricultural Statistics Service (March 2000).
http://www.usda.gov/nass/

Land Valuation: Adjustment Procedures and Assignments

**Irrigated and Non-Irrigated Cropland: Average Value per Acre,
by State, 1997-00 [1]**

State and Land Type	1997	1998	1999	2000	Change 99-00
	Dollars	Dollars	Dollars	Dollars	Percent
ID Cropland	1,320	1,370	1,420	1,490	4.9
Irrigated	1,700	1,760	1,820	1,900	4.4
Non-Irrigated	660	680	730	770	5.5
MT Cropland	458	463	461	458	-0.7
Irrigated	1,290	1,310	1,310	1,320	0.8
Non-Irrigated	340	343	340	335	-1.5
NV Cropland	1,700	1,850	1,900	1,900	0.0
Irrigated	1,700	1,850	1,900	1,900	0.0
NM Cropland	1,330	1,380	1,420	1,370	-3.5
Irrigated	2,400	2,490	2,550	2,480	-2.7
Non-Irrigated	247	255	260	245	-5.8
UT Cropland	2,300	2,390	2,610	2,740	5.0
Irrigated	2,700	2,800	3,080	3,250	5.5
Non-Irrigated	700	730	700	670	-4.3
WY Cropland	744	777	781	815	4.4
Irrigated	900	940	940	980	4.3
Non-Irrigated	220	230	245	260	6.1
Pacific:					
CA Cropland	5,080	5,260	5,700	5,960	4.6
Irrigated	5,400	5,600	6,100	6,400	4.9
Non-Irrigated	1,830	1,700	1,580	1,450	-8.2
OR Cropland	1,430	1,430	1,520	1,570	3.3
Irrigated	2,000	2,000	2,100	2,150	2.4
Non-Irrigated	980	980	1,050	1,100	4.8
WA Cropland	1,340	1,430	1,410	1,340	-5.0
Irrigated	3,200	3,400	3,600	3,500	-2.8
Non-Irrigated	790	840	760	700	-7.9

[1] States not listed make all cropland estimates only.

Source: United States Department of Agriculture, National Agricultural Statistics Service (March 2000).
http://www.usda.gov/nass/

Property Observation Checklist

APPRAISAL INSTITUTE®

PROPERTY OBSERVATION CHECKLIST

LIMITED SCOPE ANALYSIS

The Property Observation Checklist is a limited scope analysis voluntarily prepared by the appraiser during the normal course of his/her inspection of the subject property in the preparation of a real estate appraisal. In completing the checklist, only visual observations are recorded. The intent of the checklist is to identify possible environmental factors that could be observable by a non-environmental professional. The appraiser did not search title, interview the current or prior owners, or do any research beyond that normally associated with the appraisal process, unless otherwise stated.

The user of this checklist is reminded that all responses to the questions are provided by an appraiser who is not an environmental professional and is not specifically trained or qualified to identify potential environmental problems; therefore, it should be used only to assist the appraiser's client in determining whether an environmental professional is required. The checklist was not developed for use with single-family residential or agricultural properties.

The appraiser is not liable for the lack of detection or identification of possible environmental factors. The appraisal report and/or the Property Observation Checklist must not be considered under any circumstances to be an environmental site assessment of the property as would be performed by an environmental professional.

GENERAL INSTRUCTIONS

The appraiser should distinguish, as appropriate, between the physical presence of possible environmental factors and the economic effect such factors may have in the marketplace or on the value estimate. In completing the checklist, the appraiser should attach reports, photographs, interview records, notes, public records, etc., as documentation for specific observations. The instructions for each section of the checklist specify the kinds of documentation required.

If, for any reason, this checklist is prepared as a stand-alone document, it must be accompanied by an attached statement of limiting conditions and certification of the appraiser's qualifications.

TERMINOLOGY AND APPRAISAL STANDARDS

The following checklist terms appear in *The Dictionary of Real Estate Appraisal,* Third Edition (Chicago: Appraisal Institute, 1993) and are specifically referenced in the Property Observation Checklist: *adjoining properties; environmental professional; environmental site assessment;* and *pits, ponds, or lagoons.* Please refer to *The Dictionary of Real Estate Appraisal,* Third Edition, for discussions of these terms.

Please refer to Guide Note 8, "The Consideration of Hazardous Substances in the Appraisal Process," *Guide Notes to the Standards of Professional Appraisal Practice* (Chicago: Appraisal Institute, 1995); Advisory Opinion G-9, "Responsibility of Appraisers Concerning Toxic or Hazardous Substances Contamination, " *Uniform Standards of Professional Appraisal Practice* (Washington, D.C.: The Appraisal Foundation, 1995 ed.); and other appropriate statements in the professional standards documents for additional information.

Describe the appraiser's on-site inspection of the subject property and, as applicable, the adjoining properties:

_____
_____
_____
_____

| **SECTION 2** | Possible Environmental Factors Observed by the Appraiser |

Indicate below if any of the following possible environmental factors were observed during the appraiser's visual inspection(s) of the subject property and, as applicable, the adjoining properties. A written description of possible environmental factors should be provided for all questions where "Yes" is checked.

1. Did the appraiser observe an indication of current or past industrial/manufacturing use on the subject property or adjoining properties?

   ○ Yes   ○ No   **If observed, describe below:**

_____
_____

2. Did the appraiser observe any containers, storage drums, or disposal devices not labeled or identified as to contents or use on the subject property?

   ○ Yes   ○ No   **If observed, describe below:**

_____

3. Did the appraiser observe any stained soil or distressed vegetation on the subject property?

   ○ Yes   ○ No   **If observed, describe below:**

_____

4. Did the appraiser observe any pits, ponds, or lagoons on the subject property?

   ○ Yes   ○ No   **If observed, describe below:**

_____

5. Did the appraiser observe any evidence of above-ground or underground storage tanks (e.g., tanks, vent pipes, etc.) on the subject property?

   ○ Yes   ○ No   **If observed, describe below:**

_____
_____

6. Did the appraiser observe any flooring, drains, or walls associated with the subject property that are stained or that emit unusual odors?

○ Yes   ○ No   **If observed, describe below:**

_____

_____

7. Did the appraiser observe any water being discharged on or from the subject property?

○ Yes   ○ No   **If observed, describe below:**

_____

_____

8. Did the appraiser observe any indication of dumping, burying, or burning on the subject property?

○ Yes   ○ No   **If observed, describe below:**

_____

_____

9. Did the appraiser observe any chipped, blistered, or peeled paint on the subject property?

○ Yes   ○ No   **If observed, describe below:**

_____

_____

10. Did the appraiser observe any sprayed-on insulation, pipe wrapping, duct wrapping, etc., on the subject property?

○ Yes   ○ No   **If observed, describe below:**

_____

_____

11. Did the appraiser observe any transmission towers (electrical, microwave, etc.) on the subject property or adjoining properties?

○ Yes   ○ No   **If observed, describe below:**

_____

_____

12. Did the appraiser observe any coastal areas, rivers, streams, springs, lakes, swamps, marshes, or watercourses on the subject property or adjoining properties?

○ Yes   ○ No   **If observed, describe below:**

_____

_____

13. Did the appraiser observe any other factors that might indicate the need for investigation(s) by an environmental professional?

○ Yes   ○ No   **If observed, describe below:**

_____

_____

Indicate below if in completing this assignment the appraiser was informed—verbally or in writing—of any information concerning possible environmental factors reported by others. "Others" may include the client, the property owner, the property owner's agent, or any other person conveying such information. Documentation should be provided for all instances where "Yes" is checked. If the information was presented verbally, then a written description of the source and circumstance of the communication should be attached to this checklist and/or the appraisal report. Copies of printed reports provided to the appraiser should be attached to this checklist and/or the appraisal report.

14. Has the appraiser been informed about federal- or state-maintained records indicating that environmentally sensitive sites are located on the subject property or adjoining properties?

    ○ Yes   ○ No   **If yes, provide documentation.**

15. Has the appraiser been informed about past or current violations (e.g., liens, government notifications, etc.) of environmental laws concerning the subject property?

    ○ Yes   ○ No   **If yes, provide documentation.**

16. Has the appraiser been informed about past or current environmental lawsuits or administrative proceedings concerning the subject property?

    ○ Yes   ○ No   **If yes, provide documentation.**

17. Has the appraiser been informed about past or current tests for lead-based paint or other lead hazards on the subject property?

    ○ Yes   ○ No   **If yes, provide documentation.**

18. Has the appraiser been informed about past or current tests for asbestos-containing materials on the subject property?

    ○ Yes   ○ No   **If yes, provide documentation.**

19. Has the appraiser been informed about past or current tests for radon on the subject property?

    ○ Yes   ○ No   **If yes, provide documentation.**

20. Has the appraiser been informed about past or current tests for soil or groundwater contamination on the subject property?

    ○ Yes   ○ No   **If yes, provide documentation.**

21. Has the appraiser been informed about other professional environmental site assessment(s) of the subject property?

    ○ Yes   ○ No   **If yes, provide documentation.**

Signature

Name

Date Checklist Signed

State Certification or State License #   State

4 of 4

Advisory Opinion 9

ADVISORY OPINION 9 (AO-9)

This communication by the Appraisal Standards Board (ASB) does not establish new standards or interpret existing standards. Advisory Opinions are issued to illustrate the applicability of appraisal standards in specific situations and to offer advice from the ASB for the resolution of appraisal issues and problems. They do not constitute a legal opinion of the ASB.

SUBJECT: Responsibility of Appraisers Concerning Toxic or Hazardous Substance Contamination

THE ISSUE:

Federal and state legislation has been enacted to control environmentally toxic or hazardous substances and assign responsibility for any resulting contamination. How do the *Uniform Standards of Professional Appraisal Practice* (USPAP) apply to the appraisal of property considering:

(1) recognition of contamination;
(2) remediation and compliance cost estimation; and,
(3) value opinions of interests in impacted real estate?

ADVICE FROM THE ASB ON THE ISSUE:

Honesty and professional competency are common threads throughout USPAP. The professional competency of an appraiser should not be presumed to include the knowledge or experience of a professional surveyor, architect, engineer, title lawyer, or other specialist. An appraiser that professes or implies such expertise but lacks the requisite qualifications is misleading the client, users of the appraisal report, and the public. Such misleading conduct is prohibited by the ETHICS RULE of USPAP. However, an appraiser may reasonably rely on the findings and opinions of a properly qualified specialist and may work in concert with other professionals in multidisciplinary groups assembled to address a contaminated parcel of real estate.

Recognition of Contamination

An appraiser is a trained and experienced observer of real estate, but recognizing, detecting, or measuring contamination is often beyond the scope of the appraiser's expertise. The appraiser becomes aware of contamination through disclosure by the client and known facts prior to the acceptance of an appraisal assignment, or through the normal observation and research conducted during an appraisal assignment. If an appraiser is requested to complete a checklist as part of the process for recognizing contamination, the appraiser should respond only to those questions that can be answered competently by the appraiser within the limits of his or her particular expertise in this area. In each situation, the COMPETENCY RULE of USPAP outlines the responsibilities of the appraiser.

Remediation and Compliance Cost Estimation

Remediation and compliance cost estimation involves knowledge and experience beyond that of most appraisers. These estimates are typically provided by environmental consulting specialists who are properly versed in federal and state environmental requirements and are qualified to assess and measure the materials and/or methods appropriate for remediation or compliance. Other professionals who deal with legal liabilities and business operations may also be involved in the cost estimate process. An appraiser may reasonably rely on the findings and opinions of qualified specialists in environmental remediation and compliance cost estimation.

USPAP 2000 EDITION
©THE APPRAISAL FOUNDATION

Value Opinions of Interests in Impacted Real Estate

Many clients employ experts in various disciplines separately and simultaneously, and make business decisions based on comparing the results of findings from the various experts. These clients may request an appraiser to appraise real estate that is or may be contaminated under the hypothetical condition that the real estate is free of contamination. An appraiser may appraise interests in real estate that is or is believed to be contaminated based on the hypothetical condition that the real estate is free of contamination when (1) the resulting appraisal is not misleading, (2) the client has been advised of the limitation, and (3) the ETHICS RULE of the USPAP is satisfied. To avoid confusion in the marketplace, the ETHICS RULE requires a clear and accurate disclosure of the factual contamination problem as well as a statement of the validity of and useful purpose for the extraordinary assumption that the real estate is not affected.

When qualified specialists have documented the existence of contamination and estimated the costs of remediation or compliance, an appraiser may be in a position to develop an opinion of "as is" value and should be aware of, understand, and correctly employ those recognized methods and techniques necessary to produce a credible appraisal. The value of an interest in impacted or contaminated real estate may not be measurable simply by deducting the remediation or compliance cost estimate from the opinion of value as if unaffected. Other factors may influence value, including any positive or negative impact on marketability (stigma) and the possibility of change in highest and best use.

Multidisciplinary Solutions

Some appraisers have already developed a specialization in the valuation of interests in contaminated real estate through association with environmental engineers, environmental lawyers, and related professionals in a multidisciplinary group. This type of association is commendable, provided that each of the professionals involved remains within the limits of the expertise associated with his or her profession and acknowledges the contributions of the other professionals in any specific reports that rely in part on the work of others.

This Advisory Opinion is based on presumed conditions without investigation or verification of actual circumstances. There is no assurance that this Advisory Opinion represents the only possible solution to the problems discussed or that it applies equally to seemingly similar situations.

Approved December 8, 1992
Revised September 16, 1998

Guide Note 8
The Consideration of Hazardous
Substances in the Appraisal Process

GUIDE NOTE 8

THE CONSIDERATION OF HAZARDOUS SUBSTANCES IN THE APPRAISAL PROCESS

Introduction

The consideration of environmental forces along with social, economic and governmental forces is fundamental to the appraisal of real property. Although appraisal literature has long recognized environmental forces as major determinants of value, the focus has been on the consideration of climatic conditions, topography and soil, the surrounding neighborhood, accessibility, and proximity to points of attraction. These environmental forces are readily apparent to a member of the general public who is not specifically trained as an expert in observing these forces. There is, however, a growing need to give special consideration to the impact of hazardous substances on the valuation of real property.

The growing need to consider hazardous substances is a recent trend stemming from the creation and identification of new hazards, recent federal and state legislation enacted to control and place responsibility for these hazards, and an increasing public awareness of the problems resulting from these hazards.

The presence of hazardous substances can significantly impact value. In some cases the property may have a "negative" value if remediation cost is greater than the property value after any necessary clean up.

For the purpose of this guide note the term "hazardous substances" covers any material within, around or near a property that may have a negative impact on its value. Accordingly, the principles discussed in this guide note apply equally to hazardous substances that may be contained within the property and external hazardous substances.

The purpose of this guide note is to provide guidance in the application of the Uniform Standards of Professional Appraisal Practice ("USPAP") to the appraisal of real property affected by or potentially affected by hazardous substances and, in particular, to the consideration of such hazards in the appraisal process. It is not the purpose of this guide note to provide technical instructions or explanations concerning the detection or measurement of the effect of hazardous substances.

Competency

The Competency Provision of the Uniform Standards of Professional Appraisal Practice requires the appraiser to have the knowledge and experience necessary to complete a specific appraisal assignment competently or alternatively to disclose the lack of knowledge or experience to the client, take all steps necessary or appropriate to complete the assignment competently and describe in the report the lack of knowledge or experience and the steps taken to competently complete the assignment.

The Competency Provision is of particular importance in the appraisal of real property that may be affected by hazardous substances. Most appraisers do not have the knowledge or experience required to detect the presence of hazardous substances or to measure the quantities of such material. The appraiser, like the buyers and sellers in the open market, typically relies on the advice of others in matters that require special expertise.

There is nothing to prevent a professional appraiser from becoming an expert in other fields, but the real estate appraiser is neither required, nor expected, to be an expert in the special field of the detection and measurement of hazardous substances. This guide note therefore addresses the problem of hazardous substances from the viewpoint of the appraiser who is not qualified to detect or measure the quantities of hazardous substances.

For an appraisal which develops an opinion of the effects on value of hazardous substances, most appraisers would require the professional assistance of others. For an appraisal with no separate accounting for the possible effects on value of known hazardous substances, the appraiser would not require the professional assistance of others. These alternatives are further discussed below.

The appraiser may accept an assignment involving the consideration of hazardous substances without having the required knowledge and experience in this special field, provided the appraiser discloses such lack of knowledge and experience to the client prior to acceptance of the assignment, arranges to complete the assignment competently and describes the lack of knowledge or experience and the steps taken to competently complete the assignment in the report. This may require association with others who possess the required knowledge and experience or reliance on professional reports prepared by others who are reasonably believed to have the necessary knowledge and experience. If the appraiser draws conclusions based upon the advice or findings of others, the appraiser must believe that the advice or findings are made by persons who are properly qualified. (See Guide Note 6, Reliance on Reports Prepared by Others.) It is suggested that the client, not the appraiser, choose and hire any qualified environmental professionals.

In some cases, an appraiser may be asked to complete a checklist which lists specific contaminants and questions the appraiser's knowledge of each. This is addressed in USPAP Advisory Opinion G-9 entitled "Responsibility of Appraisers Concerning Toxic or Hazardous Substance Contamination," which states, "If an appraiser is requested to complete a checklist as part of the process for recognizing contamination, the appraiser should only respond to those questions that can be answered competently by the appraiser within the limits of his or her particular expertise in this area."

Basis for Proper Valuation

In developing an appraisal based in part on the findings of others with respect to the existence and effects of hazardous substances, the appraiser must correctly employ those recognized methods and techniques that are necessary to produce a credible appraisal. The loss of value attributable to hazardous substances is sometimes measurable using the same methods and techniques that are used to measure depreciation from other causes. In other cases, more specialized techniques are indicated. However, in some cases even environmental professionals cannot agree on the level of clean up required, the appropriate method of that clean up, or the cost.

The appraiser is cautioned that the value of a property impacted by hazardous substances may not be measurable simply by deducting the typical remediation cost, or discovery cost from the total value, as if "clean." The possibility of other changes affecting value, such as a change in highest and best use, marketability, and stigma should be considered. In any analysis the appraiser should concentrate on developing an opinion of the effect on value caused by the hazardous substances.

S.R. 2-3 and S.R. 5-3 require the appraiser to include, within each written report, the name of each individual providing significant professional assistance. Accordingly, environmental engineers, inspectors and other professionals who prepare reports, furnish advice or make findings that are used in the appraisal process must be named in the certification.

The appraiser may accept an assignment that would exclude the consideration of hazardous substances, provided that: the resulting appraisal is not misleading; the client has been advised of the limitation; and the report is qualified to reflect this limitation.

When there are no known hazardous substances it is recommended, as a matter of standard practice, that the appraiser issue a disclaimer or limiting condition to the effect that the appraisal is predicated on the assumption that hazardous substances do not exist. If the property being appraised is not known[1] to be affected by hazardous substances and there is no reason to believe that it may be so affected, the issuance of such a disclaimer of limiting condition would not be considered to limit the scope of the appraisal. If the property being appraised is known to be affected by hazardous substances, or if there is reason to believe that it may be so affected, the appraiser cannot exclude the consideration of such materials without limiting the scope of the appraisal. In such appraisals, the appraiser must take great care to make sure that the limitation is not misleading. The known or suspected existence of hazardous substances must be disclosed.

If a property is known to be affected by hazardous substances, or if there is reason to believe that a property may be so affected, it may serve a valid and useful purpose to obtain an appraisal of the property, excluding the consideration of hazardous substances. Such an appraisal could be required as the logical starting point in a study of the impact of hazardous substances or in connection with legal proceedings. Whatever the purpose, such an appraisal must be properly qualified to prevent its misuse and must not be misleading. The valuation of property, as if unaffected by hazardous substances that are known to be present or are suspected of being present, would be predicated on an extraordinary assumption and therefore subject to S.R. 2-1(c) without exception. S.R. 2-1(c) requires that each written or oral real estate appraisal report must clearly and accurately disclose any extraordinary

---

1. Knowledge is being defined here to mean obvious to the untrained person or specifically communicated through a reasonably reliable source.

assumption, hypothetical condition, or limiting condition that directly affects the appraisal and indicate its impact in value. The validity of and reason for making the extraordinary assumption should also be disclosed. Similarly, S.R. 2-2(a) (xi), S.R. (b), (xi), and S.R. (c) (xi) require that the report clearly identify and explain any permitted departure from the requirements of Standard 1.

In limited assignments such as discussed above, the requirements of the Departure Provision, S.R. 2-1(c), S.R. 2-2(a) (xi), S.R. 2-2(b), (xi), and S.R. 2-2(c) (xi)) may be satisfied by including a suitable disclosure or limiting condition, an appropriate statement of purpose and properly qualified conclusions in the report. For purposes of illustration, assume that a property known to contain friable asbestos is to be appraised in accordance with the client's instructions, as if unaffected by asbestos. The report for such an appraisal would require a limiting condition, an appropriate statement of purpose and qualified conclusions similar in content to the following example.

> In accordance with the client's instructions, the value opinion reported herein reflects the total value of the subject property, as if unaffected by asbestos. It is reported that asbestos is present within the subject property. The presence of asbestos may have a negative influence on the value of the subject property, but the consideration of the effects of asbestos on the value of the subject property is beyond the purpose and scope of this appraisal. The appraiser cautions against the use of this appraisal without knowledge of the intended purpose and limited scope of the appraisal.

In addition to an appropriate limiting condition such as shown above, there should be an appropriate statement of purpose and the conclusion should be properly qualified, as illustrated below.

> The purpose of this appraisal is to develop an opinion of the market value of the subject property, as if unaffected by asbestos, as of January 1, 19XX.

> The appraiser's final opinion of the market value of the subject property, as if unaffected by asbestos, as of January 1, 19XX.

The limiting condition(s) should be stated in the letter of transmittal, if any, the body of the report, and whenever the report conclusion is stated.

Standard Disclaimers and Statements of Limiting Conditions

As previously mentioned, it is recommended practice, even in the appraisal of property where there is no reason to believe that the property is affected by hazardous substances, to include a standard disclaimer or statement of limiting conditions that pertains specifically to hazardous substances in the appraisal report. Such statements are not required by the Standards of Professional Appraisal Practice, and they are not intended to limit the scope of the appraisal to something less than would otherwise be required. Rather, they are intended to clarify the normal limits of the appraisal, disclose the appraiser's lack of expertise with respect to hazardous substances, and disclaim the appraiser's responsibility for matters beyond the appraiser's level of expertise.

The following examples are offered for illustration only.

> Unless otherwise stated in this report, the existence of hazardous substances, including without limitation asbestos, polychlorinated biphenyl, petroleum leakage, or agricultural chemicals, which may or may not be present on the property were not called to the attention of nor did the appraiser become aware of such during the appraiser's inspection. The appraiser has no knowledge of the existence of such materials on or in the property unless otherwise stated. The appraiser, however, is not qualified to test for such substances. The presence of such hazardous substances may affect the value of the property. The value opinion reported herein is predicated on the assumption that no such hazardous substances exist on or in the property or in such proximity thereto which would cause a loss in value. No responsibility is assumed for any such hazardous substances, or for any expertise or knowledge required to discover them.

Because the appraiser's value opinion is based on assessment of what a knowledgeable buyer would pay a knowledgeable seller, the appraiser needs to be aware of the steps that knowledgeable buyers and sellers now take in the market place. Under federal and most state laws, the owner of a piece of property which is contaminated and from which there is a release or threatened release, may be held liable for the cost of corrective action. Under federal and state laws, an "innocent purchaser" may avoid this liability. In order for a purchaser to qualify for the "innocent purchaser" defense, the purchaser must establish that it undertook all proper investigation of the property and the purchaser's knowledge. This has come to mean, at a minimum, that the purchaser of commercial, industrial or vacant property must conduct at least a "Phase I" investigation of the property prior to acquisition. Such an investigation entails a review of the property, its history, and available government records to determine if there is reason to believe that it may contain contamination. If a properly conducted Phase I investigation finds no likelihood of contamination, it should be sufficient to establish the "innocent purchaser" defense. If the potential for contamination is disclosed in the Phase I report, further investigation, often characterized as Phase II or Phase III investigations should be able to determine with a reasonable degree of scientific certainty whether the property is affected by contamination, and if it is, what the possible remedies and costs may be. Given the accepted practice in the marketplace, the appraiser may wish to qualify his or her appraisal as follows:

If the appraiser has been provided with a Phase I, Phase II, or Phase III report finding no evidence of possible contamination:

"The client has provided an environmental assessment for the property performed by "XXX". According to the (date of report) report describing that assessmentno adverse hazardous substances were found on the subject property. The reader of this appraisal report is urged to review the entire environmental assessment for specific detail."

If no Phase I report has been prepared or provided to the appraiser and the appraiser has no reason to suspect the existence of hazardous substances, the appraiser may wish to state specifically that:

"The appraiser has not reviewed a Phase I report of examination and such an examination is customary in the transfer of commercial, industrial or vacant real estate. The appraisal is based on an assumption of a Phase I report indicating no contamination."

Of course, if a Phase I, Phase II, or Phase III report indicates the possibility of contamination, that must be noted together with the amount of further investigation that is required by customary business practice as well as necessary to establish the "innocent purchaser" defense (such further investigation must reveal the absence of contamination to establish the "innocent purchase" defense). A statement similar to the following is suggested:

"The client has provided a Phase XX environmental assessment for the property performed by "XXXX". According to the (date of report) report describing that assessmentthe following hazardous substances are found on the subject property. The reader of this appraisal report is urged to review the entire environmental assessment for specific detail. A Phase XX environmental assessment is suggested."

There is no suggestion that the preceding statements or any other disclaimers or limiting conditions would be appropriate in all jurisdictions and circumstances. Appraisers are advised to consult their own legal counsel for assistance in developing individualized language for limiting conditions statements. Such statements may be considered in determining the extent of the appraiser's liability, if any, in connection with hazardous substances, and in determining whether the appraiser is eligible for errors and omissions liability insurance in connection with appraisals involving the consideration of hazardous substances. If the appraiser becomes aware of any information not previously disclosed by the client regarding possible hazardous substances affecting the subject, the appraiser should inform the client in writing of the possibility of the existence of a hazardous substance prior to the completion of the report.

The appraiser should note in the report any evidence of hazardous substances that is observed during the inspection of the subject property or becomes known to the appraiser through the normal research involved in performing the appraisal which would lead the appraiser to believe that hazardous substances may be present in or on the subject property, or is at variance with information or descriptions provided by others.

Unacceptable Practices

In the appraisal of property that requires the consideration of hazardous substances, but where the appraiser does not have the knowledge or experience required to detect the presence of such hazards, to measure the quantities of such hazards or to quantify the impact these hazards may have on value, the following practices are unacceptable.

1. Failure to disclose to the client the appraiser's lack of knowledge and experience with respect to the detection and measurement of hazardous substances (See Competency Provision).

2. Failure to take the necessary steps to complete the assignment competently such as personal study by the appraiser, association with another appraiser who has the required knowledge and experience or obtaining the professional assistance of others who possess the required knowledge and experience (See Competency Provision).

In the appraisal of property affected by hazardous substances, but where the purpose of the appraisal is to develop an opinion of value as if unaffected by hazardous substances, the following practice is unacceptable.

3. Failure to include in the report a qualification that reflects the limited scope of the appraisal, a limiting condition that clearly reveals the fact that the property is appraised as if unaffected by hazardous substances, an appropriate statement of purpose and properly qualified conclusions (See Departure Provision, S.R. 2-1(c), S.R. 2-2(a) (viii) and (xi), S.R. (b), (viii) and (xi), and S.R. (c) (viii) and (xi) .

4. Failure to report known hazardous substances affecting the property (See S.R. 2-1(b), S.R. 2-2(a), S.R. 2-2(b) and S.R. 2-2(c)).

In the appraisal of property affected by hazardous substances, if the appraiser relies upon the findings of other professionals with respect to the presence of, and the probable effect of, hazardous substances, the following practice is unacceptable.

5. Failure to acknowledge the professional assistance of others and to name the persons providing the assistance in the certification (See S.R. 2-3 and S.R. 5-3).

[Please note: Guide Notes to the Standards of Professional Appraisal Practice are an integral part of the Standards document. Guide Notes illustrate how the requirements of the Standards should be applied. They should not be considered without referring to the Standards of Professional Appraisal Practice.]